The talkSPORT Book of

PREMIER LEAGUE LEGENDS

BILL BORROWS

with Derek Hammond

London · New York · Sydney · Toronto · New Delhi

A CBS COMPANY

FOR MY TWO BEAUTIFUL BOYS – WILLIAM BORROWS Jr
& WILLIAM G. HALL

First published in Great Britain by Simon & Schuster UK Ltd, 2012
A CBS COMPANY

1 3 5 7 9 10 8 6 4 2

Simon & Schuster UK Ltd
1st Floor
222 Gray's Inn Road
London
WC1X 8HB

www.simonandschuster.co.uk

Simon & Schuster Australia, Sydney
Simon & Schuster India, New Delhi

All photographs © Getty Images, except for the Jimmy Floyd Hasselbaink
keyring © Andy McConachie at footballcardsuk.com

A CIP catalogue for this book is available
from the British Library.

ISBN: 978-1-84983-941-9

Typeset by M Rules
Printed and bound by CPI Group (UK) Ltd, Croydon, CR0 4YY

CONTENTS

CLUB LEGENDS   243

INTRODUCTION

YOU'LL REMEMBER the famous Nike advert: "66 WAS A GREAT YEAR FOR ENGLISH FOOTBALL ... ERIC WAS BORN.' It featured Manchester United's strutting French peacock, with his collar up on that dumb little kit with the lace-ups at the neck, circa 1994.

Just five years previously, the idea that a foreigner playing in English football – let alone a Frenchman – would be the face of a global brand trying to make in-roads into a game that had just hosted the Hillsborough Disaster would have been risible. The creation of the Premier League made this possible.

You can take the date of birth of the Premier League as the publication of the Football Association's *Blueprint For The Future Of Football* in June 1991 that advocated the creation of an FA 'Premier League', a direct response to the Lord Taylor report (on the aftermath and causes of Hillsborough) 18 months earlier. Or alternatively, you could say it was the *en masse* resignation of all 22 First Division clubs from the Football League and the subsequent formation of the new Premier League as a limited company on 27 May 1992.

But why don't we leave all that to the historians for now? The purpose of this book is to celebrate 20 years of top-flight football in England and the 100 'Legends' (plus 45 'Club Legends') that have made our game the envy of the world and *we* are taking Saturday 15 August 1992 as our starting point.

At about 3.05pm that afternoon, Sheffield United striker Brian Deane glided between Steve Bruce and Gary Pallister to head a flick-on past Peter Schmeichel. Deane had just scored the first Premier League goal. Aston Villa winger Marc Albrighton scored the 20,000th in December 2011.

Essentially the same product, despite the best attempts of FIFA to change halves into quarters and make the nets bigger, football in England was broken down, rebuilt and repackaged with a big-budget advertising campaign based around the slogan 'It's a whole new ball game.' It certainly was ...

One of the ads featured a player from every team in the inaugural season. It was an unlikely line-up featuring household names of the time such as Peter Beardsley (Everton), Lee Sharpe (Manchester United) and Vinnie Jones (Chelsea), alongside others that would never quite live up to their star billing – Carl Bradshaw (Sheffield United), Alan Kernaghan (Middlesbrough) and Ian Butterworth (Norwich City) perhaps.

The ad, filmed in a huge mansion, featured a shower scene with eight naked players including Tim Sherwood (Blackburn Rovers) and Gordon Durie (Tottenham), Gordon Strachan (Leeds) having a massage and being offered built-up training shoes, David Seaman and Anders Limpar (both Arsenal) playing football in the garden and being brought breakfast in bed by a glamorous woman, respectively, and Paul Stewart (in transit between Tottenham and Liverpool at the time) driving his own Porsche.

The message was simple. Football was the new rock 'n' roll and footballers the new mega-rich celebrity superstars.

The turnover after the end of the first season of the new Premier League in 1993 was £46 million – less than Chelsea paid for Fernando Torres last year – with an aggregate attendance of 9.75 million. In 2012, the organisation signed a new TV deal worth £3.018 billion (ten times the first deal), excluding world rights, while the season before last, despite rising ticket prices and a global recession, posted an aggregate attendance of 13.4 million.

But it was not all blind optimism on that sunny day 20 years ago when the Premier League kicked off. England had just failed at yet another major tournament, and the best English players were moving abroad (Gary Lineker to Japan; David Platt, Des Walker and – eventually – Paul Gascoigne all to Italy).

Off the pitch, hooliganism was on the wane, but there were plenty of fans who resented the move away from terracing to all-seater stadia, the new back-pass rule, rescheduled matches (Everton even offered to refund all season ticket-holders who could not make a Monday night game) and the fact that, after the exclusive deal negotiated by BSkyB, they would now have to pay to watch live football from their armchair.

Indeed, Paul Hawksbee (then editor of seminal football weekly *90 Minutes* magazine and now one half of the brilliant Hawksbee and Jacobs afternoon talkSPORT show) had a moan in his '90 Minutes Say ...' slot in the week BSkyB announced the fixtures they planned to broadcast up until Christmas.

He was upset about the 'hassle and expense of having a satellite dish fitted (*and* having to fork out six quid a month for a subscription to Sky Sports – they kept quiet about that didn't they?)' and had trouble seeing 'the likes of Ford and Gillette clambering to bag a half-time slot in a Monday night QPR v Oldham showdown'. He has since revised his opinion.

A Premier League launch event at the Midland Hotel in Manchester, however, was a glitzy affair with attractive young ladies in the kits of the 22 clubs handing out goody-bags to the assembled reporters – of whom I was one. Inside the bag was a transistor radio branded with the new Premier League logo. Today it would be an iPad. You have no idea how old that makes me feel.

On that first round of games in August 1992, there were only 12 foreign players (not including the Republic of Ireland) representing Premier League clubs*, in the 2011-12 season just over 60 per cent of the players starting Premier League matches on any particular weekend were foreign, and much of the best talent in the world now comes here. Many of those have made our list of 100 'Legends', some just failed to make the cut. Robert Pires (Arsenal) was unlucky. As was English born-and-bred Neil 'Razor' Ruddock (clubs various).

A 'Legend' in this instance is someone who excites debate and/or who

---

*They were: Eric Cantona, Andrei Kanchelskis and Peter Schmeichel (all Manchester United); Craig Forrest (Ipswich Town); Gunnar Halle (Oldham Athletic); John Jensen and Anders Limpar (both Arsenal); Roland Nilsson (Sheffield Wednesday); Ronnie Rosenthal (Liverpool); Hans Segers (Wimbledon); Michel Vonk (Manchester City) and Robert Warzycha (Everton).

changed the game and is impossible to forget. If it were based purely on footballing ability and honours won, then there would be places for Jens Lehmann (Arsenal), Denis Irwin (Manchester United) and Michael Essien (Chelsea), but it's about more than that.

A Premier League 'Legend' has to have made a major contribution to the game as it is celebrated today. Be it through breathtaking brilliance at a world-class level (almost all of the 100 main entries, to be honest), sheer impact (Tony Yeboah springs to mind) and consistency (Brad Friedel, perhaps) – sometimes a combination of all three. Perhaps full-backs have been unfairly discriminated against in this list, but the two who made the top 100 are/were undoubtedly the best in the world in that position in their prime – besides, the 'Club Legends' section might be worth a look.

But it is not just about players. Managers, chairmen, owners and broadcasters all feature. There's even a referee in there. Sorry about that.

And that is because the Premier League is not all about the superstars and their WAGs. They may grab the headlines, but every club has its own 'Legends' and so there is a separate section at the back of the book featuring one person from every club to have played at least one season in the Premier League. Selected with the help of the many fan forums on the net (in 1992, you would have had to set the video to record *Inspector Morse* and attend supporters' club meetings up and down the country) these are not just here to make up the numbers. They are 'Legends' in their own right.

Some were only given a brief time to shine, but they took their moment and will live on in the hearts and minds of the people who loved to watch them play and/or owe them a debt of gratitude. Your personal favourite may not be there but, as seasoned cliché-watchers will attest, football is all about opinions – like the decision to leave out Joey Barton (QPR), who certainly excites debate but is hardly a 'Legend' (even though he would probably disagree), and there are already too many words written about him – usually by old 'Hashtag' himself.

For a large percentage of the last 20 years, Paul Gascoigne has been the most famous English player, but his exclusion is due to the fact that it is what you achieved in the Premier League that counts – when reference is made of heroic cup and European feats, and there are many, it is taken that the player concerned is representing a Premier League club.

Gazza left in 1992 and reappeared only when he was past his glorious best. Other players you may feel have missed out, such as Joe Hart and David Silva (Manchester City), Gareth Bale (Tottenham) or Danny Welbeck (Manchester United), have not had long enough, but, at the current rate of progress, will surely be included in the book to celebrate the 'Legends' of the last 25 years.

We've used ten writers and, like spectators, they take different things from the game. Some prefer the drama, some the sense of occasion or the absurd and others the stats, but I've tried to provide as broad a spectrum as possible. Every entry also pinpoints when the person concerned became a 'Legend', something you didn't know about them and a quote that hits the nail on the head.

Enjoy the book.

Bill

Bill Borrows

talkSPORT STARS' LEGENDS

IAN 'THE MOOSE' ABRAHAMS

All-time Premier League Legend?
Paolo di Canio

Why him?
He had incredible skill, unpredictability and could produce a moment of skill unlike anybody else.

Most memorable Premier League moment?
Di Canio's volley against Wimbledon.

Who shouldn't be on the list?
Graham Poll, with respect to Graham: when did anyone ever pay money to see him?

Favourite Premier League moment?
Eric Cantona's kung-fu kick and his 'Seagulls follow the trawler' comments.

My all-time Premier League XI
Peter Schmeichel; Gary Neville, Tony Adams, Rio Ferdinand, Ashley Cole; David Beckham, Dennis Bergkamp, Ryan Giggs; Paolo di Canio, Eric Cantona, Gianfranco Zola. Subs: Thierry Henry, Cristiano Ronaldo, Paul Scholes.

ALAN BRAZIL

All-time Premier League Legend?
Dennis Bergkamp

Why him?
He had everything: great touch, vision and he was the best all-round player of the last 20 years.

Most memorable Premier League moment?
Bergkamp making Newcastle United's Dabizas look stupid, the cheek of it ...

Who shouldn't be on the list?
Stan Collymore – because he makes me feel old.

My all-time Premier League XI
Peter Schmeichel; Gary Neville, Sol Campbell, Rio Ferdinand, Ashley Cole; Paul Scholes, Roy Keane; Matt Le Tissier; Alan Shearer, Dennis Bergkamp, Thierry Henry. Subs: Patrick Vieira, Gianfranco Zola, Ryan Giggs.

STAN COLLYMORE

All-time Premier League Legend?
Gianfranco Zola

Why him?
He was a superb striker and changed the way we thought about foreign players. He had that little something else, more than magic – he was like [Thierry] Henry plus unpredictability.

Most memorable Premier League moment?
I'm going to have to be a little self-indulgent here. It has to be the 4–3 against Newcastle for Liverpool. Sometimes when you play in a fantastic game, you come off the pitch and know you've been involved in something special. It was two sets of teams full of attacking talent. Both teams were still going for the title and there it was, the winner in the last minute, right in front of the Kop.

Who shouldn't be on the list?
Vinnie Jones – It was Wimbledon–Liverpool and there was a massive ruck … Jones came over and threw a haymaker and was sent off. He subsequently had his red card overturned because the ref didn't see it, but let me assure you he did it all right [laughs]. I was drinking through a straw for a week.

Favourite Premier League moment?
Just because about three or four teams have dominated the Premier League for so long, I think I'm going to go for Manchester City winning the title at the Etihad last year. I was commentating and the fans were crying around us, thinking 'Here we go again', but just as you were thinking 'this can't happen', it happened. Incredible. From despair to disbelief. It was surreal.

My all-time Premier League XI
Peter Schmeichel; Gary Neville, Nemanja Vidic, Rio Ferdinand, Ashley Cole; David Beckham, Patrick Vieira, Steven Gerrard, Ryan Giggs; Thierry Henry, Alan Shearer. Subs: Gianfranco Zola, Dennis Berkamp, Frank Lampard.

IAN DANTER

All-time Premier League Legend?
Dennis Bergkamp

Why him?
His impact at Arsenal was so subtle yet so influential over time – Gunners fans knew how special he was, but the rest of us discovered the same thing by degrees. Possessed possibly the best first touch of any footballer I've ever seen.

Most memorable Premier League moment?
That incredible piece of skill at St James' Park in 2002. He touched the ball with the outside of his boot and, as it ran on, he pirouetted around a bewildered Nikos Dabizas and finished emphatically.

Who shouldn't be on the list?
David Ginola – not because he wasn't a great, skilful player, because he was. It's just because he once turned down my perfectly reasonable request to interview him after he'd scored a winner for Villa. No need for that … unless he knew I was a Bluenose, that is.

Favourite Premier League moment?
The Sergio Aguero goal to win the title for Manchester City in 2012. I was at Stoke, filing a report off-air as Bolton had been relegated. It went something like: 'Sorensen did brilliantly late on to deny Tim Ream's firm header from a … F*CKING HELL FIRE HE'S DONE IT!!!!'

My all-time Premier League XI
Peter Schmeichel; Gary Neville, Sol Campbell, John Terry, Ashley Cole; David Beckham, Patrick Vieira, Steven Gerrard; Dennis Bergkamp, Alan Shearer, Ryan Giggs. Subs: Eric Cantona, Christian Dugarry, Thierry Henry.

ADRIAN DURHAM

All-time Premier League Legend?
Steven Gerrard

Why him?
He's English, he's influential, he's iconic, he's a leader and a brilliant footballer. Not many in the list have all those qualities. He's a consistently brilliant performer and arguably the greatest player ever to play for one of England's biggest clubs.

Most memorable Premier League moment?
Gerrard's hat-trick in a Mersey derby in 2011-12. It didn't contribute to anything spectacular, but it was a big moment for a scouser.

Who shouldn't be on the list?
Jeff Stelling. Great guy and great at what he does, but he's not talkSPORT and didn't play in the Premier League.

Favourite Premier League moment?
The stunning climax to the 2011-12 season. Manchester City scoring two goals in injury time to seal a title Manchester United thought was theirs. Incredible.

My all-time Premier League XI
Peter Schmeichel; Sol Campbell, John Terry, Jaap Stam; Darren Anderton, Roy Keane, Frank Lampard, Paul Scholes; Thierry Henry, Michael Owen, Steve McManaman.

ANDY GRAY

All-time Premier League Legend?
Alan Shearer

Why him?
As a goalscorer I'm always looking for people who can score goals – and he was one of them. He is the Premier League's top goalscorer of all time, and the only person in Premier League history to score 30 league goals three years running.

Most memorable Premier League moment?
When Shearer was at Blackburn and battling Manchester United for the title. It was the year Blackburn won the race and it was their biggest test. Alan Shearer scored the header for them to win the title – a great moment.

Who shouldn't be on the list?
I wouldn't throw anyone off the list.

Favourite Premier League moment?
Liverpool v Newcastle. Kevin Keegan was going for the title, Newcastle went to Anfield in midweek and there was a goal in the first minute, and a winner by Stan Collymore in stoppage time, plus five other goals in between. A brilliant game.

My all-time Premier League XI
Peter Schmeichel; Gary Neville, Tony Adams, John Terry, Ashley Cole; Cristiano Ronaldo, Steven Gerrard, Paul Scholes, Ryan Giggs; Alan Shearer, Thierry Henry. Subs: Rio Ferdinand, Roy Keane, Gianfranco Zola.

PAUL HAWKSBEE

All-time Premier League Legend?
David Ginola

Why him?
Because he's worth i ... Sorry. Because, for three glorious years, he lit up White Hart Lane, reminded me why I became a Spurs supporter in the first place and almost made my season ticket feel like a bargain. Almost.

Most memorable Premier League moment?
Delia. No need to explain any further. 'A message to the greatest football supporters in the world. Where are you?' Gold.

Who shouldn't be on the list?
Vinnie Jones. For *that* tackle on Gary Stevens – and for *Smokin' Aces 2: Assassin's Ball.*

Favourite Premier League moment?
Beckham's halfway line goal against Wimbledon in 1996. I don't think any of us realised at that moment what a huge figure he would become, or how he and his missus would dominate our every waking hour for the next 15 years.

My all-time Premier League XI
Peter Schmeichel; Gary Neville, Ledley King, Paul McGrath, Ashley Cole; David Beckham, Roy Keane, Steven Gerrard, David Ginola; Gianfranco Zola, Thierry Henry. Subs: Alan Shearer, Ryan Giggs, Matt Le Tissier.

MATT HOLLAND

All-time Premier League Legend?
Ryan Giggs

Why him?
The only player to have played and scored in every Premier League season. He has the most Premier League titles (12) and has the most appearances and assists in Premier League history.

Most memorable Premier League moment?
When Roy Keane stuck up for Gary Neville in the tunnel at Highbury and confronted Patrick Vieira, saying we'll sort it out on the pitch. United went on to win the game 4-2.

Who shouldn't be on the list?
Delia Smith. I am sure she is a lovely lady, and would cook me a great meal, but the fact she is connected to the team across the border [Norwich] means she has to go!

Favourite Premier League moment?
It was actually voted the best goal in Premier League history. I was at the game commentating when Wayne Rooney scored his overhead kick against Manchester City at Old Trafford.

My all-time Premier League XI
Peter Schmeichel; Gary Neville, Tony Adams, Rio Ferdinand, Ashley Cole; Cristiano Ronaldo, Roy Keane, Paul Scholes, Ryan Giggs; Thierry Henry, Alan Shearer. Subs: Eric Cantona, Steven Gerrard, Patrick Vieira.

ANDY JACOBS

All-time Premier League Legend?
Jose Mourinho

Why him?
He's the greatest manager in Chelsea's history, and he brought the club its first league title in 50 years.

Most memorable Premier League moment?
The time when Mourinho threw away his league medal after Chelsea won a second successive Premier League title.

Who shouldn't be on the list?
Thierry Henry – I couldn't stand the way he celebrated – he looked so arrogant.

Favourite Premier League moment?
Sergio Aguero's goal to win the title for Manchester City last season.

My all-time Premier League XI
Petr Cech; Lee Dixon, Ricardo Carvalho, John Terry, Ashley Cole; Frank Lampard, Steven Gerrard, Paul Scholes; Didier Drogba, Thierry Henry, Gianfranco Zola. Subs: Rio Ferdinand, Wayne Rooney, Emile Heskey.

ALVIN MARTIN

All-time Premier League Legend?
Thierry Henry

Why him?
Because he was special over so many years. At his best, he looked like a man playing among boys. He had grace, pace and was not solely reliant on good service to be effective.

Most memorable Premier League moment?
Phillipe Albert's chip versus Manchester United when Newcastle won 5-0.

Who shouldn't be on the list?
Duncan Ferguson – he broke my nose.

Favourite Premier League moment?
Dennis Bergkamp's goal versus Newcastle – sheer class.

My all-time Premier League XI
Peter Schmeichel; Gary Neville, John Terry, Nemanja Vidic, Ashley Cole; Steven Gerrard, Paul Scholes; Cristiano Ronaldo, Alan Shearer, Thierry Henry, Ryan Giggs. Subs: Tony Adams, David Beckham, Didier Drogba.

MICK QUINN

All-time Premier League Legend?
Alan Shearer

Why him?
He's been the most complete striker in the Premier League. All strikers have strengths and weaknesses, but he had an all-round game: a good head, good on the ball, and he could get you 20 goals or more a season while bringing others into play.

Most memorable Premier League moment?
When Shearer turned down Manchester United to join his hometown club, Newcastle United.

Who shouldn't be on the list?
Eric Cantona – I don't agree with kung-fu kicking the crowd.

Favourite Premier League moment?
When Keegan lost it with Alex Ferguson on live TV – Manchester United challenged Newcastle for the title, the pressure was on and Keegan lost the war of words and his head live on TV.

My all-time Premier League XI
Brad Friedel; Gary Neville, Rio Ferdinand, Tony Adams, Ashley Cole; Steven Gerrard, Patrick Vieira, Cesc Fabregas; Cristiano Ronaldo, Alan Shearer, Wayne Rooney. Subs: Jamie Carragher, Ian Wright, Ryan Giggs.

MARK SAGGERS

All-time Premier League Legend?
Eric Cantona

Why him?
He had everything and more, plus attitude. He also knew when it was time to finish.

Most memorable Premier League moment?
After the kung-fu kick, Cantona's goal against Liverpool at Old Trafford on his return from suspension and community service showed he could cope with a pressure moment.

Who shouldn't be on the list?
Throw out Keys and Gray. When did they play?

Favourite Premier League moment?
When Rupert Murdoch had the vision to change the live TV football format from a tired, out-of-date First Division to a brand new exciting Premier League. Without it none of the rest would have happened.

My all-time Premier League XI
Peter Schmeichel; Gary Neville, Tony Adams, John Terry, Ashley Cole; Steven Gerrard, Patrick Vieira, Roy Keane, Ryan Giggs; Ruud van Nistelrooy, Dennis Bergkamp. Subs: Petr Cech, Paul Scholes, Thierry Henry.

100 FAUSTINO ASPRILLA

PREMIER LEAGUE DEBUT:
Newcastle United v Middlesbrough,
10 February 1996

PREMIER LEAGUE CLUB:
Newcastle United

PREMIER LEAGUE APPEARANCES/GOALS:

Newcastle U	48	9
Total	48	9

PREMIER LEAGUE HONOURS:
None

COUNTRY:
Colombia (born Tulua, 10 November 1969)

EVEN IN THESE cosmopolitan times, when every Premier League squad contains players rotating furiously between central midfield and the Central African Republic, the sheer exoticism of a man from Colombia arriving in the North East deserves to be remembered. Indeed, as he appeared in the midst of a St James' Park snowstorm in a fur coat borrowed from the set of a Blaxploitation film, his arrival remains impossible to forget.

Asprilla hailed from the dreamily distant, richly associative land of cocaine, murderous drug barons and the martyred Andrés Escobar, a close friend – but this was 1996. Anyone would have thought Newcastle had never clapped eyes on a South American before, when in fact the club had already provided a stage for George Robledo (Chile) in the 1950s and Mirandinha (Brazil) in the 1980s.

THE MOMENT HE BECAME A LEGEND

He played his best-ever game for Newcastle in the 1997-98 Champions League campaign, scoring a hat-trick at St James' Park in a 3-2 victory over Barcelona. Typically, they proved the last goals he ever scored for Newcastle, as Dalglish sold him back to Parma for £6 million.

However, neither managed to inspire quite the personality cult that lay in wait for Faustino 'Tino' Asprilla.

Named for the fabled anti-hero who sold his soul to the Devil, Faustino was a self-confessed playboy with a penchant for firearms and ladies, who spoke hardly a word of English. Signed from Parma for £6.7 million to boost Kevin Keegan's attack late in 1995-96, the boss introduced his brand-new secret weapon to his table-topping team-mates over a matchday lunch.

Having downed a glass of wine and a high-protein all-you-can-eat feast (his appetite was renowned), he hand-signalled surprise at the offer of a place on the bench against Middlesbrough later the same day. Supremely unprepared, gloved and all but buried in a standard-issue XXXL shirt, he spun wearily past Boro's flabbergasted full-back to lay on the equaliser, and steal the show with his apparently lazy, eccentric skills in a great win.

Still nine points clear of Manchester United, with just 13 games to go, and a new attacking hero up front, surely nothing could go wrong with Keegan's glorious Premier League title assault ...

Sadly, the Beardsley–Ferdinand goal machine was unsettled by Asprilla's introduction, and although there were three cracking back-flipping, fist-pumping goal celebrations in the run-in, the Colombian was widely blamed for the infamous collapse. The next season ended with disappointment once more and another runners-up spot to Manchester United, punctuated with great performances in the UEFA Cup. But the following year, new manager Kenny Dalglish, intent upon breaking up the team he inherited, got rid of David Ginola, Peter Beardsley, Les Ferdinand and, of course Asprilla. Newcastle finished 13th.

Derek Hammond

IN 2004 AND with newly promoted Norwich struggling in the Premier League, Ipswich Town fanzine *Meet Me At Sir Alf* kindly brought out a T-shirt featuring the Canaries' benefactor and most famous fan, Delia Smith, wearing an Ipswich rosette in 1978, the year the Tractor Boys reached the FA Cup final. Smith is still trying to explain the incident away over 30 years later. 'Yawn, yawn,' she sighed recently, 'I was working for [children's TV programme] *Swap Shop* and the joke was my rosette and hat were turned round to reveal the Norwich colours, amidst very loud booing as we were filming in Christchurch Park in Ipswich.'

> ## THE MOMENT SHE BECAME A LEGEND
>
> 'A message for the best football supporters in the world: we need a twelfth man here. Where are you? Where are you? Let's be 'avin' you! Come on!'
>
> Delia Smith on the pitch at half time, live on Sky Sports in 2005.

The fact that she was targeted and that it is still a source of irritation demonstrates her passion for the club she effectively saved from bankruptcy in 1996 by becoming joint major shareholder with her husband Michael Wynn-Jones. The following year she created the award-winning Delia Smith Catering at Carrow Road that still provides a valuable revenue stream.

In business circles there is a phenomenon called 'The Delia Effect' – for example, a firm that made omelette pans had to increase annual production from 200 to 90,000 four months after her recommendation. In football terms, the attendances at Carrow Road have not quite undergone such a dramatic up-turn, but the highest before her involvement with the club was 21,843 and is now a fairly consistent 26,000.

The couple have also ploughed in over £12 million of their own money, earned chiefly by sales of over 21 million recipe books and several successful TV series. Norwich, after promotion to the

> ## WELL I NEVER ...
>
> The TV cook had 'had some wine with [my] lunch' and experienced difficulty walking on the pitch because she was wearing heels, but was completely sober when she made her famous 'Let's be 'avin' you' exhortation.

99 DELIA SMITH

PREMIER LEAGUE DEBUT (OWNER):
Norwich City v Crystal Palace,
14 August 2004

PREMIER LEAGUE CLUB (OWNER):
Norwich City

PREMIER LEAGUE MATCHES (OWNER*):
Norwich C   76
Total   76

PREMIER LEAGUE HONOURS:
None

COUNTRY:
England (born Woking, 18 June 1941)
* technically, she is joint major shareholder

top tier in 2003 followed by instant relegation and then relegation once more and then consecutive promotions under highly rated manager Paul Lambert, are once again a respected mid-table Premier League side.

Now 71, has her dedication to the cause begun to wane? 'If [Lambert] ever wanted to leave,' she declared last year. 'I would lie down in Carrow Road and prevent his car from leaving.' So that'll be a 'No', then – and that wasn't a speed bump he hit on the way to Villa Park.

Bill Borrows

QUOTE

'If I can share with you my own deep joy that I have, thanks to Paul Langbert [sic] and the players and the backroom staff, is that this football club is now financially secure. Next time you have a glass, just toast staying up and think of this wonderful thing, we haven't got to go in the frigging play-offs next year.'

Smith addresses the faithful from the balcony of Norwich City Hall after promotion in 2011.

98 JAY-JAY OKOCHA

PREMIER LEAGUE DEBUT:
Bolton Wanderers v Fulham,
17 August 2002

PREMIER LEAGUE CLUB:
Bolton Wanderers

PREMIER LEAGUE APPEARANCES/GOALS:

Bolton W	124	14
Total	124	14

PREMIER LEAGUE HONOURS:
None

COUNTRY:
Nigeria (born Enugu, 14 August 1973)

JAY-JAY ('So good they named him twice') Okocha was a prodigy, developing his 'Sombrero Flick' even before he joined Nigeria's Enugu Rangers as a youngster. Like so many African footballers before him, Augustine Azuka Okocha learned on the streets with anything that resembled a ball – a training that would later serve him well in a professional career that began in Germany and took in Eintracht Frankfurt before a move to Fenerbahce in Turkey in 1996.

While at the Commerzbank-Arena, he grabbed attention by way of a devastating humiliation of Karlsruhe goalkeeper Oliver Kahn – it was a goal of the season contender that left the usually super-confident German number one visibly shaken. In Istanbul, he scored 30 goals in 60 appearances, took out Turkish

THE MOMENT HE BECAME A LEGEND

That 'Sombrero Flick' against Arsenal in April 2003. He receives the ball by the corner flag in the 96th minute and pulls off an absurd, over-himself scoop, beats the second man while actually off the field before executing a shimmy to send a third opponent four feet the wrong way.

citizenship under the name of Muhammet Yavuz and then engineered a move worth over £15 million to Paris St Germain in 1998.

By 2002, the well-travelled attacking midfielder was approaching his 30s and was thought by many to be past it, so Bolton Wanderers took him on a free in the summer – perhaps the best piece of business in Premier League history. And so, in the unlikely setting of the Reebok Stadium, on a retail park at the side of the M61, Jay-Jay Okocha set about proving his boast: 'I believe when I've got the ball I decide what happens and you can never know what I'm thinking about. That's my strength.'

In his first season with Bolton, he spearheaded an improbable escape from relegation with seven goals, most of them spectacular; and in the second he was made captain. A highlights package of his time at Bolton would include a swerving free-kick with the outside of his foot against Aston Villa, another piece of trickery that simultaneously left David Beckham on his backside and Roy Keane kicking fresh air and a 60-yard run and volley against West Ham.

Okocha was the great anti-utilitarian of British football, a living rebuke to those dunderheaded Gradgrinds in the wretched fool's gold mine of the ten-yard square pass. There is a reason it's called the beautiful game, and it has nothing to do with Vinnie Jones or Ray 'Butch' Wilkins.

Frank Carney

WELL I NEVER ...

Okacha is name-checked in the song 'Paper Planes' by M.I.A. (feat. Afrikan Boy): 'I'm a legend, something like Jay-Jay Okocha.' The former national team captain also has a stadium named after him in the Delta State region of Nigeria.

QUOTE

'I created that one, it's my move and I can tell you exactly where [Luís Nazário de Lima] Ronaldo picked it up from, it was during the Olympic Games in 1996 and I did it against Brazil, that's where he saw it.'

Okocha trademarks his famous 'roll and step' move.

FOOTBALL TENDS to nurture two broad categories of goalkeeper. Perhaps the most prominent are the error-prone sensationalists (think David Seaman) and then there are the pragmatists – unheralded players with an innate understanding of angles (and even the meaning of the sigmoid curve), an unflappable disposition and often a ledger detailing their career statistics. They might not earn their team points with a stoppage-time wondersave, but they won't lose them any by chucking one in their own net either. Think Brad Friedel.

Saying that the American first arrived on these shores for a trial with Nottingham Forest in 1993 only becomes notable when you realise that, at that time, anxious goalkeepers were coming to terms with the fact that the new back-pass rule meant that they suddenly needed to be able to control a ball with their feet. Then there was the physical contest. 'When I first arrived, if you ventured one millimetre out of your six-yard box it was fair game,' Friedel recently recalled. 'People could smash you all over the place.'

He survived, though, and longevity has since become the key feature of his career. The 41-year-old is by a distance the holder of the record for the most consecutive appearances in the Barclays Premier League; having last missed a game on 15 May 2004, he reached the landmark of 300 consecutive Premier League matches on 14 April 2012 (Pepe Raina is his nearest rival, and he managed just 183 consecutive games). It is a remarkable statistic, even more so given the fact that before his £1.7 million move to Liverpool in 1997, he had been denied a work permit to play for Newcastle United and, later, Sunderland.

He briefly found gainful employment in Denmark and Turkey, and, already a United States international, he returned to England with Liverpool. His lack of first-team action at

> ## THE MOMENT HE BECAME A LEGEND
>
> February 2004. Blackburn Rovers trail 2-1 to Charlton Athletic at The Valley as the clock ticks into the 90th minute. In a desperate search for an equaliser, Friedel goes forward for a corner and adroitly redirects Paul Gallagher's shot into the net from eight yards. Alas, seconds later, Charlton scored again.

> ## WELL I NEVER ...
>
> Friedel was a college contemporary of sprinter Carl Lewis in California and was part of the US team for the 1992 Olympic Games.

PREMIER LEAGUE DEBUT:
Liverpool v Aston Villa, 28 February 1998

PREMIER LEAGUE CLUBS:
Liverpool, Blackburn Rovers, Aston Villa, Tottenham Hotspur

PREMIER LEAGUE APPEARANCES/GOALS:

Liverpool	25	0
Blackburn R	261	1
Aston Villa	114	0
Tottenham H	38	0
Total	438	1

PREMIER LEAGUE HONOURS:
None

COUNTRY:
USA (born Lakewood, 18 May 1971)

Anfield (he made around 30 appearances in all competitions) was due to the managerial flux at the club as much as anything else. Souness (for whom he had played at Galatasaray) had no doubts over his reliability and moved to bring him to Blackburn Rovers early in the 2000-01 season, when the Lancashire side was trying to regain Premier League status.

It was there that he began to cement his reputation; a man-of-the-match display in the 2002 League Cup final victory over Spurs lingering in the mind. An equally fulfilling move to Aston Villa followed in 2008, Friedel maintaining both his flawless appearance record and his consistency, before Harry Redknapp lured the veteran to White Hart Lane in the summer of 2011 and installed him as his first-choice keeper.

Who needs sensational when a man into his fifth decade can make a claim like that?

Richard Winton/Graham Stephenson

> QUOTE
>
> 'Friedel must have got changed in a telephone box. I wouldn't be surprised if when he takes his shirt off there's a blue jersey with an "S" on underneath it.'
>
> Disgruntled Southampton boss
> Gordon Strachan in 2002.

96 EMMANUEL PETIT

PREMIER LEAGUE DEBUT:
Arsenal v Leeds United, 9 August 1997

PREMIER LEAGUE CLUBS:
Arsenal, Chelsea

PREMIER LEAGUE APPEARANCES/GOALS:

Arsenal	85	9
Chelsea	55	2
Total	140	11

PREMIER LEAGUE HONOURS:
1 (1997-98)

COUNTRY:
France (born Dieppe, 22 September 1970)

THE TALL, handsome man with long blond hair strolled into a Monte Carlo casino. It had been a good summer. He'd won the Premier League and FA Cup Double with Arsenal in his first season playing in England. Then he'd helped his nation to their first World Cup win, scoring in the final as France beat Brazil 3-0. He popped a speculative franc into a fruit machine ... and won the equivalent of £17,000. He already had two Mercedes convertibles, a Monaco apartment with a sea view and a stunning former cabaret dancer fiancée. No wonder Emmanuel Petit was dubbed the 'Luckiest Man Alive' in that summer of 1998.

But his fame and fortune almost never happened ...

THE MOMENT HE BECAME A LEGEND

Scoring the third goal in a 3-0 win over Brazil in the 1998 World Cup final.

When he was 18 and had just signed for AS Monaco, his elder brother Olivier collapsed and died while playing football. The family were devastated and Petit almost allowed it to ruin his own life. He stopped seeing his parents and remaining brother, got divorced, and took little interest in his game. 'I hated anything to do with football,' he remembered later. 'I lost all my spirit and became an average player.'

Fortunately, he had a patient and understanding manager at his club in Arsène Wenger, who persisted with a player that he knew was gifted and slowly managed to get him back to a level where he was picking up winners' medals and French caps.

In 1997, Wenger brought Petit to Highbury, converted him from a centre-half into a defensive midfielder and teamed him up with fellow Frenchman Patrick Vieira. The result was instant, glorious success, with the Gunners clinching the Double and Petit repaying his debt to the coach who had kept faith in him.

> ## WELL I NEVER ...
>
> Petit admits he went off the rails after his successes of 1998, witnessing 'unbelievable debauchery' on rich Arabs' yachts and in 'the parallel world of Parisian nights – private soirées, swapping clubs'.

Given that familiar image of the pony-tailed Petit elegantly emerging from a challenge with the ball before indulging in a spot of classy distribution, it seems remarkable that he made only 85 Premier League appearances in three seasons at Arsenal, and never added any further medals to that first flourish.

In the summer of 2000, he moved to Barcelona for £7 million, but a positional move back to defence, a poor relationship with coach Serra Ferrer and a series of injuries made for a miserable season at the Nou Camp. The Premier League was Petit's true stage and after his gap year in Spain he returned to London, retaining his £7 million valuation with a move to Chelsea. In this spell, he was only occasionally at his best. A knee injury eventually brought his career to an end in 2005, but as he could readily appreciate there were worse things in life than retiring with a dodgy knee and a fortune in the bank.

> ## QUOTE
>
> 'I love England, one reason being the magnificent breasts of English girls.'
>
> Petit brings his own interpretation to the *entente cordiale*.

Gary Silke

JAAP STAM stood in the showers as the opening game of the Premier League season raged outside. As water cascaded around him, the intermittent gasps and groans of the Old Trafford crowd offered an audible reminder of what he was missing. The disconsolate Dutchman had failed to emerge for the second half of his league debut.

Signed in a club record £10.6 million deal just weeks earlier, the 26-year-old had endured an inauspicious introduction in a Charity Shield defeat by Arsenal – an unconvincing display remembered chiefly for his inability to shackle Nicolas Anelka – and here he was, the following weekend, being replaced at half time after being taught a lesson by 33-year-old Tony Cottee of Leicester City.

Alex Ferguson had, by common consent, made a terrible mistake. Or so it seemed. By October, however, nobody would remember those difficult early days, as Stam grew into a defensive colossus, the rock upon which any number of attacks foundered. His dead-eyed stare, and the fact that he looked like he just might have been thrown out of the Hell's Angels for unreasonable behaviour, chilled the blood of many a striker.

Stam was, however, much more than a hard man. Recruited to give United a more adaptable defensive presence in continental competition, the Dutchman was excellent positionally, capable of decent distribution and surprisingly quick across the ground for a man of such domineering proportions. He was not without technical gifts, either – consider his solitary goal for the club, an accomplished cushioned volley in a 6-2 rout at Filbert Street.

His celebration of that effort spoke somewhat of his personality. No raised arms or dance-studio choreography, Stam simply sprinted back towards his centre-back position with his bewildered team-mates in tow and his manager chuckling benevolently.

Unfortunately for both parties, the relationship eroded after three

---

THE MOMENT HE BECAME A LEGEND

Highbury, August 1999. A tense Premier League encounter is tied at 1-1 when Roy Keane rattles into Patrick Vieira, causing a confrontation. Within seconds, Stam is upon the Arsenal midfielder, the Dutchman's flared nostrils and crazed eyes sufficient warning for the home players to hurriedly haul their cowering team-mate from danger.

WELL I NEVER ...

In 1998, Mrs Stam had her baby daughter induced two weeks early so she could give birth between the Netherlands' World Cup campaign and Manchester United's pre-season training camp.

95 JAAP STAM

PREMIER LEAGUE DEBUT:
Manchester United v Leicester City, 15 August 1998

PREMIER LEAGUE CLUB:
Manchester United

PREMIER LEAGUE APPEARANCES/GOALS:

Manchester U	78	1
Total	78	1

PREMIER LEAGUE HONOURS:
3 (1998-99, 1999-00, 2000-01)

COUNTRY:
Netherlands (born Kampen, 17 July 1972)

seasons during which the club lifted three titles, an FA Cup and an Intercontinental Cup as well as the Champions League, Ferguson allowing Stam to leave amid unfounded reports of a rift caused by comments in the serialisation of his autobiography in the *Daily Mirror*.

Stam may have alleged that Ferguson made an illegal approach for him and told players to dive in European competition, but that had nothing to do with the decision to sell him two weeks later. 'At the time [Stam] had just come back from an Achilles injury and we thought he had just lost a little bit. We got the offer from Lazio: £16.5 million for a centre-back who was twenty-nine. It was an offer I couldn't refuse.' This time Ferguson really did make a mistake. Unusually perhaps, he has even said so himself.

And so Stam went to Italy, a league for which he had little regard, even if he served both Lazio and AC Milan with distinction – albeit his spell there was marred by a four-month ban after testing positive for nandrolone – before returning home to end his career at Ajax. Not bad for a player who was almost chased out of the Premier League within a week of his arrival.

RW

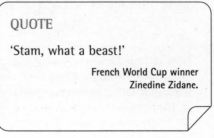

QUOTE

'Stam, what a beast!'

French World Cup winner
Zinedine Zidane.

94 IAN HOLLOWAY

PREMIER LEAGUE DEBUT (MANAGER):
Blackpool v Wigan Athletic, 14 August 2010

PREMIER LEAGUE CLUB (MANAGER):
Blackpool

PREMIER LEAGUE APPEARANCES (MANAGER):
Blackpool   38
Total   38

PREMIER LEAGUE HONOURS:
None

COUNTRY:
England (born Bristol, 12 March 1963)

BACK IN 1937-38, reigning champions Manchester City scored more goals than any other First Division side and, at the end of the season, were relegated for their troubles. It always seemed a bizarre record that could never be threatened in the modern era – until 2010-11, and the devil-may-care campaign waged by Premier League first-timers Blackpool.

Cue the occurrence of another jaw-dropping football phenomenon: the Seasiders' maverick managerial wild-card, Ian Holloway.

THE MOMENT HE BECAME A LEGEND

After Charlie Adam's midfield vision and goalscoring touch had lit up Blackpool's season, it was Ollie's final word that stole the limelight: 'If he's worth four million pounds, I'm a Scotsman called McTavish.' We've no idea either.

As a player, the left-sided up-and-downer demonstrated a fierce determination and loyalty (Holloway spent no less than three spells with his local side Bristol Rovers, spanning 11 of his 18 years as a player, before graduating from player-manager to manager). Not necessarily the best player on the pitch, he made sure there was never any need for a team-talk.

As manager of Queens Park Rangers, Plymouth Argyle and Leicester City, he developed a certain reputation for tactical boldness, a perfect side dish to his *à la carte* eccentricity. After-match quotes from 'Ollie' are part Zen, part idiot-savant, wholly off-message – we knew that, but nothing prepared us for his season-long end-of-pier performance on the Golden Mile, and the ultimate top-flight rollercoaster ride.

On the eve of the season, press reports of Holloway's resignation over his tiny working budget were denied as he introduced four last-gasp signings he'd lured into his patchwork squad of apparent no-hopers: 'Before anyone asks a question,' he said. 'I just want to make sure you can see me – you can see me here and I'm not a cardboard cut-out ...'

Almost incredibly, after the opening match, the Premier League table showed the Seasiders joint top with Chelsea, having thrashed Wigan 4-0. Blackpool weren't here just to make up the numbers. Spanked by six and four by Arsenal and Chelsea, away wins at Newcastle United and Liverpool revealed Holloway's audacious masterplan. Lacking the basic ability to defend against the onslaught of billionaire outfits, Blackpool would go down with all guns blazing, aiming simply to score more than they leaked.

As such, Blackpool became the second team of every English football fan. To gentlemen of a certain age, it was to hell with 'Roy of the Rovers' stuff. This was pure 'Billy's Boots', every game a magical, amateurish, high-scoring bonanza – sound-tracked by the random thoughts of a bald eccentric man from Bristol wearing a big orange tie.

With 15 points from their first 13 matches, Blackpool lost star goalie Matt Gilks to long-term injury, and his slow, elderly, lower-league defence began to creak. Despite the best efforts of the inspired journeymen and Charlie Adam, the Tangerines went down fighting time and again. There were headline wins against the likes of Spurs and Liverpool (again) but, tellingly, Blackpool conceded more goals after the 75th minute than any other team.

Finally going down 4-2 away to Manchester United, no side had ever scored as many goals in a Premier League season – 55, the same as sixth-placed Spurs – and still been relegated. Holloway's attack-attack-attack tactical gambit goes down in history as a glorious but unforgettable failure.   DH

WELL I NEVER ...

Ian and his wife Kim are converts to the self-sufficiency movement, keeping horses, chickens, turkeys and ducks as well as two dogs. 'The fixation started when I got the sack at Leicester. We wanted to be a bit self-sufficient like Tom and Barbara [Good – the characters in 1970s sitcom *The Good Life*].'

QUOTE

'If you're a burglar, it's no good poncing about outside somebody's house, looking good with your swag bag ready. Just get in there, burgle them and come out. I don't advocate that obviously, it's just an analogy.'

Holloway stops digging a hole halfway through and then, in typical style, attempts to climb out.

BORN AND BRED in Leeds, David Batty always held a special place in the hearts of everyone at the club, specifically the fans. He was Leeds United through and through. Leeds Leeds Leeds. Scowling, aggressive, hot-headed – and that's the first time a row of adjectives has ever been employed to describe Batty that neglected to use the term 'terrier-like'. A Yarksher terrier, like. From Leeds.

The association with the club was powerful from the day of his debut, aged 18, when manager Billy Bremner threw his young protégé into the middle of the park. He was instantly accepted as the embodiment of the 'Mighty Leeds' of old. 'I think he saw a lot of himself in me,' Batty has said. 'It was a bit embarrassing at times. I mean, he did genuinely love me. People obviously likened me to him, but it was a great honour to be mentioned in the same breath.'

Having won the last-ever First Division title with Leeds in a midfield that also starred Gary McAllister, Gordon Strachan and Gary Speed, Batty was snapped up by Blackburn Rovers in 1993 to assist in Uncle Jack's ultimately successful pursuit of silverware. He helped the side to runners-up spot in his first season and then, of course, they won the title in 1995; but, sidelined with a broken foot, he refused a medal for his five-game contribution, referring to it as 'minimal'.

Switching to Newcastle United, the England regular's tenacity, work-rate and underrated passing ability once again earned Batty runners-up medals in both 1995-96 and 1996-97. But, like Blackburn, Newcastle just wasn't

> ## THE MOMENT HE BECAME A LEGEND
>
> He failed to score for almost four seasons – 145 games in his initial spell at Leeds. Every time he got the ball in the opponent's half, the entire Leeds crowd would shout at Batty to 'Shooooooooooooot!' – and even miscues would get exaggerated 'Oooohs' and ovations.

> ## WELL I NEVER ...
>
> Batty's dad was a Leeds binman. And David used to help him on his round right up to the close-season of 1991, just before he won his first England cap.

93 DAVID BATTY

PREMIER LEAGUE DEBUT:
Leeds United v Wimbledon, 15 August 1992

PREMIER LEAGUE CLUBS:
Leeds United, Blackburn Rovers,
Newcastle United, Leeds United

PREMIER LEAGUE APPEARANCES/GOALS:

Leeds United	129	1
Blackburn R	54	1
Newcastle U	83	3
Total	266	5

PREMIER LEAGUE HONOURS:
None (refused medal in 1994-95)

COUNTRY:
England (born Leeds, 2 December 1968)

Leeds. And so it came to pass (and tackle, and snap) that the prodigal son returned to Elland Road in 1998 for a second six-year spell at a resurgent Leeds under David O'Leary for £4.4 million. Tellingly, every successive transfer involving Batty saw his value increase.

Despite being hampered by injuries, it was a more mature Batty who helped the club back into the Premier League limelight and to the semi-finals of the UEFA Cup and the Champions League. Back where they belonged – for a brief time. Injury dictated that he played his last game in 2003-04, the season his beloved Leeds were relegated after a spectacular financial collapse. DH

> QUOTE
>
> 'As soon as I came off the pitch I forgot about it. There's more to life than football. Although I was disappointed we were going out, of course ... I just thought I'd get home and see the kids.'
>
> Batty fails to gauge the reaction of the nation after his penalty miss against Argentina at France 98.

92 | STEVE McMANAMAN

PREMIER LEAGUE DEBUT:
Liverpool v Nottingham Forest,
16 August 1992

PREMIER LEAGUE CLUBS:
Liverpool, Manchester City

PREMIER LEAGUE APPEARANCES/GOALS:

Liverpool	240	41
Manchester C	35	0
Total	275	41

PREMIER LEAGUE HONOURS:
None

COUNTRY:
England (born Liverpool, 11 February 1972)

WITH HIS floppy mop of ginger hair, his pale, weedy frame and seemingly oversized boots, Steve McManaman looked an unlikely candidate to terrorise Premier League defences. But when the ball rolled to his feet and he slammed into gear, he was unstoppable. He was also gloriously consistent.

His stock-in-trade was to cut in from the wing, make a bee-line towards goal, a hapless defender three yards ahead with no idea whether he was going left or right, and arrive at the edge of the box before casually letting loose a rocket that always – or always seemed to – go in off the inside of the post. That was unless, of course, McManaman – the player who until 2011 held the record for most career Liverpool assists – laid the ball directly into the path of Robbie

THE MOMENT HE BECAME A LEGEND

His on-field handbags with Bruce Grobelaar in September 1993 when he was accused by the Liverpool keeper of a very poor clearance, which led to an Everton goal in the derby.

Fowler or Michael Owen to achieve exactly the same result with a more perfunctory finish from five yards out.

This is how McManaman should be remembered: a brilliant winger and the creative driving force of the Liverpool side from the beginning to the end of the 1990s. His manager Roy Evans called him 'a genius'.

However, in February 1995, an interview with himself and Fowler appeared in a lads' mag and, when the papers got hold of it, helped to start a backlash against the newly wealthy Premier League stars. 'If you see something in a shop you fancy,' McManaman explained with childlike wonder, 'You can just go in and buy it.' Along with Fowler's pension plans, that didn't play well with the fans.

> ## WELL I NEVER ...
>
> McManaman was a dyed-in-the-wool Evertonian as a kid. And still is. 'If I had a son, I would bring him up an Everton fan.'

But the tabloids didn't focus on 'Macca's' naïve alignment with Liverpool fans – 'We're all the same people, no matter what anyone says.' Instead, the legend of the Anfield 'Spice Boys' was born: white Armani suits at the 1996 FA Cup final, fast cars, debauched Christmas parties but, most of all, no serious silverware to silence the critics. Oh, and McManaman shared an agent with the Spice Girls ...

Having arrived at Anfield just as Liverpool's era of league domination ended, McManaman eventually won the trophies to match his talent at Real Madrid, but only after a protracted contractual saga that did nothing for his popularity on Merseyside. He returned to the Premier League in 2003, when Kevin Keegan signed him for Manchester City. Already at the club were Robbie Fowler and David James, leading to inevitable 'Spice Boys Reunion' headlines.

GS

> ## QUOTE
>
> 'He reminds me of me when I was playing. I wish there were more dribblers like him.'
>
> Sir Stanley Matthews on McManaman's display in the 1995 League Cup final.

THERE AREN'T too many appearances made by bottom-half dwellers in this cavalcade of big-league barnstormers. If you've got what it takes in the heroic stakes and happen to play for a club outside the Top 10, tradition now demands that you tend to sign up sharpish for a more powerful club's 50-man squad, gratefully taking your place as a small cog in a large, slowly rotating machine.

During his five-year Premier League pomp, Bullard was anything but a bit-part player. His hair a tousled, sweaty mop, his knees like knots in cotton, this pasty-faced son of East Ham roved around the pitch on the lookout for fancy-dan scalps, unlikely shooting opportunities and unbridled fun. Pure fizzing danger, he tackled, he dribbled, he shot and sometimes even scored from unfeasible distances.

But one tell-tale characteristic immediately set him apart: just when it seemed as though all the character, all the wide-eyed swagger and irreverence was being drained from the game, here was a geezer acting the giddy goat. Rejected by West Ham United, his boyhood team, he was picked up, appropriately enough, by Barry Fry at Peterborough United. On to Wigan Athletic and up to the Premier League in 2005, Bullard instantly caught the eye with his inspirational, feel-good drive and good old-fashioned high jinks.

How we treasure that all-time favourite *Soccer AM* clip of Bullard looking up like a school kid at the bristling Duncan Ferguson, unsure whether to go for a joke and lighten the mood, or to run and hide. And that

THE MOMENT HE BECAME A LEGEND

When the floodlights failed against Arsenal in February 2006, Bullard ran the length of the Wigan pitch so that when the lights came back on he was standing alone with the ball on the Gunners' goal line.

WELL I NEVER ...

While golfing in Portugal in the 2006 close season, scratch player Jimmy drove into the garden of a villa, from which Newcastle United's Scott Parker emerged unexpectedly to point out his tricky lie. Three games into the season, another chance meeting between the pair resulted in the dislocation of Bullard's kneecap. There is no suggestion that two events were related.

91 JIMMY BULLARD

PREMIER LEAGUE DEBUT:
Wigan Athletic v Chelsea, 14 August 2005

PREMIER LEAGUE CLUBS:
Wigan Athletic, Fulham, Hull City

PREMIER LEAGUE APPEARANCES/GOALS:

Wigan Ath	36	4
Fulham	39	6
Hull City	15	5
Total	90	15

PREMIER LEAGUE HONOURS:
None

COUNTRY:
England (born Newham, 23 October 1978)

headlong stage-dive over a mound of bodies against Everton. And scoring the equaliser at Manchester City before proceeding to mime the half-time on-pitch dressing down the Hull team had received from Phil Brown.

Three world-class games into his Fulham career in 2006, he suffered cruciate knee ligament damage. Worse still, the dislocation injury and other problems with his knees and long lay-offs were recurrent, striking again at Hull City, his next Premier League club, where he arrived in 2009. Despite four squad call-ups from Fabio Capello, the England team was ultimately robbed of a player the fans could not only get behind but actually relate to.

DH

> QUOTE
>
> 'We love Jimmy Bullard. He's one of our favourite players, 'cos first and foremost it is quite clear that he just loves playing football. He loves everything about the game.'
>
> Helen Chamberlain, *Soccer AM* presenter, speaks for the general football public.

90 RAFA BENITEZ

PREMIER LEAGUE DEBUT (MANAGER):
Liverpool v Tottenham Hotspur,
14 August 2004

PREMIER LEAGUE CLUB (MANAGER):
Liverpool

PREMIER LEAGUE APPEARANCES (MANAGER):
Liverpool   228
Total   228

PREMIER LEAGUE HONOURS:
None

COUNTRY:
Spain (born Madrid, 16 April 1960)

LESS THAN TWO weeks after joining Liverpool, Rafael Benitez touched down in sun-drenched Lisbon where unsettled captain Steven Gerrard was reported to have been embroiled in lucrative contract discussions with Chelsea, during Euro 2004. The Spaniard's powers of persuasion eventually shone through, as he left Portugal basking in a significant first triumph in charge. Gerrard was to remain Red.

Three months later, it was Chelsea toasting victory when Liverpool succumbed to a third defeat in seven league games, leaving Benitez and his team cut adrift from a coveted Champions League spot. Qualification eventually arrived, after Liverpool came back from three goals down at half time to beat AC Milan in the Champions League final of 2005. Despite Liverpool's final

THE MOMENT HE BECAME A LEGEND

Half time at the Ataturk Stadium in Istanbul, 25 May 2005. With Liverpool 3-0 down, Benitez changed the formation to play five across the middle and galvanised his team, led by his captain and Man of the Match Steven Gerrard, to take the game to extra time and then win on penalties.

league position of fifth, UEFA felt moved to reward them with the opportunity of defending their title.

Benitez quickly atoned for his early domestic shortcomings by becoming Liverpool's most successful Premier League boss, pushing Manchester United to within four points of glory in 2008-09 and collecting a new club Premier League record of 86 points in the process. Players admired the meticulous pre-match briefings but found the manager difficult to please at times; Gerrard himself confessing to longing for a 'well done' after virtuoso performances.

Unfortunately for Benitez, who had twice lifted La Liga at Valencia ahead of Barcelona and Real Madrid, he found the task of dislodging United and Chelsea beyond him. But he was, at least, prepared to fight. With Liverpool top of the table in January 2009, his passionate rant bemoaning the authorities' apparent preference towards Sir Alex Ferguson, repeatedly referring to his own assertions as 'facts', was well received for echoing what many others had long felt.

There was no fairytale ending, however, and Benitez's reign deteriorated in tandem with his relationship with Liverpool's unpopular new owners, George Gillett and Tom Hicks, until a seventh spot finish in 2009-10 – the first season he'd failed to qualify for Europe's premier competition – resulted in a mutual parting of ways.

Having already accepted a new post at Internazionale, by way of a farewell, he donated £96,000 to the Hillsborough Family Support Group in June 2010 and retains a family home on Merseyside. He has spoken of a dream return to his beloved Liverpool, where the Premier League title remains an elusive goal. As indeed, since his departure, has Champions League qualification.   Chris Mendes

---

WELL I NEVER ...

Benitez has played and studied the game of chess since he was 13, introducing aspects of its strategy into football management.

QUOTE

'I have learnt more from Rafael Benitez than any other coach I have worked with. I am a much better player for the time I've spent working with him and if I do go on to manage at some point in the future, he's the model I'll use in my career.'

An unusually effusive Craig Bellamy
sings the praises of Benitez.

'Ooooooo Balotelli
He's a striker
He's good at darts
He's got an allergy to grass
But when he plays he's f*cking class
He drives around Moss Side with a wallet full of cash'

WELL HE'S certainly made a mark. And nobody can deny that – least of all
the Academy player who allegedly felt one of said projectiles thrown from
a window at the club's Carrington training facility, after which Balotelli
was fined. Then there was Scott
Parker who received, in the words
of Tottenham manager Harry
Redknapp, 'A lovely cut ... a
backheel to the head. I don't
know why you'd do that on a
football pitch ... It's there for
everybody to see; it's not the first
time he's done it.' Balotelli was
fined and suspended.

As Harry says, it's not the first
time he's done several things ...

The word 'allegedly' will oft be
used in this piece, so let's get on with a few of them. Just for legal reasons,
and because it is almost impossible to separate fact from fiction where
Balotelli is concerned, let's just assume everything is alleged. And not
necessarily true. Got it? So here are some of the things he is alleged to
have done:

- Paid over £10,000 in parking fines and had (various) cars impounded
  over 30 times
- Won £25,000 in a casino before giving £1000 to a homeless person
- Became involved in an altercation with several bouncers after
  breaking the no-touching rule at a gentleman's establishment
- Went into a woman's prison in
  Italy because he was 'curious'
  to see what it was like
- Converted the back garden of
  his rented posh Cheshire
  mansion into a quad-bike
  track

Still with me? Thought you might
be. He is the most talked-about
foreign footballer in the top
division since Eric Cantona.

THE MOMENT HE BECAME A LEGEND

When he revealed the famous
'Why always me?' T-shirt after
scoring against Manchester United
in the 6-1 victory at Old Trafford
in October 2011.

WELL I NEVER ...

The 2011 annual fireworks display
at Edenbridge, Kent, witnessed
the burning of a 12ft effigy of the
striker – traditionally, it features a
figure in the public eye who has
'disgraced' himself that year.

89 MARIO BALOTELLI

PREMIER LEAGUE DEBUT:
Manchester City v Arsenal,
24 October 2010

PREMIER LEAGUE CLUB:
Manchester City

PREMIER LEAGUE APPEARANCES/GOALS:

Manchester C	49	19
Total	49	19

PREMIER LEAGUE HONOURS:
1 (2011-12)

COUNTRY:
Italy (born Palermo, 12 August 1990)

- When stopped by the police and asked to explain why he had a pile of cash in his car replied, 'Because I'm rich'
- Drove around Manchester high-fiving City fans after the 6-1 win at Old Trafford in 2011-12
- And, of course famously, as the 'face' of a safety fireworks campaign, either set his house on fire by letting fireworks off in the bathroom, or was certainly in there when his friends perpetrated the deed

But all that's off the pitch. On it, he's got a ratio of almost one goal every two games for City. Given that the 2012 Premier League was won on goal difference, former-player-turned-pundit Gary Neville's prediction ('That lad will either win City the title or lose it for them') may be considered to be prescient. His two against United at Old Trafford were certainly influential. A powerful striker and expert penalty-taker, Balotelli scares the life out of the opposition. And probably some of his team-mates.

Of Ghanaian origin, his birth parents could not afford to look after him, so he was fostered by the Balotellis, an Italian family. Whatever he goes on to do, alleged or otherwise, he will be forever remembered at the Etihad Stadium for providing the assist for Sergio Aguero before the latter won the Premier League for Manchester City against QPR, 44 years after their last title success.

BB

88 SCOTT PARKER

PREMIER LEAGUE DEBUT:
Charlton Athletic v Wimbledon,
26 December 1998

PREMIER LEAGUE CLUBS:
Charlton Athletic, Chelsea, Newcastle United,
West Ham United, Tottenham Hotspur

PREMIER LEAGUE APPEARANCES/GOALS:

Charlton Ath	110	8
Chelsea	15	1
Newcastle U	55	4
West Ham U	109	9
Tottenham H	29	0
Total	318	22

PREMIER LEAGUE HONOURS:
None; FWA Footballer of the Year 2010-11

COUNTRY:
England (born Lambeth, 13 October 1980)

SCOTT PARKER claims to have been born in 1980, but it's hard to believe he isn't an impostor from another footballing age. Just look at the man: the absence of tattoos and jewellery, the smart side parting, the two-shaves-a-day face, the firm jaw that might have been clenched through a hundred German bombing raids as he gathered his young family around him in an Anderson shelter.

And in keeping with his 1950s film-star looks, Parker plays in an old-fashioned manner. There's a pleasing selflessness about the way he scurries, covers, blocks, intercepts, steals, tackles, fills in, stands on the goal-line, puts himself on the line; generally does all the inglorious labouring that allows Bale and Co to reap the plaudits of those who fail to

THE MOMENT HE BECAME A LEGEND

Hammers fans named him their Player of the Year three times in a row starting in 2008-09, the first player since Trevor Brooking to achieve this accolade.

realise that while, in football, possession is nine parts of the law, the other tenth, dispossession, is also vital. Parker is currently England's best dispossesser, a serial offender when it comes to robbing his opponents.

Like Barry, his England rival, at his present club Parker constrains his game for the sake of the team – transforming himself into an ego-free football version of Geoffrey Boycott. He has not, however, always played the modest role he fulfils at Spurs. In lesser teams, he had to be both stopper and creator, not only Stiles with teeth, but also Gascoigne with sense. Parker is now a superlative holding midfielder, the English Makelele.

In addition to his beautifully timed tackling, he is calm, courageous and smart; he turns quickly in the overcrowded madness of the modern midfield, has fine ball control and rarely fails to find his man. Moreover, when distributing the ball, unlike many in his position, he is not torn between the rules of association football and rugby. He can pass forwards as well as back.

His quiet virtues have paid off. At Chelsea, despite playing infrequently on account of their EU midfielder mountain, he was named PFA Young Player of the Year. In 2006, Sky nominated him as the second-best player in England and for the 2010-11 season he was named Footballer of the Year by the Football Writers' Association. He is the finest 1950s half-back to play Premier League football.

Back in the present, Tottenham have won again. As his team-mates don their Italian cashmere and climb into their tank-sized cars, Parker belts up his mac and adjusts his bicycle clips. When the maximum wage goes, he'll upgrade to ten gears.   FC

WELL I NEVER ...

In 1994, the 13-year-old Parker appeared in a McDonald's advert, doing keepy-uppies in his garden.

QUOTE

'We were diabolical, but at half time Scott was inspirational. If you were there, you would have had a tear in your eye.'

Carlton Cole on Parker's half-time talk at Upton Park in 2008-09 when the Hammers were losing 3-0 to West Bromwich Albion. It was either that or an outbreak of conjunctivitis. Either way, they ended up drawing 3-3.

87 JEFF STELLING

PREMIER LEAGUE DEBUT:
Sports Saturday, 20 August 1994

PREMIER LEAGUE CLUBS:
None

PREMIER LEAGUE HONOURS:
None; SJA Sports Broadcaster of the Year (five times)

COUNTRY:
England (born Hartlepool, 15 March 1955)

AS SERIAL rock wife Patsy Kensit once opined while giving a guided tour of her house to a style magazine, 'That's where Liam [Gallagher] sits on Saturday afternoon ... he is mesmerised by that mad programme on Sky where everyone is watching football on tellies you can't see. Honestly, that is the weirdest show I've ever seen – and both my husband and my eldest son are riveted to it every week.'

She was, of course, talking about *Gillette Soccer Saturday*, the show anchored by the ineffably charming and professional Jeff Stelling. And – with four cocksure ex-professional footballers to control, while watching live feeds from a bank of screens, reading out scores from all over the country and bringing in obscure stats about every team from Manchester United to Raith Rovers (or Roath Ravers as he once called them in an extremely rare gaffe) – it takes some anchoring.

'He'll keep at you until you've got nowhere to run,' explains

THE MOMENT HE BECAME A LEGEND

Some time around 2004 when his catchphrase, 'It's all doom and gloom' accompanied by a baleful look to camera, became the basis for a Saturday afternoon drinking game.

former Arsenal great and regular pundit 'Champagne' Charlie Nicholas. 'When [ex-Aston Villa and Bayern Munich player] Alan McInally said somebody was "one of the most unique", Jeff wouldn't let him get away with it. It became a running gag for the rest of the series ... his knowledge is remarkable.' As McInally confirms, 'He's a feisty little bugger. He has all this information coming into his headphones and then he has to stop us laughing and make sure we shut up at the right time. He makes it look easier than it is.'

And, if Stelling's haul of Sports Broadcaster of the Year Awards is any guide, that would seem to be the trick. He has managed to marry authority with an engaging personality and a passion for what he calls, 'Quite simply, the best job in the world.'

After a career in newspapers and local and national radio, he arrived at Sky in 1992 and presented a range of live sports including snooker, darts and horse-racing. 'I'd been round the houses,' is how he puts it. 'But I was in the right place at the right time and when the opportunity arose I thought, "I know just the man for the job" and, thankfully, my boss agreed. It's like most things in life, you need a lot of luck.'

In the show's present format, he's been in the seat for six hours every Saturday since 1998 and is simply irreplaceable.

BB

IT COULD easily have been a strip out of *Scorcher and Score*. A hugely talented, tiny midfield dynamo of just 5ft 5in wings in to England from São Paulo in exotic Brazil. He has the pick of any club in any city in Europe, and yet elects for grey, post-industrial Middlesbrough and their team of eternal losers. He plays football with the kids in the street, and swiftly becomes the greatest player in Boro's history ...

> ## THE MOMENT HE BECAME A LEGEND
>
> A 4-1 home win against Manchester City in December 1995 when Juninho scored his first goal and the Boro fans began to realise just how good he was.

After well over a century of gritty, trophy-less football, recently promoted Middlesbrough suddenly went all glam under Bryan Robson in the mid-1990s. With fellow Brazilian Emerson anchoring Juninho's incredible running and passing, and the Italian Fabrizio 'The White Feather' Ravanelli banging in the goals, Boro more than held their own in the Premier League. And they didn't just reach their first-ever cup final, but also their second in the same season.

In April 1997, Boro met Leicester City in the League Cup final at Wembley. Three weeks earlier, Juninho had destroyed Leicester in a Premier League game at Filbert Street with a performance that made manager Martin O'Neill realise: 'Any notion of leaving Juninho to run free in the final was well and truly put in its place.' He was a marked man, literally. 'They wouldn't let me play!' said Juninho after the game, close to tears of frustration.

After a 1-1 draw, Boro lost the replay at Hillsborough, going on to experience yet more bitter disappointment in the FA Cup final with defeat to Chelsea. Still worse, they suffered an eminently avoidable relegation due to their failure to fulfil a fixture at Blackburn. Fearing that second-tier football would damage his

> ## WELL I NEVER ...
>
> Juninho moved his mum and dad over to live with him in Middlesbrough. We're sure they were very pleased.

86 JUNINHO

PREMIER LEAGUE DEBUT:
Middlesbrough v Leeds United,
4 November 1995

PREMIER LEAGUE CLUB:
Middlesbrough

PREMIER LEAGUE APPEARANCES/GOALS:
Middlesbrough 125 29
Total   125 29

PREMIER LEAGUE HONOURS:
None

COUNTRY:
Brazil (born São Paulo, 22 February 1973)

1998 World Cup prospects with Brazil, the golden boy moved on to Atlético Madrid for £12 million, and the Juninho/Boro love affair was over ... for a while, at least.

Sadly, Juninho broke his leg and missed the World Cup anyway, but was loaned back to Teesside for 24 games in the 1999-00 season, Boro having bounced back into the Premier League. He never quite recaptured that early electrifying form after his break, but the return of the 'Little Fella', as he was known, gave the fans a fantastic lift.

In true comic-book style, he returned to the Riverside once again in the summer of 2002, now with a World Cup winners' medal to his name, enjoying two more seasons in a red shirt. And that's when Boro finally broke their trophy duck, landing the League Cup in 2004 with a 2-1 win over Bolton Wanderers at the Millennium Stadium. It was a victory that an emotional Juninho admitted meant more to him than winning the World Cup.

GS

> QUOTE
>
> 'Why have you included a schoolboy?'
>
> Midfielder Dunga to manager Mario Zagalo when he first saw Juninho training for Brazil.

FOR AN ENTIRE generation of Premier League defenders, the gruesome image of Kevin Davies scrubbing blood off the walls of a butcher's stall and discarding animal carcasses somewhere in the North of England would act as an entirely fitting metaphor for his career.

Happily, it is also how the Bolton Wanderers striker earned a few pounds in his youth. To many of the division's more delicate souls, his role has hardly evolved in the intervening years, but there is much more to his game than just being a big man up front.

Granted, the Premier League's most-booked player remains more than capable of throwing his not unsubstantial bulk around and occasionally voices his disdain for the 'unmanly' sin of diving, but it is easy to forget that Davies barged his way into the national consciousness not as a brawny target man but as a winger in the Chesterfield team that reached the semi-finals of the 1997 FA Cup.

Indeed, it was not until he earned a move to Southampton later that year that he began to play centrally, nine goals in 25 matches attracting the attention, and the apparently unlimited largesse, of Blackburn Rovers. The £7.5 million move was disastrous, Davies scoring just once in 23 matches as the Ewood Park club were relegated. 'It was a poor dressing room, with too many cliques, and I was never happy,' he has since explained. 'Me and Chris Sutton didn't get on.' He returned to Southampton for only a sixth of the fee that they had sold him for. Then, enter Big Sam in 2003.

Allardyce envisaged the by then ample Davies as the pivot around which his Bolton side could be built, and worked on rebuilding his confidence to huge success. His emergence as the man who committed more fouls than anyone else in Premier League

THE MOMENT HE BECAME A LEGEND

April 2008. In a game against West Ham United at the Reebok, one of Davies' fingers became horribly dislocated in a challenge. Unperturbed, he instructed the physio to yank it back into place and went on to score his 100th career goal a few minutes later.

WELL I NEVER ...

His late father Cyril represented Britain in the 1965 Deaflympics in Washington DC.

85 KEVIN DAVIES

PREMIER LEAGUE DEBUT:
Southampton v Bolton Wanderers,
9 August 1997

PREMIER LEAGUE CLUBS:
Southampton, Blackburn Rovers,
Southampton, Bolton Wanderers

PREMIER LEAGUE APPEARANCES/GOALS:

Southampton	107	19
Blackburn R	21	1
Bolton W	316	67
Total	444	87

PREMIER LEAGUE HONOURS:
None

COUNTRY:
England (born Sheffield, 26 March 1977)

history (1000+ and counting) – as well as being one of the most sinned against – eventually led to an England call-up for a European Championships qualifier against Montenegro in 2010.

His brief substitute appearance at Wembley was a window to a different world, one in which England literally brushed aside pesky foreign visitors, as indeed they used to before those damned Hungarians and their intelligent football ruined everything. The view, though, proved not to Fabio Capello's liking. 'I got a call after the squad was announced for the next game explaining they wanted to look at other things,' Davies said. 'I argued back and said I didn't feel I had been given a chance, but I'm delighted to have had even one cap.'

RW

> QUOTE
>
> 'People might look at him and think he's not "England", that he's not fashionable, but he's a proper centre-forward.'
>
> Former Tottenham Hotspur manager Harry Redknapp tells it as it is. As usual.

84 EMILE HESKEY

PREMIER LEAGUE DEBUT:
Leicester City v Queens Park Rangers,
8 March 1995

PREMIER LEAGUE CLUBS:
Leicester City, Liverpool, Birmingham City,
Wigan Athletic, Aston Villa

PREMIER LEAGUE APPEARANCES/GOALS:

Leicester C	124	33
Liverpool	150	39
Birmingham C	68	14
Wigan Ath	82	15
Aston Villa	92	9
Total	516	110

PREMIER LEAGUE HONOURS:
None

COUNTRY:
England (born Leicester, 11 January 1978)

'A DEATH ROW prisoner has been allowed to choose his firing squad ... He has chosen Emile Heskey.'

'Emile Heskey gets a job at a zoo taking care of the tortoises ... Later, the keeper pops back to see how Emile is doing and finds him standing by an empty enclosure, sobbing. "Where have all the tortoises gone?" asks the keeper. Emile shrugs: "I just opened the door and *whooooossh!*."'

'Emile Heskey plans to open a pub when he retires ... He's great at putting shots over the bar.'

Few England internationals have ever split fans' opinion like Emile William Ivanhoe Heskey. As a 'battering ram' front-runner, his game may flatter to deceive; or maybe it is just sadly unappreciated

THE MOMENT HE BECAME A LEGEND

How would the large, shy kid cope with Premier League defences? In Leicester's first home game of the 1996-97 season, he fired home both goals in a 2-1 win against Southampton, including one into the top right-hand corner.

by all except the likes of Martin O'Neill and Fabio Capello. Is Heskey deceptively slow or deceptively fast, sure-footed or clumsy? An £11 million transfer from Leicester City to Liverpool followed by 23 goals in 2000-01 failed to end the argument, as did 62 England caps over 11 years – under four different bosses.

The fans who witnessed Heskey emerge from the Leicester City youth team and explode onto the Premier League scene just don't get the wisecracks. Even before he'd signed pro forms, Heskey had made a low-key debut for a flu-ravaged side as a 17-year-old in a Premiership defeat at QPR. As the old saw has it, he was good enough and so he was old enough.

Being 6ft 3in and already weighing in as a heavyweight boxer possibly helped, but 'Bruno' (as he was almost inevitably known) began to fulfil his potential the following season under new boss O'Neill, ending the season at Wembley and helping City to victory over Crystal Palace in the First Division play-off final. The victory sparked a golden age for Leicester, and Emile was the top scorer and provider in a side that managed four top-half finishes, reached two more League Cup finals and played in Europe.

From the status of hero at Leicester, Heskey's subsequent reputation for club and country has been unfathomably mixed for a striker who has played in the Premier League for 14 unbroken seasons, with transfer fees totalling over £25 million. The majority of fans just don't get Heskey, but a string of top managers and fellow strikers – Houllier, Cottee, Owen – sing his praises as a great player and an unselfish partner. How do you solve a problem like Emile? The answer seems to be, sign him for a club record fee and stick him up front.

GS

> QUOTE
>
> 'He's not David Beckham, not Paul Scholes, not Michael Owen, but his strength is that he's good in the air, he can keep the ball and score goals. He has his own kind of quality.'
>
> Former England manager Sven-Goran Eriksson makes it obvious, all of a sudden.

ROBERTO MANCINI was asked on Italian TV programme *Le Iene* in 2003 to describe himself in one word. He was the manager of Lazio at the time and, despite incredible financial constraints (the best players were sold, the others had to take huge pay cuts and he is reputed to have worked for a period without pay), he had taken them to the semi-finals of the UEFA Cup.

In his time as manager at Fiorentina, Lazio, Internazionale and now Manchester City, he has never failed to take a team to the semi-final of at least one major competition every season. That is indeed a remarkable record, but it still fails to establish him as a team-builder nonpareil. A club-rebuilder some would argue. Internazionale ill-advisedly dispensed with his services after he had taken them to three successive titles (their first since 1989), but failed to win the Champions League.

But that's the game, and Mancini would have known that, as he had intended to be a manager since breaking into the Bologna team aged 17 in 1981. Sampdoria snapped him up a year later. He eventually played as a second striker, just behind the front man. He established a remarkable partnership with Gianluca Vialli and was good enough to be capped by Italy 36 times.

As an 18-year-old, he was precocious enough to start a fight with star Sampdoria signing Trevor Francis, a man ten years his senior, another with Liam Brady, eight years older, and then, later, with Juan Sebastian Veron, 11 years younger, after a row on the pitch with his team-mate continued into the dressing room. Mancini was stripped off to the waist and waiting to take the

---

THE MOMENT HE BECAME A LEGEND

Delivering the FA Cup for Manchester City in 2011 after a wait of 35 years for a trophy.

WELL I NEVER ...

He shares his birthday, 27 November, with Ernie Wise, Jimi Hendrix and *Enter the Dragon* kung-fu star Bruce Lee.

QUOTE

At Sir Alex Ferguson's 25th anniversary celebration dinner, less than two weeks after his team had been mauled 6-1 by City at home, he was asked how many City managers there had been during his time in the job. He didn't know. 'Fourteen,' he was told. 'I wish it was fifteen,' was all he said. That was a compliment.

83 ROBERTO MANCINI

PREMIER LEAGUE DEBUT (PLAYER):
Leicester City v Arsenal, 20 January 2001

PREMIER LEAGUE DEBUT (MANAGER):
Manchester City v Stoke City,
26 December 2009

PREMIER LEAGUE CLUB (PLAYER):
Leicester City

PREMIER LEAGUE CLUB (MANAGER):
Manchester City

PREMIER LEAGUE APPEARANCES/GOALS:

Leicester C	4	0
Total	4	0

PREMIER LEAGUE APPEARANCES (MANAGER):

Manchester C	97
Total	97

PREMIER LEAGUE HONOURS:
1 (2011–12)

COUNTRY:
Italy (born Jesi, 27 November 1964)

matter further when Veron got there. 'He is not an easy person, you know,' the Argentine has said. 'He has this complicated personality.'

As many of the current Manchester City squad can attest, not least Carlos Tevez, that is certainly the case. The stories are that if players are not playing for whatever reason, he has no time for them. The *Guardian* reported one unnamed source at the club who called him, 'The hardest bastard you'll ever meet.' Probably one of the best dressed as well.

When he was just 28, he was on the interview panel at Sampdoria that selected his mentor Sven-Goran Eriksson as manager. He later followed him to Lazio. 'He wanted to be a manager even while he was a player,' Eriksson remembers. 'He was the coach, he was the kit man, he was the bus driver, everything. But that's how he was.'

Oh and that one-word description of himself on Italian TV: 'Genius.'

BB

82 EDWIN VAN DER SAR

PREMIER LEAGUE DEBUT:
Fulham v Manchester United,
19 August 2001

PREMIER LEAGUE CLUBS:
Fulham, Manchester United

PREMIER LEAGUE APPEARANCES/GOALS:

Fulham	127	0
Manchester U	186	0
Total	313	0

PREMIER LEAGUE HONOURS:
4 (2006-07, 2007-08, 2008-09, 2010-11)

COUNTRY:
Netherlands (born Voorhout,
29 October 1970)

FEW FANS would quibble with the nomination of Sir Alex Ferguson as the greatest manager of the Premier League era, though many have raised an eyebrow over the years at the great man's apparent Achilles heel – his questionable taste in number ones.

First on the charge sheet would be archetypal Scottish goalie Jim Leighton followed by Raimond 'Who?' van der Gouw, troubled Aussie Mark Bosnich (twice), Massimo 'The Blind Venetian' Taibi, Fabien Barthez and disaster-prone Roy Carroll. Even Tim Howard and Ben Foster looked distinctly shaky on duty for the Reds.

And on the other side of the ledger? There's no doubt Ferguson got it dead right with 'The Great Dane' Peter Schmeichel and, in more recent years, with another of the finest keepers of all time – the towering, frequently flying Dutchman Edwin van der Sar.

In retrospect, it seems over-

THE MOMENT HE BECAME A LEGEND

His penalty save from Nicolas Anelka that won the Champions League for Manchester United, one rainy night in Moscow, 2008. Watch it back, he is smiling before the ball hits his hands.

generous to give the United manager too much credit for 'spotting' a hugely respected goalie who stood 6ft 5in in his bright orange socks, already well on his way to earning the record number of Dutch caps. However, after winning the UEFA Cup and his first Champions League medal during a nine-year spell at Ajax, then going on to star for Juventus, there was a sense that van der Sar was past his peak when he signed for Fulham for £7.1 million in 2001.

His form was excellent during four years at Craven Cottage, yet even van der Sar had doubts about the future. 'I remember watching Chelsea's Champions League matches against Bayern Munich and Barcelona,' he admitted later, 'and thinking it would be great to be playing those kind of games again.'

Enter Sir Alex in 2005, clutching a cheque made out for a derisory figure of around £2 million for the 34-year-old. Taken by van der Sar's 'football mentality', he was impressed most by the veteran's constant communication that kept defenders on their toes, as well as his 'temperament, professionalism and performance levels'.

And so the keeper entered a new phase of his career and one in which he would double his glittering haul of four league titles and a Champions League medal. Statistically alone, his unbeaten span of 1,311 minutes on the way to the 2009 title was not just a Premier League record but a world single-season record at the top level; and when he lined up for the final match of his career, it was a record fifth time for the same goalkeeper to be playing in a Champions League final. All that remains now is for Sir Alex Ferguson to find a replacement.

DH

> ## WELL I NEVER ...
>
> He had a special handshake he used to intimidate opponents. 'He gives you his hand then crushes your thumb,' revealed biographer Jaap Visser. 'He once showed me how he does it and I had to check I still had all my fingers afterwards.'

> ## QUOTE
>
> 'I'm sorry, I'm just not very rock 'n' roll.'
>
> Admirable understatement from the Dutchman.

81 GRAHAM POLL

PREMIER LEAGUE DEBUT:
Southampton v Sheffield United,
2 October 1993

PREMIER LEAGUE APPEARANCES:
329

PREMIER LEAGUE HONOURS:
None

COUNTRY:
England (born Tring, 29 July 1963)

IT'S A SHAME that arguably the most competent referee in the Premier League's history will be remembered for showing Croatia's Josip Simunic a second yellow card at the 2006 World Cup, and then failing to follow it up with a red. Poll admitted that his decision to retire from the game a year later was partly influenced by crowd chants in England of, 'World Cup/And you f*cked it up.'

Aside from the day job refereeing the biggest games in the Premier League for 16 years with a minimum of fuss, Poll was also in the middle for the 2000 FA Cup final between Chelsea and Aston Villa, the 2002 League Cup final between Spurs and Blackburn Rovers, the 2005 UEFA Cup final, and two Championship play-off finals.

He was widely respected by players and managers alike for his ability to control fractious games, while at the same time being chatty and cheerful, but it wasn't just the chants that pushed him towards a sooner-than-expected retirement.

THE MOMENT HE BECAME A LEGEND

He dealt with the serially abusive loudmouth Neil Warnock at half time of the 2003 Arsenal–Sheffield United FA Cup semi-final by calmly smiling at him.

In November 2006 he sent off John Terry at Stamford Bridge in a derby match against Tottenham, prompting Terry to claim in the media that Poll was 'out to get' Chelsea. Poll issued a strenuous denial, but the FA took so long to deal with the matter, before fining Terry £10,000, that the official felt he was lacking the necessary support from the governing body, and that his integrity had been questioned.

His only 2002 World Cup game, between Italy and Croatia, prompted Italian striker Francesco Totti to complain that Poll was typically English in not giving enough free-kicks in his favour. Perhaps Poll had studied footage of Totti's tendency to fall over for seemingly little reason. But apart from one more appearance as a fourth official, it was the only game he took at the tournament.

In 2006, Croatia versus Australia was his third game at that World Cup, and the most highly charged. The Simunic error was seen by the watching world, and even the confident Poll found it hard to take. Later, though, he managed to joke about the incident as an after-dinner speaker, and is now an occasionally egregious media pundit.

Ian Plenderleith

WELL I NEVER ...

When he blew the whistle to start the South Korea versus Togo game at the 2006 World Cup, it was at the exact moment he'd married wife Julia 14 years earlier.

QUOTE

'There is nothing worse than driving home after a game knowing you made a mistake and that millions of people know it, too ... that sort of thing doesn't happen in most people's jobs.'

Poll speaks from the heart.

IN THE SUMMER of 1996, Middlesbrough audaciously signed a storied Italian player who had lifted the European Cup for Juventus just a few weeks earlier. Looking back, it was the Premier League equivalent of David Beckham signing for LA Galaxy over a decade later. Except it was in Middlesbrough not Los Angeles.

The arrival on glamorous Teesside of the tall, distinctively grey-haired 'White Feather' was the moment when fans of all clubs thought, 'If [expletive deleted] 'Boro can sign Fabrizio Ravanelli, then the sky's the limit.' Gifted foreigners were no longer an exotic species on English fields, they were about to become a requirement for any club with ambition.

> ## THE MOMENT HE BECAME A LEGEND
>
> Scoring a hat-trick for Middlesbrough on his Premier League debut at home to Liverpool in a 3-3 draw.

Ravanelli's stay in Middlesbrough was short but eventful. That season at the Riverside, neither he nor the sylph-like Brazilian playmaker Juninho could prevent their team from being relegated. However, they took them to two cup finals, where they lost to Leicester City in the League Cup and Chelsea in the FA Cup.

A man used to continental training and dietary regimes, Ravanelli caused tensions when he publicly expressed his surprise at the primitive methods of manager Bryan Robson. Given that he was the league's highest paid player at the time, many thought he should keep his mouth shut and play, but he was a man ahead of his time and kick-started the disappearance of English top-flight football's lager-swilling norms.

On the field, meanwhile, he had an immediate impact, scoring a hat-trick on his debut at home to Liverpool. They weren't brilliant goals, by any means – a penalty, a close-range tap-in, and

> ## WELL I NEVER ...
>
> Since retiring, Ravanelli has embarked upon a part-time career as a model, and has walked down the catwalk in swimwear and, at 2010 Milan Fashion Week, menswear for Belgian designer Dirk Bikkembergs.

80 FABRIZIO RAVANELLI

PREMIER LEAGUE DEBUT:
Middlesbrough v Liverpool, 17 August 1996

PREMIER LEAGUE CLUBS:
Middlesbrough, Derby County

PREMIER LEAGUE APPEARANCES/GOALS:

Middlesbrough	33	16
Derby Co	31	9
Total	64	25

PREMIER LEAGUE HONOURS:
None

COUNTRY:
Italy (born Perugia, 11 December 1968)

a snap shot after an ugly defensive scramble – but they typified Ravanelli's predatory talents.

The Italian may have been built like a target man, but he was also a clever player who could hold up the ball and lay it off with precision. He also knew when to set up his team-mates and in that one season he scored 31 goals in 48 appearances in all competitions – players for teams such as Hereford (beaten 7-0 by Middlesbrough in the League Cup, with Ravanelli scoring four) and Chester (6-0 in the FA Cup, a brace for the 'White Feather') must have wondered if they were dreaming when they saw the man who'd just scored in a European Cup final bearing down on them.

Following relegation, he played only twice in the Championship before moving to Marseille and then Lazio, before returning for a second Premier League spell at the age of 32 at Derby in the 2001-02 season, a campaign that also ended in relegation. IP

> QUOTE
>
> 'I started the shirt-lifting thing, and I'm still the best at it.'
>
> Ravanelli makes a potentially confusing claim while at Derby, with reference to his habit of covering his face with his shirt after scoring.

AMONG HIS many talents, Niall Quinn possesses a nice line in self-deprecation. Once asked to define his playing career, a familiar grin spread across the garrulous Irishman's face as he suggested that he had 'nicked a living playing caveman football'. His game might have lacked some of the haughty refinement that characterises others in this list, but the imposing target-man has earned everything the game has given him.

His reputation as Saint Niall is well established; he donated the proceeds of his 2002 testimonial to children's charities in the North East and Ireland, and paid £8000 in taxi fares to ensure a group of 100 stranded supporters could get home from a Sunderland match in Bristol after their flight was cancelled. He is loved by the fans of every club he has represented – that is to say: Arsenal, Manchester City and Sunderland.

Yet among all that acclaim, it is easy to forget the ferocious boozer and gambler who washed up in George Graham's Arsenal side of the late 1980s and early 1990s. Indeed, Quinn offers an entertaining anecdote of regularly leaving his bus fare in a garden near Haringey dog track, so that he would be able to get home after a day out. The tactic worked until he took to retrieving the money so he could stake it on the last race.

He might have enjoyed some success with Arsenal and Manchester City, but it was not until Peter Reid took him to the North East for a club record £1.3 million in the summer of 1996 that the Republic of Ireland international truly established himself. Once he recovered from the knee injury that robbed him of six months of his debut season, Quinn struck up a partnership with Kevin Phillips that helped the club to promotion and a continued stay in the top flight.

The Irishman was under-rated with the ball to feet and possessed an innate understanding of the game that enabled him to play until 2003 – helping his country

> ## THE MOMENT HE BECAME A LEGEND
>
> 15 August 1997: Sunderland v Manchester City. Quinn seized upon an errant back pass and calmly slid the ball into the net to record the first goal scored at the Stadium of Light.

> ## WELL I NEVER ...
>
> While at Sunderland as a player, Quinn bought four cows and named them Dempsey and Makepeace and Cagney and Lacey.

79 NIALL QUINN

PREMIER LEAGUE DEBUT:
Manchester City v Queens Park Rangers, 17 August 1992

PREMIER LEAGUE CLUBS:
Manchester City, Sunderland

PREMIER LEAGUE APPEARANCES/GOALS:

Manchester C	121	30
Sunderland	129	29
Total	250	59

PREMIER LEAGUE HONOURS:
None

COUNTRY:
Republic of Ireland (born Dublin, 6 October 1966)

to the last 16 of the World Cup in 2002 – then allowed him to move into the administrative side of the game in 2006. He fronted the Drumaville consortium, a group of Irish businessmen he met at the Cheltenham Festival, and persuaded them to invest in Sunderland despite financial advice to the contrary.

He became chairman of Sunderland and thrived at that, too, after an ill-starred stint as caretaker-manager in 2006-07 in which he lost his first four league matches and a cup tie at Bury. 'At least I won a pre-season friendly,' he recently recalled, his ready self-deprecation to the fore once again. He might also have mentioned that his 'Disco pants' (a song dedicated to him by Manchester City fans) are still the best. But then they go up from his ...   RW

> QUOTE
>
> 'I learned my trade at Arsenal, became a footballer at Manchester City, but Sunderland got under my skin. I love Sunderland.'
>
> Niall Quinn looks back on his career.

78 XABI ALONSO

PREMIER LEAGUE DEBUT:
Liverpool v Bolton Wanderers,
29 August 2004

PREMIER LEAGUE CLUB:
Liverpool

PREMIER LEAGUE APPEARANCES/GOALS:

Liverpool	143	15
Total	143	15

PREMIER LEAGUE HONOURS:
None

COUNTRY:
Spain (born Tolosa, 25 November 1981)

WHEN LIVERPOOL sold Xabi Alonso to Real Madrid in the summer of 2009 for a cool £30 million, they made almost three times more than they'd paid Real Sociedad five years earlier. In the intervening time, he had not only become a European champion with his native Spain, but had proven his worth for Liverpool several times over as a poised and creative holding midfielder. Think Graeme Souness without the studs up.

Alonso defies the stereotype of holding midfielders as stubby, rugged enforcers only good for breaking down play and hoofing the ball clear of danger. He reads the game so well that he's more likely to intercept a pass than clatter into an opponent and give away a free-kick in a dangerous position. And once he has the ball at his feet, the range and accuracy of his passing are breathtaking. Much like Steven Gerrard, he could have slotted into any Liverpool team of the 1970s or 1980s.

The only criticism of Alonso

> ## THE MOMENT HE BECAME A LEGEND
>
> When he scored Liverpool's third goal in the 2005 Champions League final.

seems to be that he doesn't score enough goals, but, when he does strike, the end result tends to be memorable. He forged his name into Liverpool's rich history by scoring the third goal in the astonishing comeback victory against AC Milan in the 2005 Champions League final, following up his own penalty to slam in the rebound and make the score 3-3. And then there were the trademark long-range efforts from inside his own half.

Most players would be happy to score one goal from inside their own half in the course of a professional career. Alonso not only managed two, he scored them within the same calendar year. The first was late on in an FA Cup win at Luton and then, nine months later, having not scored for his club in between, he caught Newcastle keeper Steve Harper off his line. 'I was waiting for Alonso to pass and I would have spoken to him about it,' said manager Rafael Benitez. 'But after he scored I said to him, "Good, fantastic goal."' Indeed.

Inexplicably, it was the same Benitez who attempted to offload Alonso to either Arsenal or Juventus in 2008 in a bid to raise cash for the ultimately unsuccessful purchase of Gareth Barry. At that moment, the player resolved to leave Anfield but stayed for another season and performed to the same high standard ('I do my talking on the pitch and that's that') before leaving for the Bernabeu the following summer. In 2010 he picked up a World Cup winner's medal.

IP

RECRUITED FROM Atlético Madrid, as soon as Torres touched the pitch the glamour-starved Kopites knew he was different. He stood out – a peacock among crows. He took the field in a halo of Mediterranean light; while not quite boasting the physique of Rafael Nadal, he certainly had the skin of Penelope Cruz. Whenever he left the field chatting to fellow-countrymen Alvaro Arbeloa and Xabi Alonso, it was as the romantic lead with two less delicate supporting actors.

Moreover, he was that great rarity, an exquisitely skilful all-round striker, the goal-scoring equivalent of Didier Drogba who stayed on his feet whenever he could. He scored with both feet, his head, from distance and inside the six-yard box, he could outrun any defender, dribble, pass and tackle – a veritable Spanish Roy of the Rovers. In his first season, he scored an astonishing 33 goals in 46 appearances. He also liked netting against Manchester United, always popular with the Anfield contingent.

Liverpool supporters spent a large proportion of every game standing up – as soon as he was in possession, 45,362 plastic seats snapped into the upright position. Even his goal celebrations were perfect – neither smug nor hysterical. Just right.

Off-field it was the same exemplary picture. He quickly acquired impressive fluency in English and came across as a model husband and devoted

THE MOMENT HE BECAME A LEGEND

14 March 2009: Manchester United 1 Liverpool 4. Having scored the equalising first goal, Torres puts Liverpool ahead by stealing the ball from Vidic, running clear and finishing coolly. He knows he's going to score. So does everyone else in the ground, especially Vidic.

WELL I NEVER ...

Understandably aggrieved at the transfer of 'El Niño' to Chelsea, Nick Miners, a 38-year-old Liverpool fan, created HasTorresScoredForChelsea.com. The site comprised one page with the word 'NO' in huge type, and in the 903 minutes pitch time during which the striker failed to score for his new club the site attracted more than 850,000 visitors.

77 FERNANDO TORRES

PREMIER LEAGUE DEBUT:
Liverpool v Aston Villa, 11 August 2007

PREMIER LEAGUE CLUBS:
Liverpool, Chelsea

PREMIER LEAGUE APPEARANCES/GOALS:

Liverpool	102	65
Chelsea	46	7
Total	148	72

PREMIER LEAGUE HONOURS:
None

COUNTRY:
Spain (born Madrid, 20 March 1984)

family man. He lived quietly in a suburb for professional people, in the same street as Pepe Reina. Even in the heyday of News International's phone-hacking frenzy and teams of dustbin-rummagers, nobody dared suggest that Torres had become embroiled in a nightclub fracas or broken the seventh commandment.

A run of injuries starting in the build-up to the 2010 World Cup may have taken their toll, but the Latin glow persisted; he was more handsome than ever. He went to Chelsea for £50 million in the January transfer window in 2011, but the goals failed to follow him. Only last week, the *Liverpool Echo* reported that a portrait has been found in a Woolton attic of 'a man hideously ugly, his face a battleground of wrinkles and liver spots'. Torres himself is as angelically youthful-looking as ever, but it's the man in the painting who scores the goals. FC

> QUOTE
>
> 'My commitment and loyalty to the club and to the fans is the same as it was on my first day when I signed.'
>
> Torres pledges his loyalty to the cause. Six months before joining Chelsea.

76 DARREN ANDERTON

PREMIER LEAGUE DEBUT:
Tottenham Hotspur v Southampton, 15 August 1992

PREMIER LEAGUE CLUBS:
Tottenham Hotspur, Birmingham City

PREMIER LEAGUE APPEARANCES/GOALS:

Tottenham H	299	34
Birmingham C	20	3
Total	319	37

PREMIER LEAGUE HONOURS:
None

COUNTRY:
England (born Southampton, 3 March 1972)

'DEAR DARREN, I am writing to inform you that Tottenham Hotspur Football Club will not be offering you terms of re-engagement upon the expiry of your contract on 30 June 2004.' Just like that, Darren Anderton's 12-year Tottenham career came to an end. There was 'Good luck for the future', of course. It was, he has admitted, 'A blow.' The loyal forward-playing midfielder had been with the club since he was 20.

There were, of course, happier times and Darren Robert Anderton had already started making a name for himself at Portsmouth under Jim Smith – his goal had put the South Coast club within minutes of the 1992 FA Cup final at the expense of Liverpool and the cup run had engendered a

THE MOMENT HE BECAME A LEGEND

He lit up Euro 96 – it seemed Anderton was going to be an England fixture for at least the next two World Cups – but perhaps his determination to never give up confirms his place in this list.

number of suitors for the young player who was either languid or elegant, according to taste.

Terry Venables, by now chief executive, eventually coaxed him to White Hart Lane just in time for the Premier League's inaugural season for a fee of £2 million. Anderton was, indeed, one of the first poster boys for the Premier League and even appeared in Sky Sports' television promo doing sit-ups in a gym – an ironic choice of location in retrospect – as the station ushered in a new era for football.

As a club, however, Tottenham contrived to stay in bed for the brave new dawn and ended the first two campaigns in eighth and 15th spots, a period of stasis as frustrating to their young forward as the first of his many injury setbacks. The arrival of Ossie Ardiles as manager in June 1993, however, saw him flourish during the 1994-95 season as one of the 'Famous Five' frontline, alongside Nick Barmby, Ilie Dumitrescu, Teddy Sheringham and Jürgen Klinsmann.

> ## WELL I NEVER ...
>
> His last five England caps were given to him by five different managers. Glenn Hoddle selected him in 1998, Howard Wilkinson in 1999, Kevin Keegan and Peter Taylor in 2000 and Sven-Goran Eriksson in 2001.

Venables, who had become head coach of England in January 1994, had introduced him into the England set-up by this time, but the following campaign he was again plagued by injuries – a by no means exhaustive list of his problems since joining the club would include three hernia operations, a recurring groin injury and a hamstring problem. Cue the nickname 'Sicknote'.

It was a label he was never able to shake, but by the time he eventually left Tottenham in 2004, he was able to boast that he had turned down the chance to join Manchester United, won the League Cup in 1999 and played in 299 Premier League matches – winning 30 caps for England in the meantime. It could and should have perhaps been so much more.

He retired at 36, coming off the bench to score the winner for Bournemouth in his final game in 2008.   Damian Mannion

> ## QUOTE
>
> 'To me, he was a champion. People talk about stars, but stars only come out at night. There are few champions about.'
>
> Terry Venables, as quoted in the foreword to Anderton's 2010 autobiography *Take Note!*.

WELL, THERE ARE double acts and double acts. And Keys and Gray may not be Laurel and Hardy or Morecambe and Wise – but like all great double acts, they are known simply by their surnames. In truth, they are former *TV-am* presenter Richard Keys and former Aston Villa, Wolves, Everton and Scotland striker Andy Gray. The former is a consummate broadcaster with a non-regionally divisive mid-M6 accent and Andy Gray is Andy Gray. If it's last orders in a pub in the arse-end of Glasgow and Gray is telling you it is, it almost certainly is.

The Sky Sports publicity machine used to define them as 'the driving force behind Sky Sports' rise to football supremacy' and claimed that they were synonymous with 'the rise of Premiership football throughout the world'. In other words, the anchorman (Keys) was the voice of reason, while his broadcasting partner (Gray) provided authority with a hint of menace. The combination served to provoke comment in front rooms and pubs up and down the country. All over the world, in fact. It worked from 1992 to 2011.

And then Keys resigned and Gray was dismissed by Sky after some sexist old nonsense about a female assistant referee off-air. Moz Dee, the Sony Award-winning talkSPORT controller, pounced to sign them up for the radio station and put it like this: 'If you'd told me a year ago that we would have Keys and Gray on the station, I would have said you were f**king insane ... They are a brilliant addition to the station.' The listeners certainly love them, and in May 2012 they picked up a gold Sony Award for Best Sports Programme.

The radio format remains the

75 KEYS AND GRAY

PREMIER LEAGUE DEBUT (ON TV):
Nottingham Forest v Liverpool,
16 August 1992

PREMIER LEAGUE CLUBS:
n/a

PREMIER LEAGUE APPEARANCES/GOALS:
n/a

PREMIER LEAGUE HONOURS:
n/a

COUNTRY:
Richard Keys – England (born Coventry,
23 April 1957)
Andy Gray – Scotland (born Glasgow,
30 November 1955)

same: Gray insisting that, as a former international footballer of some repute, he has an opinion worth listening to, while Keys cajoles and asks the questions we all want to know the answers to. In many ways, they are the odd couple, but Keys covered more than 1000 games for Sky and Gray cannot have been far behind.

Along with Martin Tyler, they were the voice of the Premier League for almost two decades. Alan Smith? Do me a favour.

BB

QUOTE

Keys to former Liverpool manager Roy Evans: 'Well Roy, do you think that you'll have to finish above Manchester United to win the league?'
Evans: 'You have to finish above everyone to win the league, Richard.'

A fair point well made.

Gray: 'People say footballers have terrible taste in music, but I would dispute that. In the car at the moment I've got The Corrs, Cher, Phil Collins, Shania Twain and Rod Stewart.'

No comment.

74 GEORGI KINKLADZE

PREMIER LEAGUE DEBUT:
Manchester City v Tottenham Hotspur,
19 August 1995

PREMIER LEAGUE CLUBS:
Manchester City, Derby County

PREMIER LEAGUE APPEARANCES/GOALS:

Manchester C	37	4
Derby Co	65	3
Total	102	7

PREMIER LEAGUE HONOURS:
None

COUNTRY:
Georgia (born Tbilisi, 6 July 1973)

THE BREVITY of Kinkladze's stay in the Premier League belies the fact that he was one of the most technically gifted players English football had seen since George Best. His misfortune was to be signed by a very average Manchester City side in July 1995, two months after they had only just escaped relegation by beating Liverpool and the eventual winners of the title, Blackburn Rovers, in successive matches. A pearl before swine, perhaps.

Oasis frontman Noel Gallagher witnessed his debut against Tottenham and predicted that the little Georgian would either lead City to win the European Cup or help take the team down to the Third Division. He was closer than he realised, and three years later City were in the third tier of English football for the first time in their history.

THE MOMENT HE BECAME A LEGEND

In March 1996 during a boring 1-1 draw against Southampton at Maine Road, Kinkladze picked up the ball on the right just past the halfway line, beat five men in a jinking run before lifting the winning goal over Dave Beasant. BBC commentator Jon Champion described it as 'mesmeric' and it came runner-up in the Goal of the Season competition.

Signed on the strength of a Georgia versus Wales video seen by then chairman Francis Lee, the club was in the process of appointing a new manager to replace the sacked Brian Horton when the player arrived for £2 million from Dinamo Tbilisi. Alan Ball was to be the unknowing beneficiary of this astute bit of business.

When Kinkladze was six, he joined Dinamo's junior side. He was a prodigy driven by his father, who made his son climb the stairs to the family's seventh-floor apartment juggling the ball without using his hands, and enrolled him in ballet lessons that served to improve his balance – such a key factor in his destruction of opposition defences.

City started the following season with two points from the first nine games, but gradually Kinkladze brought his influence to bear and things improved for a spell before the club were eventually relegated on the last day of the season. As is traditional, he left the pitch in tears, but stayed another two seasons with City, responding to the urgent entreaties of the Maine Road faithful to provide them with something worth watching. Eventually, he left for Ajax before returning to the Premier League with a struggling Derby County side who were eventually relegated in 2002.

He was the club's player of the season in 2002-03, his last season there, an honour he had received twice at Manchester City, but his career can be seen as one of unfulfilled promise compromised by the poor quality of the teams for whom he inevitably starred.

BB/GSt

> ## WELL I NEVER ...
>
> Kinkladze was headhunted for Boca Juniors by Diego Maradona and spent a month on loan in Buenos Aires before joining Manchester City.

> ## QUOTE
>
> 'He became a legend before he became a player.'
>
> Manchester City manager Joe Royle delivers a back-handed compliment to a player he regarded as 'a weak link'.

73 MARC OVERMARS

PREMIER LEAGUE DEBUT:
Arsenal v Leeds United, 9 August 1997

PREMIER LEAGUE CLUB:
Arsenal

PREMIER LEAGUE APPEARANCES/GOALS:
Arsenal   100   25
Total   100   25

PREMIER LEAGUE HONOURS:
1 (1997-98)

COUNTRY:
Netherlands (born Emst, 29 March 1973)

ARSENAL'S 1997-98 Double-winning team resembled football's equivalent of a Formula One car: founded on an English chassis and supported by some of Europe's finest specialist components. Tony Adams determined the team's structure, Patrick Vieira powered the engine and Dennis Bergkamp manoeuvred play with his precision passing – the acceleration was fuelled by Marc Overmars.

But the man known as 'Meep Meep' for his trademark *Roadrunner*-style runs down the touchline was more than just a speed merchant. Despite being right-footed, he played on the left where he could beat opponents for pace on the outside or cut inside with a subtle shift of the shoulders. He was the ideal wing-man for close friend and compatriot Bergkamp – and he could score goals, too. Important ones.

THE MOMENT HE BECAME A LEGEND

Arsenal overcame a 13-point deficit against Manchester United to win the title in 1998 and the most crucial psychological blow in that comeback was Overmars' goal on 79 minutes at Old Trafford to give the Gunners a decisive 1-0 victory.

After being signed for £5.5 million from Ajax in the summer of 1997, a typically astute piece of business from the Arsène Wenger school of economics, Overmars had a sensational first season. He scored 12 league goals, including a decisive strike against title rivals Manchester United at Old Trafford and a brace against Everton that effectively ensured that the title would return to North London.

However, the goal that is most often appreciated by Arsenal fans came two weeks later against Newcastle in the 1998 FA Cup final. Overmars latched on to a long-ball, left Alessandro Pistone for dead and toe-poked the opener through Shay Given's legs to set the Gunners on their way towards a memorable Double.

> **WELL I NEVER ...**
>
> Peter 'Pete' Sutcliffe pretends to be an astronaut called 'Captain Marc ... Overmars' in an excruciating role-playing scenario with his wife Dawn designed to reignite their sex life in an episode of *Gavin and Stacey*. It fails.

Those heights were always going to be difficult to scale consistently and, although he ultimately scored 41 goals in 142 appearances in all competitions, a series of injuries lessened his impact over the next two seasons, where the team came close to winning silverware without ever actually getting to smoke the cigar.

Nonetheless, his performances in this country convinced Barcelona to spend £25.5 million in an effort to replace Luis Figo in 2000. But, eventually, injuries were the only opponent that could catch up with him and he was forced to retire with a knee complaint in 2004 – gaining respect at the Nou Camp for his dignified refusal to be compensated for the final year of his contract.

Ever since Wenger converted Arsenal from artisans to artistes, pace has been synonymous with their counter-attacking style of play – featuring speed demons from Thierry Henry and Robert Pires to Theo Walcott and Alex Oxlade-Chamberlain. But, the original mould was set by (yet another) flying Dutchman who could have given anyone in the history of the Premier League a run for their money.

Overmars made a brief comeback for his first Dutch club, Go Ahead Eagles, after impressing in Jaap Stam's testimonial four years following his retirement from Barcelona. His return was ended by a broken leg, but he remains a director at the club.

Richard Arrowsmith

> **QUOTE**
>
> 'If I don't have a fried breakfast in the morning, I won't play or train well.'
>
> Overmars was not a fervent disciple of Wenger's strict dietary regime.

IF ONLY CRAIG Bellamy could evade his reputation the way he dodges defenders. If only a furious burst of acceleration could leave behind a history of fracas, fisticuffs and fallings-out and allow a picture to form of a player rather than a persona, then the Welshman could be more readily judged on his substantial footballing merits. As is stands, subjective judgements are irrevocably coloured by his past.

The bald facts are these: Bellamy has played for nine clubs (six in the Premier League), one of them twice; he has largely averaged almost a goal every three games; he has won two major trophies; and he has endured nine major operations in a career blighted by injuries. Strip the biographical details from the equation and you are left with an effective, if unfortunate, striker whose talents have yielded a respectable return.

Yet therein lies the rub. The numbers speak of an ordinary player; it is his past that makes Bellamy a legend. The incidents are legion. He has been sent off for head-butting opponents at club level and using his elbow at international level; he once took a golf club to team-mate John Arne Riise in a karaoke-related incident; he has been involved in numerous breaches of club discipline and had more problems in the tunnel than the escapees from Stalag Luft 3.

Sir Bobby Robson, one of the few managers able to channel the striker's aggression, described him as 'a great player wrapped round an unusual and volatile character' and it is easy to see why. Behind him lies a trail of broken relationships with characters such as Graeme Souness, Alan Shearer and Roberto Mancini, but dig through the wreckage and a kernel of validation can often be found in Bellamy's stance.

Take the latter, for example. Despite the striker having enjoyed a splendid season prior to his arrival, Mancini demanded he abandon his specialised training programme – created to protect a lingering knee

72 CRAIG BELLAMY

PREMIER LEAGUE DEBUT:
Coventry City v Middlesbrough, 19 August 200

PREMIER LEAGUE CLUBS:
Coventry City, Newcastle United, Blackburn Rovers, Liverpool, West Ham United, Manchester City, Liverpool (loan)

PREMIER LEAGUE APPEARANCES/GOALS:

Coventry C	34	6
Newcastle U	93	27
Blackburn R	27	13
Liverpool	54	13
West Ham U	24	7
Manchester C	40	13
Total	272	79

PREMIER LEAGUE HONOURS:
None

COUNTRY:
Wales (born Cardiff, 13 July 1979)

complaint – and do the same work as the rest of the squad. A series of injuries ensued, swiftly followed by Bellamy's departure.

Then there is the sentimental side to his character, be it joining boyhood heroes Cardiff City on loan, investing around £1.2 million – and rising – in his own football foundation in Sierra Leone, or returning to Liverpool for a second time in the summer of 2011, citing the club's return to the approach that thrilled him as a child. That is an image of Bellamy that most people would not recognise. Maybe it is about time they did.

RW

> QUOTE
>
> 'People say, "If you take the anger out of Craig Bellamy, he wouldn't be half the player." It's bollocks. You know what? I'd be a better player. I would be actually thinking more rationally.'
>
> Craig Bellamy in default forthright/ contrary mode.

ADEBAYOR WAS unable to walk until he reached the age of four. The story is that he was 'cured' when a football bounced into the church where the congregation was praying for him. As his mother remembers it, 'Emmanuel tried to get up, tried to walk towards it. He was crying, wailing but he finally got the ball. The next day he could walk. I knew then he was destined to be a footballer.' She might have added that he was also destined to cry and wail because, as a player, his career has been characterised by a series of outbursts that have, on occasion, overshadowed his ability as one of the best strikers in the world.

> ## THE MOMENT HE BECAME A LEGEND
>
> Scoring the winner for Arsenal against Manchester United in 2006.

An unused substitute for Monaco in the 2004 Champions League final, Adebayor's career really took off when he arrived at Arsenal for £7 million in 2006. Arsenal fans did not have to wait long to see the kind of complicated player they would grow to worship and then despise – he scored 21 minutes into his debut against Birmingham City, but was sent off in a bad-tempered Carling Cup final against Chelsea in February 2007.

In season 2007-08 he netted 24 times in 36 league appearances, but in the middle of enjoying his most successful season with the club, he also left team-mate Nicklas Bendtner with a bloodied nose. That year, he scored *Match of the Day*'s Goal of the Season against Spurs (one touch and a right-foot volley into the top corner) and was named BBC African Footballer of the Year.

By the end of 2008-09, and despite being the club's second highest scorer that season and executing a brilliant bicycle kick against Villareal in the Champions League, he was signed for Manchester City in July 2009 for £25 million on a rumoured wage of £170,000 per week. Again, he scored on his debut and followed it up with goals in each of the

> ## WELL I NEVER ...
>
> The computer game *Bad Adebayor!*, based on his celebration after scoring for City against Arsenal in the fourth game for his new club, requires the participant to click the mouse every 0.5 seconds to run towards clearly aggrieved Arsenal fans, stamp on Van Persie's head using the SPACE bar (for extra points) and then dodge the objects thrown by angry Gooners during an extended slide towards the away end.

71 EMMANUEL ADEBAYOR

PREMIER LEAGUE DEBUT:
Arsenal v Birmingham City, 4 February 2006

PREMIER LEAGUE CLUBS:
Arsenal, Manchester City, Tottenham Hotspur (loan)

PREMIER LEAGUE APPEARANCES/GOALS:

Arsenal	104	46
Manchester C	34	15
Tottenham H	33	17
Total	171	78

PREMIER LEAGUE HONOURS:
None

COUNTRY:
Togo (born Lomé, 26 February 1984)

next three games, including (infamously) one against Arsenal. His celebration, sprinting the length of the pitch towards the away fans was later deemed to be 'over the top' by several stuffed shirts.

Although technically still a City player at the end of the 2011-12 season, he has not played for them since November 2010, with Sergio Aguero, Mario Balotelli, Edin Dzeko and Carlos Tevez all ahead of him in the pecking order. He had a disagreement with boss Roberto Mancini and was forced to train with the youth team during the 2010-11 campaign. He was loaned out first to Real Madrid for the rest of the season and then joined Tottenham in August 2011 on loan, where he impressed with a goal every two games.   GSt

QUOTE

'We were singing on the bus, but ended up carrying out dead bodies ... when you realise you were so close to dying, you don't want to argue about small things any more.'

Adebayor reflects on the terrorist attack on the Togo team coach on the way to an African Cup of Nations game in Angola in January 2010.

70 JACK WALKER

PREMIER LEAGUE DEBUT (OWNER):
Blackburn Rovers v Crystal Palace,
15 August 1992

PREMIER LEAGUE CLUB (OWNER):
Blackburn Rovers

PREMIER LEAGUE MATCHES (OWNER):
Blackburn R   278
Total   278

PREMIER LEAGUE HONOURS:
1 (1994-95)

COUNTRY:
England (born Blackburn, 19 May 1929)

WHEN JACK WALKER died, aged 71, just after the turn of the millennium, there was an outpouring of emotion in Blackburn that recalled the demise of many a powerful mill-owner during the Lancashire town's Victorian industrial heyday. The difference in this latter-day case was that the townspeople's tears and massed marks of respect were heartfelt, the words of the eulogies actually true.

With a £600 million fortune founded in steel and bolstered by an airline (now known as flybe) based in Jersey – tax haven heaven you might even be tempted to say – the almost reclusive Walker remained resolutely uninterested in profit margins when it came to piloting his precious Blackburn Rovers.

Even as the dawn of the Premier League promised a cash bonanza for owners (as well as venture capitalists, agents, players, corporate sponsors, investors and everyone else involved in the game), to the most successful club owner of his day, the revolving pound signs were meaningless.

THE MOMENT HE BECAME A LEGEND

As Rovers' majority shareholder – not as chairman or even as a director of the club (although he was, nominally, the vice-president) – Walker back-handed the club a lorryload of cash, and publicly threatened to make Manchester United look 'cheap'.

For years, the otherwise hard-nosed businessman had slipped the club cash for the odd signing; but when he finally took over the helm in 1991, he reacted like a kid in a sweetshop. Ex-Liverpool boss Kenny Dalglish was tempted from the golf course and armed with a blank chequebook. Rovers scraped into the big league via the play-offs, thanks to the likes of Colin Hendry, Mike Newell and David Speedie.

Having renovated Ewood Park and revitalised the town, 'Uncle Jack' set his sights yet higher for 1992-93, smashing the British transfer record to land 22-year-old striker Alan Shearer for £3.5 million – and ended up finishing fourth. England regulars Graeme Le Saux, Tim Flowers and David Batty were among the next to join 'The Team That Jack Built'. Rovers made runners-up behind Double-winners Manchester United in 1994.

They might have made it to the top even quicker had a bid for Gary Lineker paid off, or if Roy Keane had not changed his mind and joined United instead. But for 1994-95, the transfer record was topped again, bringing Chris Sutton from Norwich for £5 million. And Rovers pulled off the big one, with the SAS (Shearer and Sutton) scoring 49 goals to fire them to the title.

Jack Walker goes down as the last of football's great local benefactors, the last hometown chairman ever to lift a club up by the bootlaces and bankroll them to the title. And all for about £30 million, the same price as a modern star's packed lunch. Oh, lest we forget, both Shearer and Sutton, job done, were sold for an enormous profit.

DH

> **WELL I NEVER ...**
>
> In order to close a business deal in America in 1960, he persuaded a taxi driver to take him 1,000 miles through category 4 Hurricane Donna on the eastern seaboard. The deal was done and Walker rewarded the driver with a huge tip.

> **QUOTE**
>
> 'He followed Rovers all his life and was a bread-and-butter fan,' said Rovers legend Simon Garner. 'Luckily, he had a lot of money.'
>
> Hopefully, and for comedic effect, there was a pause between those two statements.

'**BALD, BEAUTIFUL** and brilliant!' was the verdict of most Liverpool fans at the end of the 2000-01 season, after Gary McAllister played a major role in helping the team win three cups in a rollercoaster year. The most incredible stat of that season? McAllister was 36 years old and playing the best football of an already distinguished career.

The most talented Scottish midfielder of his generation, McAllister's man-of-the-match performance saw him setting up three goals and scoring one in Liverpool's 5-4 win against Alaves in the 2001 UEFA Cup final, just four days after coming on as a substitute against Arsenal in the FA Cup final and helping to turn a 0-1 deficit into a 2-1 victory.

> ## THE MOMENT HE BECAME A LEGEND
>
> Just a month before the 2001 FA and UEFA Cup final wins, his 44-yard free-kick in the fourth minute of added time at Goodison Park saw Liverpool win a dramatic derby game 3-2.

'The Enforcer' won over not just Liverpool fans sceptical about his age, but supporters at Leeds United and Coventry City, his other two Premier League clubs in a career that started in his native Motherwell and took him to Elland Road and a league winner's medal via a five-year stay at Leicester City. Combative, quick and canny in his distribution, McAllister boasted the qualities that endear a player to the paying spectator – he was humble, passionate, loyal, and after scoring he usually acknowledged those celebrating in the stands before turning to his team-mates.

The Scotsman's trademark goal was a neatly chipped free-kick placed with preternatural accuracy into the top corner, but he also specialised in steely long-range shots and volleys that rippled, if not ripped, the fabric of nets across the whole country. He captained Leeds at Wembley when they lost the 1996 League Cup final to Aston Villa, and also led Coventry to their 'miracle' escape from relegation at the end of the 1996-97 season, when they drew at Arsenal, beat Chelsea at home, and won at both Liverpool and Tottenham during a tough run-in.

He missed the 1990 and 1998 World Cups through injury, but was an integral part of the Scotland squad that impressed at

> ## WELL I NEVER …
>
> He once turned up for an interview with Brian Clough wearing cowboy boots, prompting Clough to question his sexuality.

69

GARY McALLISTER

PREMIER LEAGUE DEBUT:
Leeds United v Wimbledon, 15 August 1992

PREMIER LEAGUE CLUBS:
Leeds United, Coventry City, Liverpool

PREMIER LEAGUE APPEARANCES/GOALS:

Leeds U	151	24
Coventry C	119	20
Liverpool	55	5
Total	325	49

PREMIER LEAGUE HONOURS:
None

COUNTRY:
Scotland (born Motherwell,
25 December 1964)

the 1992 European Championships – that is to say, unlike England, they did not finish bottom of their group. Four years later at Euro 96, he missed a penalty with Scotland 1-0 down at Wembley. McAllister uncharacteristically aimed his spot-kick down the middle of the goal, and David Seaman parried it over with his elbow.

'I know there are more important things in life than football,' McAllister said afterwards. 'But if you cut me open and looked inside me right now it wouldn't be a pretty sight. I don't know if I can sink any lower.' And yet his career in the top flight was only just ready for take-off.

IP

> QUOTE
>
> '[McAllister] was my most inspirational signing,' explained former Liverpool boss Gerard Houllier, before adding that if the club had signed him ten years earlier they would have won the Premier League.

68 VINNIE JONES

PREMIER LEAGUE DEBUT:
Chelsea v Oldham Athletic, 15 August 1992

PREMIER LEAGUE CLUBS:
Chelsea, Wimbledon

PREMIER LEAGUE APPEARANCES/GOALS:

Chelsea	7	1
Wimbledon	177	12
Total	184	13

PREMIER LEAGUE HONOURS:
None

COUNTRY:
Wales (born Watford, near Wales,
5 January 1965)

IN THE LATE 1980s, the outlook for fans of ultra-violence was unpromising. The golden age of terrace aggro was over, the government was making killjoy noises about video nasties, and Kubrick's withdrawal of *A Clockwork Orange* was still dampening the spirits. Then Wimbledon's droogs arrived to restore the fun – in Vinnie Jones' own phrase, to take violence off the terraces and onto the pitch.

Wimbledon played a game loosely based on association football, combining the strategic sophistication of parks soccer with the more extreme tactics of Rollerball and the Crazy Gang's chief lunatic was Jones – who admitted to fewer scruples than Lady Macbeth – and presumably is a close friend of Guy Ritchie's.

The rules state that a tackle is

THE MOMENT HE BECAME A LEGEND

Already holder of the record for the fastest booking (three seconds for Chelsea against Sheffield United in the 1992 FA Cup), the Premier League was less than three months old when Jones released a bestselling video entitled *Soccer's Hard Men*, just to make sure everybody knew that he had been invited to the party. He received a record £20,000 fine from the FA.

illegitimate if the tackler uses careless, reckless or excessive force. Jones wasn't careless. It is impermissible to kick, trip, jump or charge at, strike or push an opponent. It's clear that he was one of the few players who knew these laws – no offence was absent from his unmatched repertoire. When Wimbledon came to play your team, the result was immaterial; you prayed for the home side to surrender meekly and live to fight another day.

No one wanted their gifted No 10 to exit the ground in flatpack form, or leave the game altogether – in the style of Spurs' Gary Stevens during the pre-Premier League era perhaps, after a disagreement over possession was settled decisively in Jones' favour in a challenge that was hard but did not even result in a free-kick being awarded.

Actually, no one will ever know whether our hero could play football – the well-oiled pub contrarian in the snug may be confused by the classy way the midfield hit-man would hold an elegant, sculptural pose after successfully completing a routine ten-yard pass. But then that would be to forget that Jones was a born actor.

However, violence has its own weird integrity, and Vinnie was no mercenary, brawling gratis on at least two continents in bar and airport. Post-football, Jones stuck to his guns, resourcefully making his reputation pay in films where he played what seemed always to be a version of himself. Some representative titles: *Tooth and Nail*; *The Midnight Meat Train*; *The Bleeding*; *Kill the Irishman*. His roles have included Juggernaut; Killer (twice); The Extractor; Bullet-tooth Tony; Mongrel; Brick – and, most terrifyingly, Himself.

FC

> **WELL I NEVER ...**
>
> Jones' favourite band is Coventry death metal merchants Bolt Thrower.

> **QUOTE**
>
> 'Well, stone me! We've had cocaine, bribery and Arsenal scoring two goals at home. But just when you thought there were truly no surprises left in football, Vinnie Jones turns out to be an international player!'
>
> Jimmy Greaves reacts to the news that, due to the birthplace of his maternal grandfather, Jones was set to represent Wales.

67 ROBBIE KEANE

PREMIER LEAGUE DEBUT:
Coventry City v Derby County, 21 August 1999

PREMIER LEAGUE CLUBS:
Coventry City, Leeds United, Tottenham Hotspur, Liverpool, Tottenham Hotspur, West Ham United (loan), Aston Villa (loan)

PREMIER LEAGUE APPEARANCES/GOALS:

Coventry C	31	12
Leeds U	46	13
Tottenham H	238	91
Liverpool	19	5
West Ham U	9	2
Aston Villa	6	3
Total	349	126

PREMIER LEAGUE HONOURS:
None

COUNTRY:
Republic of Ireland (born Dublin, 8 July 1980)

PLENTY OF people will tell you Robbie Keane should be nowhere near this list; that he is little more than a cocksure chancer, a snapper-up of unconsidered trifles in front of goal with one eye on his next signing-on fee. Some will recall a 17-year-old who, during his first Republic of Ireland training session, arrogantly dribbled round senior players demanding, 'So who is this John Aldridge?' Others will cite his ten different clubs and retirement to Los Angeles Galaxy, his second spell at Tottenham having ended in ignominious marginalisation.

It often seems to have been the way with Keane: signed amid

THE MOMENT HE BECAME A LEGEND

When Marcello Lippi lured the then 19-year-old to Internazionale from Coventry City for £13 million, feting Keane as one of the best young players in the world.

fanfare, then quietly ushered out of the door after falling from the first team.

Yet, for all those perceived flaws, he is never short of suitors. For more than a decade, managers have regularly competed for the right to harness the impetuosity of a player who regularly responds with early bunches of goals. Approximately £77 million has been invested in his quick feet, sharp mind and agile movement, with those who show faith in Keane rewarded with performances rich in endeavour and effervescence; ask Harry Redknapp, whose decision to pair the Irishman with Dimitar Berbatov heralded the most pleasing period of the striker's career.

During that spell at White Hart Lane, the team adapted to suit him. Given licence to roam from the front line, dropping deep or peeling out wide and making rapier bursts into the area, Keane thrived in much the same way that he has always done at international level. Although underappreciated by some, the captain's 53 goals in 116 appearances for the Republic not only include some of the most memorable efforts in the country's recent past, but also make him one of the most prolific international strikers of his time.

As a renowned good trainer, hard work has been part of Keane's game from his start at Wolves, through Coventry and Leeds United, to his two spells at Tottenham. Even his perceived failures at Internazionale and Liverpool seem to be attributable to a case of the wrong player being signed at the wrong time, while his swashbuckling loan spell at Celtic is one the Dubliner will long cherish. In this, as in much else, he shares a great deal with Craig Bellamy – not least the fact that, despite being well travelled and being perceived to be 'difficult', the supporters of the clubs both have represented rarely have a bad word to say about them.   RW

> ## WELL I NEVER ...
>
> Having signed Keane from Tottenham for £20 million, former Liverpool owner George Gillett wanted to meet the player. Having been introduced to him he announced, 'Jeez, you're not very big for all that money we spent on you, are you?'

> ## QUOTE
>
> 'Why would I pay £500,000 for him only to sit him in the reserves?'
>
> Alex Ferguson's response when it was suggested he might move for Keane when he was a teenager at Wolves.

PUT YOURSELF, if you will, in the shoes of a Manchester United superstar-in-waiting, freshly knackered from running round the pitch 47 times. From the training methods employed, it's clearly some time between 1981 and 1995. Ron Atkinson or Alex Ferguson taps you on the shoulder and says you're one of the captains in a full-scale training game. The lads line up along the touchline. So who's your first pick?

Cantona? Not in the mood. Keane? A liability. Robson? Injured. The self-styled gubernatorial Ince? Nope. If you want to win, it will be Mark 'Sparky' Hughes.

THE MOMENT HE BECAME A LEGEND

Ferguson corrected Ron Atkinson's blunder and re-signed Hughes from Barcelona in 1988. He scored on his second debut, and went on to become Manchester United's first-ever PFA Player of the Year.

Away from the training ground, Hughes scored the goals that twice captured the Premier League and no player in the 20th century collected more FA Cup winners' medals. On the pitch, he offered pace, power, clever running, leadership, a target and a killer touch. He was the centre-forward no centre-half ever wanted to play against, and Ferguson knew his value well enough to keep hold of him until he had found an adequate replacement in Andy 'Andrew' Cole. Glenn Hoddle took full advantage and signed him for Chelsea in 1995.

WELL I NEVER ...

Hughes has had the nickname 'Sparky' since he was eight years old. He and his friends decided to choose nicknames after comics in circulation at the time. He had a mate called 'Beano'.

'I went there just at the right time, as they were starting to take off,' Hughes has said. He was 31 at the time and central to their FA Cup success under Ruud Gullit in 1997 and also the Cup-Winners' Cup triumph under Luca Vialli a year later. He was a player's player. A winner. It was always his intention to go into management, and with typically individualistic élan he went into international management first (with Wales) before graduating to the day-to-day business of running a club.

So far he has managed Blackburn Rovers, Manchester City, Fulham and QPR. He has been sacked only once, at Manchester City just before Christmas 2009 to make way for

QUOTE

'What a strange man Mark Hughes is.'

Fulham owner Mohamed Al-Fayed, the man behind the club's much-admired statue of Michael Jackson.

66 MARK HUGHES

PREMIER LEAGUE DEBUT (PLAYER):
Manchester United v Sheffield United, 15 August 1992

PREMIER LEAGUE DEBUT (MANAGER):
Blackburn Rovers v Portsmouth, 18 September 2004

PREMIER LEAGUE CLUBS (PLAYER):
Manchester United, Chelsea, Southampton, Everton, Blackburn Rovers

PREMIER LEAGUE CLUBS (MANAGER):
Blackburn Rovers, Manchester City, Fulham, Queens Park Rangers

PREMIER LEAGUE APPEARANCES/GOALS:

Manchester U	111	34
Chelsea	95	25
Southampton	52	2
Everton	18	1
Blackburn R	50	6
Total	324	68

PREMIER LEAGUE APPEARANCES (MANAGER):

Blackburn R	147
Manchester C	55
Fulham	38
QPR	18
Total	258

PREMIER LEAGUE HONOURS:
2 (1992-93, 1993-94)

COUNTRY:
Wales (born Wrexham, 1 November 1963)

Roberto Mancini. The players he signed – Kompany, de Jong, Barry et al and others that continue to light up the Premier League including Adebayor, Bellamy, Given ... and Tevez, famously stolen away from United – were all inherited by Mancini as he helped City end their 35-year trophy drought.

Now put yourself, if you will, in the shoes of whoever decides upon the successor to Sir Alex Ferguson. Cantona? Not in the mood. Keane? Shown wanting. Robson? Not delivered. Ince? Not good enough at the highest level. Once again, if they want to win, it could very well be Mark 'Sparky' Hughes.

DH

65 STEVE BRUCE

PREMIER LEAGUE DEBUT (PLAYER):
Manchester United v Sheffield United,
15 August 1992

PREMIER LEAGUE DEBUT (MANAGER):
Birmingham City v Arsenal, 18 August 2002

PREMIER LEAGUE CLUB (PLAYER):
Manchester United

PREMIER LEAGUE CLUBS (MANAGER):
Birmingham City, Wigan Athletic, Sunderland

PREMIER LEAGUE APPEARANCES/GOALS:

Manchester U	148	11
Total	148	11

PREMIER LEAGUE APPEARANCES (MANAGER):

Birmingham C	165
Wigan A	63
Sunderland	89
Total	317

PREMIER LEAGUE HONOURS:
3 (1992-93, 1993-94, 1995-96)

COUNTRY:
England (born Newcastle, 31 December 1960)

DESPITE PLAYING for Wallsend Boys and representing Newcastle Schools, both notable recruiting grounds for footballing talent in the North East, Steve Bruce slipped through the net of both Sunderland and Newcastle United, the team he used to jump the turnstiles to support as a boy. The probable reason for this improbable oversight? Even as a youth, Bruce was an unlikely shape for a footballer – his torso a giant up-turned analogue TV perched on the legs of Zola Budd.

He was about to give up on his dreams and sign up to be an apprentice plumber at the Swan Hunter dockyard when Gillingham stepped in to save him from a career of metal-bashing, weekends in William Hill's and premature redundancy. He did, though, eventually team up with a Sparky (Hughes) in 1987 when, via Norwich City, he arrived at an average

Manchester United side in the initial stages of transformation under former Aberdeen manager Alex Ferguson.

Twenty-five years later, the club are arguably the most successful in English history (with only Liverpool able to raise an objection). Ferguson, as you might expect, has been garlanded, but on the field it is usually the fabled 'Class of '92' – the Beckham-Butt-Giggs-Nevilles-Scholes generation – who are held to be the catalyst. Some greybeards might nod in the direction of Mark Hughes, Paul Ince and Eric Cantona, but the real motor in the engine of United's comeback was the partnership of Bruce and Gary Pallister.

The best centre-back never to play for England, Bruce was cool, brave and, considering his height, superb in the air. And he scored goals (including an astounding 19 in all competitions in 1990-91). Typically, he would employ his stadium-sized chest at every opportunity, deflecting shots, intercepting aerial passes and controlling the ball in tight situations. In 1993-94, he became the first English captain in the 20th century to win the Double. A host of other honours followed as United came to dominate the English game.

Subsequently, and despite winning promotion to the Premiership for Birmingham on two occasions, his career as a manager has been an anti-climax to date. He became a permanent fixture around the top flight's discomfort zone with several teams, but maintained his dignity; his battered face, enough to drive a plastic surgeon to early retirement, featuring in countless cheerful post-mortems after another 0-1 home defeat. However, behind the sweet reasonableness, and that tuneful Geordie accent, there is a man of shipyard steel. It took a chest that big to accommodate his heart. **FC**

THE MOMENT HE BECAME A LEGEND

10 April 1993. Two headed goals in injury time (or Fergie time) rescue an unlikely 2-1 win over Sheffield Wednesday during the title run-in. With momentum behind them, United go on to win their first league title since 1967.

WELL I NEVER ...

He has published three novels, *Sweeper!* (sample line: 'There was no doubt I was going to die. And not even in Newcastle. Not even Premier League. In Halifax, of all places, with a club in the Third Division'), *Defender!* and *Striker!*.

QUOTE

'I'm not really into tactics.'

Shortly after taking charge at Sunderland, Steve Bruce was asked whether he would consider playing in a Christmas Tree formation.

64 RUUD GULLIT

PREMIER LEAGUE DEBUT (PLAYER):
Chelsea v Everton, 19 August 1995

PREMIER LEAGUE DEBUT (MANAGER):
Chelsea v Southampton, 18 August 1996

PREMIER LEAGUE CLUB (PLAYER):
Chelsea

PREMIER LEAGUE CLUBS (MANAGER):
Chelsea, Newcastle United

PREMIER LEAGUE APPEARANCES/GOALS:
Chelsea   49   4
Total   49   4

PREMIER LEAGUE APPEARANCES (MANAGER):
Chelsea   63
Newcastle U   41
Total   104

PREMIER LEAGUE HONOURS:
None

COUNTRY:
Netherlands (born Amsterdam,
1 September 1962)

GROOVY, LAID-BACK and possibly just a little bit nasty might be the best way to describe Ruud Gullit, one of the most enigmatic Dutch footballers of all time. Groovy in terms of his effortlessly mesmerising ability with the ball, laid-back as a pundit in the studio as he delivers cool, cutting analysis, and nasty if you played under him as a manager and fell out of favour. As Newcastle defender Alessandro Pistone put it, 'When he went, I had a little party.'

Before coming to the Premier League in 1995, the 1987 European Footballer of the Year (an award he dedicated to the then-incarcerated Nelson Mandela) was known to the world as a frighteningly skilful midfielder and forward for the Netherlands and AC Milan. Alongside equally gifted countryman Marco van Basten, he was a key player in the wondrous Dutch team that won the 1988 European Championship and the Milan team that famously humiliated Real Madrid 5-0 in the semi-final second leg on their way to lifting the 1989 European Cup.

Signed by Glenn Hoddle from Sampdoria, Gullit first played for Chelsea as a sweeper, but the outspoken player complained that his team-mates were unable to read his passes. He had more success in central midfield, and finished runner-up as Footballer of the Year behind Eric Cantona. When Hoddle left to manage England, Gullit took over as player-manager and led the team to FA Cup glory over Middlesbrough, becoming the first overseas manager to win a major domestic trophy in England.

His second season brought more success, but not enough for chairman Ken Bates, who fired Gullit despite Chelsea being second in the Premier League, and making good progress in the European Cup-Winners' Cup and the League Cup (they subsequently went on to win the latter two). Bates, without a trace of irony, moaned about Gullit's high wage demands and his arrogance.

It was a charge that followed him to Newcastle when he took over in 1998; infamously, Alan Shearer was benched for a derby against Sunderland and club captain Robert Lee was denied a squad number. Gullit resigned early in the 1999-00 season, and has since continued to struggle as a manager, with Feyenoord, LA Galaxy and Terek Grozny. As a TV pundit, however, he remains refreshingly forthright and untroubled by concerns of sporting politesse. IP

THE MOMENT HE BECAME A LEGEND

Already long established as a legend by the time he arrived in the Premier League, his dribble and stunning shot for Chelsea against Manchester City on a wet Tuesday night in March 1996 served to reinforce the view that the English top flight was on the rise.

WELL I NEVER ...

A huge fan of 1970s BBC sitcom *It Ain't 'Alf Hot, Mum*, as manager at Chelsea he called his players 'My lovely boys'. Allegedly.

QUOTE

'Ruud loved conflict. He enjoyed being at loggerheads with certain players. And he was just so arrogant. His ego was as big as Amsterdam and he didn't even try to disguise it.'

Rob Lee, on being managed by Gullit at Newcastle.

THERE'S AN enduring image of John Barnes, in the all-red of Liverpool, calmly and dismissively back-heeling a banana into touch. He did it with the insouciance one might expect from the son of a colonel and military attaché. 'I grew up in a middle-class family in Jamaica, I had no self-worth issues whatsoever,' he has said. 'For someone to call me a nigger and call me worthless doesn't register with me.' But then Barnes was never defined by the startling ignorance of some football fans, rather by the quality of the football he produced.

When flying into Britain from Jamaica for the first time, he was amazed at the number of pitches he could see from the window. From park football ('I looked at John Barnes for ten minutes,' recalled Watford chief scout Bertie Mee, 'and I said, "I want his phone number and address"'), he went straight into the Watford team in 1981, aged just 17. Within a few years a modest George Best was reflecting, 'Barnes has the ability to become the best, the most exciting winger in British soccer since me.'

Liverpool swooped in 1987 and Barnes left to join a truly great side alongside the likes of Beardsley, Houghton and Rush. It is from this period that he is chiefly remembered, pulling full-backs apart and jinking down the flanks with muscular grace. But, arguably, it was in the era of the Premier League that he became the complete player. Despite a stormy relationship with new manager Graeme Souness, Barnes performed an invaluable role at Anfield, bringing along the new generation of players and sitting deeper in midfield, linking up with Jamie Redknapp and Steve McManaman.

Robbed of his explosive pace after an Achilles' tendon injury, he subsequently blossomed under Roy Evans to become a visionary playmaker, a string-puller. It was a job description he developed when former Liverpool team-mate

THE MOMENT HE BECAME A LEGEND

A stunning goal against Brazil in the Maracana in 1984. Barnes ran 40 yards through the heart of Brazil's defence before prodding the ball home for one of England's greatest ever goals.

WELL I NEVER ...

Watford's sale of Barnes for £900,000 was a decent return on their original investment, having 'bought' him for a full set of playing kit from Middlesex league team Sudbury Court.

63 | JOHN BARNES

PREMIER LEAGUE DEBUT:
Liverpool v Queens Park Rangers,
23 November 1992

PREMIER LEAGUE CLUBS:
Liverpool, Newcastle United, Charlton
Athletic

PREMIER LEAGUE APPEARANCES/GOALS:

Liverpool	162	22
Newcastle U	27	6
Charlton A	12	0
Total	201	28

PREMIER LEAGUE HONOURS:
None

COUNTRY:
England (born Kingston, Jamaica, 7
November 1963)

and boss Kenny Dalglish snapped him up for Newcastle in 1997. With belief enough to play him even further out of position, as striker in place of the injured Alan Shearer and the departed Les Ferdinand, Barnes ended the season as top scorer (with six goals).

In a slightly disappointing denouement, the arrival of Ruud Gullit saw Barnes eventually frozen out and he ended his Premier League career with a brief cameo at Charlton Athletic, but his reputation was assured. He is now a respected and eloquent voice on all the 'big' issues within the modern game.

GS

> QUOTE
>
> 'You two scousers are always
>   yappin'
> I'm gonna show you some serious
>   rappin'
> I come from Jamaica, my name is
>   John Bar-nes
> When I do my thing the crowd go
>   bananas.'
>
> 'The Anfield Rap', Liverpool FC 1988.

62 DWIGHT YORKE

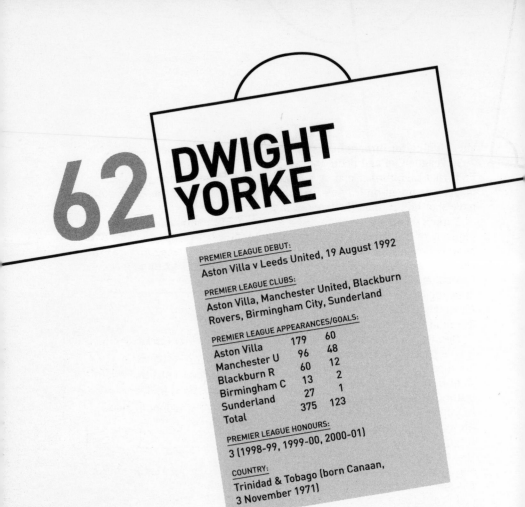

PREMIER LEAGUE DEBUT:
Aston Villa v Leeds United, 19 August 1992

PREMIER LEAGUE CLUBS:
Aston Villa, Manchester United, Blackburn Rovers, Birmingham City, Sunderland

PREMIER LEAGUE APPEARANCES/GOALS:

Aston Villa	179	60
Manchester U	96	48
Blackburn R	60	12
Birmingham C	13	2
Sunderland	27	1
Total	375	123

PREMIER LEAGUE HONOURS:
3 (1998-99, 1999-00, 2000-01)

COUNTRY:
Trinidad & Tobago (born Canaan, 3 November 1971)

IN A CAREER that has seen more changes in direction than the wind, there has always been one constant in Dwight Yorke's life – and that is the smile that has never left his face. For the self-proclaimed 'small island boy' who had travelled from the poor beaches of the Caribbean to find fame and fortune in the Premier League, what was there not to beam about?

Yorke was famously discovered by Graham Taylor, then Aston Villa manager, on a tour of the West Indies and signed for £10,000. Most Villa fans still hold Yorke in high esteem (despite him

THE MOMENT HE BECAME A LEGEND

St James' Park, 30 September 1996. Yorke's first hat-trick for Villa may have ended in a 4-3 defeat to Newcastle, but the fight-back from 3-1, and a man, down was inspired.

later signing for Birmingham City) for exploits that included winning the 1996 League Cup and being the last person to score in front of the Holte End. That said, former manager John Gregory, upon hearing that the player was intent on leaving for Manchester United, commented, 'I would have shot him if I had [had] a gun in the office.'

Yorke's debut season at United – a snip at £12.6 million – was the pinnacle of his career. As the more cheerful member in a partnership with polar opposite Andrew Cole, he scored 29 goals in all competitions as the club won an unprecedented Treble of Premier League, FA Cup and Champions League titles in dramatic circumstances. Inevitably perhaps, it was all downhill from there.

Despite winning another two league titles, Yorke seemed to lose his appetite for the game and he went from creating football history to making tabloid headlines – mostly for a playboy lifestyle that saw him squander fortunes on fast cars and even faster women. He has admitted sneaking girls into his room before United games and Sir Alex Ferguson has blamed him for the premature greying of his hair.

Eventually, of course, the United manager finally tired of nocturnal tales involving wild parties with Mark Bosnich and his tempestuous relationship with pneumatic glamour model Jordan, and Yorke was cast out into the comparative Premier League wilderness. He upset another Scottish manager in Graeme Souness at Blackburn, who was unimpressed with his commitment during a training session. He later played for former United stars Steve Bruce and Roy Keane, at Birmingham and Sunderland respectively, in between reinventing himself as a midfielder during a successful spell Down Under with Sydney FC.

Dwight Yorke admits to having made some mistakes, but few could doubt that he seemed to enjoy himself along the way.   RA

> **WELL, I NEVER ...**
>
> During the 1999 Cricket World Cup, Yorke was often seen bringing drinks onto the field of play for the West Indies team featuring his childhood friend Brian Lara.

> **QUOTE**
>
> 'To be quite honest, I think it's a myth that sex before games is bad. Each to his own. Gary Neville says forty-eight hours for sex before a match. Actually for him it's probably a week.'
>
> Dwight Yorke explains how he manages that difficult bedroom/training ground balance.

IT WAS ONLY when taking the job at the Stadium of Light that it emerged that, growing up as a kid in Kilrea, County Derry, young Martin O'Neill's favourite team was Sunderland. It was a predictably unpredictable choice of team for a young man in Northern Ireland at the time. His idol was the man who had broken all the goal-scoring records for the club (63 in 74 games) and managed their youth team before, incredibly, going on to manage him at Nottingham Forest less than 15 years later.

> ## THE MOMENT HE BECAME A LEGEND
>
> He maintained Leicester City's top ten Premier League place for four seasons from 1997, and steered them to three League Cup finals.

Brian Clough's playing career effectively ended on Boxing Day 1962. 'I remember shedding a few tears that day and I shed a few tears with him since, but not over his injury,' O'Neill recently revealed. 'I can see him now. I never once phoned him for advice [as a manager] because I know he would have said, "You got yourself into this mess, you get yourself out of it."'

As a player, O'Neill spent ten years in the Forest midfield under Clough – the latter five taking in the title, two League Cup and two European Cup wins – before departing for Norwich City. As a manager he cut his teeth at Shepshed Charterhouse and Wycombe Wanderers before joining and then abruptly leaving Norwich for Leicester City where, on a shoestring budget, he assembled a surprisingly slick team in his own stubborn, passionate, eccentric image.

Much like Clough, he took players previously overlooked and dragged them into the top flight: Kasey Keller, Matt Elliott, Muzzy Izzet, Robbie Savage, Neil Lennon, Pontus Kaamark, Steve Guppy. They were all internationals when he'd finished with them, and the winners of two League Cups. And so to Celtic, his other boyhood team, who he successfully steered to domestic glory and the final of the 2003 UEFA Cup; but just two years later his wife Geraldine's illness put his career on indefinite hold.

> ## WELL I NEVER ...
>
> A former trainee lawyer, O'Neill employs the psychological skills of a criminologist to get the best out of his players. He has visited the scenes of several infamous crimes, and attended the trial of the Yorkshire Ripper at the Old Bailey.

61 MARTIN O'NEILL

PREMIER LEAGUE DEBUT (MANAGER):
Leicester City v Sunderland, 17 August 1996

PREMIER LEAGUE CLUBS (MANAGER):
Leicester City, Aston Villa, Sunderland

PREMIER LEAGUE APPEARANCES (MANAGER):

Leicester C	152
Aston Villa	152
Sunderland	25
Total	329

PREMIER LEAGUE HONOURS:
None

COUNTRY:
Northern Ireland (born Kilrea, 1 March 1952)

Returning to manage Villa in 2006, O'Neill's characteristic bounce, swagger and doublethink seemed hampered by expectations and finances. He resigned. However, after a spell of sofa-bound incisive punditry, he is now back in the Premier League, fully four feet off the ground at any shot on goal, preaching, pondering, praying – positively willing the ball into the net – at Sunderland, where his characteristic magical aura has instantly returned.

He may not be the smartest, the most driven or the most tactically astute of all Premier League managers, but, as his mentor might have put it, he's in the top one. **DH**

> ## QUOTE
>
> 'It's with a sense of relief that we are back in the business of friendliness and enjoyment here at the Dovecote. Those who matter know and, further than that, we have no comment.'
>
> The Shepshed Charterhouse chairman's programme notes after his sacking of Martin O'Neill in 1989.

60 PETER CROUCH

PREMIER LEAGUE DEBUT:
Aston Villa v Bolton Wanderers,
30 March 2002

PREMIER LEAGUE CLUBS:
Aston Villa, Southampton, Liverpool,
Portsmouth, Tottenham Hotspur, Stoke City

PREMIER LEAGUE APPEARANCES/GOALS:

Aston Villa	37	6
Southampton	27	12
Liverpool	85	22
Portsmouth	38	11
Tottenham H	72	12
Stoke C	32	10
Total	291	73

PREMIER LEAGUE HONOURS:
None

COUNTRY:
England (born Macclesfield, 30 January 1981)

IT'S HARD TO BELIEVE, but the 6ft 7in pipe-cleaner figure of Peter Crouch failed to catch the eye at Spurs around the turn of the millennium. The powers-that-be decided that their target man, though useful enough with a ball pinged at his head, was unlikely to become either a top-drawer Premiership striker or the trophy boyfriend of a glamorous underwear model.

Offloaded to QPR for a paltry £60,000, he was instantly dubbed 'Rodney' by the Loftus Road faithful (after the gormless *Only Fools & Horses* character, rather

THE MOMENT HE BECAME A LEGEND

Those robot-dancing celebrations after his first England goal against Hungary in May 2006 gave the big man *Heat* magazine celebrity appeal.

than former QPR star Rodney Marsh). However, there were a few promising signs – a deft touch with the ball to feet, the ability to arrive unnoticed in the box (eat your heart out David Blaine) and a hitherto undiscovered ability to turn even the best defenders.

Crouch scored ten goals in his year at Rangers, before moving on to Pompey for a more respectable £1.5 million fee. Less than a year later, he was on the move again, this time to Aston Villa, 18 goals having elevated his price tag to £5 million. There was a momentum building and so it went on, this gradual accrual of spiralling cash value.

A successful loan period at promotion-winning Norwich increased public recognition and brought forth the affectionate chant: 'He's tall, he's lean, he's a freaky goal-machine.' Via Southampton and a first England cap, Crouch arrived at Anfield with a £7 million price tag that weighed heavily at first. No longer a 'freaky goal-machine', the Kop had a new song for him: 'He's big, he's red, his feet stick out the bed ...'

By the end of the season, he had an FA Cup winner's medal and was in the England World Cup squad. As he has said since, 'I never lost belief at any stage.' The following year, he appeared in a Champions League final (against Milan) and finished as the club's leading goalscorer in all competitions, before returning to Portsmouth in 2008 (£9 million plus a potential further £2 million) and then Tottenham a year later – both homecomings orchestrated by Harry Redknapp.

Ever thrown away a beloved sticker album during an over-zealous clear-out before buying it back on eBay several years later? Well, that's exactly how Spurs must have felt, having to match the £9 million shelled out by 'Arry at Portsmouth just to reclaim their lanky reject turned multi-millionaire celebrity international striker, with a goal ratio better than one in two over 42 appearances for England. His combined transfers, freshly topped up by Stoke's record punt of £10 million in August 2011, now add up to £43,560,000. It's all about playing the long game.

GS

59 NICOLAS ANELKA

PREMIER LEAGUE DEBUT:
Arsenal v Chelsea, 5 April 1997

PREMIER LEAGUE CLUBS:
Arsenal, Liverpool (loan), Manchester City,
Bolton Wanderers, Chelsea

PREMIER LEAGUE APPEARANCES/GOALS:

Arsenal	65	23
Liverpool	20	4
Manchester C	89	37
Bolton W	53	21
Chelsea	125	38
Total	352	123

PREMIER LEAGUE HONOURS:
2 (1997-98, 2009-10)

COUNTRY:
France (born Versailles, 14 March 1979)

NICOLAS ANELKA'S legendary status is a two-headed beast. His consistent goalscoring feats mark him out as one of the most feared forwards in the Premier League's two decades. Yet his perpetual discontent has landed him with the nickname 'Le Sulk'. And that moniker's putting it kindly. His 18-match ban for France, after being sent home from the 2010 World Cup, followed a verbal broadside aimed at coach Raymond Domenech that caused salty fishwives to blush like virgin angels.

Anelka is the archetypal modern pro, though perhaps not a model one. Apparently misunderstood by fans, managers and the media alike, the lanky young prospect who could turn on an apple seed burst on to the

THE MOMENT HE BECAME A LEGEND

Scoring a first-half hat-trick as a 19-year-old for Arsenal against Leicester City in a 5-0 shellacking.

'Tino' Asprilla found out halfway through the game that Newcastle were thinking about extending his contract in the North East.

Four-time all-Norfolk speed-dating champion, Gilo 'The Viper' Blennerhasset, 53, pictured here beating his personal best of 36.4 seconds in somewhat controversial fashion.

Friedel: 'What do I think about Pepe Reina's attempt to take my record for consecutive Premier League appearances?'

The Cone Hotline was inundated. 'Where,' they wanted to know, 'do you get one of the those "Ian Holloways"?'

At first, Batty was reluctant to challenge the petulant, French millionaire, 20-year-old Arsenal superstar Nicolas Anelka. But he soon got over it.

Bullard: 'What do you mean, I'm not Phil Brown enough? Well, maybe I'm allergic to creosote, how about that?'

In the online version of the *Illustrated Children's Dictionary*, this is what you get when you type in, 'What is a rhetorical question?'

Joey Barton: 'Hang on mate, I'm an England international.'
Scott Parker: 'Yeah, I heard you got two caps. Your first and your last.'

Nobody could accuse Middlesbrough of being a one-man team.

Just to prove that Kevin Davies was also occasionally on the painful end of a bad tackle.

A voice in the crowd: 'Jesus Christ, he's deaf as well.'

'They can take their "Walking in a Mancini Wonderland" and . . .'

Niall Quinn: 'And this is your wish list . . .'
Steve Bruce: 'Yep.'
Quinn: 'Well, I think we can stretch to that . . . Does it have to be Ben and Jerry's or will Tesco own-brand ice cream do?'

'Final offer . . . Torres and a scarf . . . £48 million and I'm cutting my own throat here . . .'

And in a parallel universe, Darren Anderton attempted to tackle Xabi Alonso.

The remake of *Reservoir Dogs*, starring Keys and Gray, was not a complete success . . . Not least because they kept smiling at the wrong times.

To Arsenal fans at the City of Manchester Stadium in 2009: 'I'm also looking for a Toys R Us garden table to go with it, one about this big, that seats between six and eight.'

Ryan Shawcross: 'Why don't you pick on somebody your own size?' Craig Bellamy: 'I can't. They're seven years old.'

'This is the man all tattered and torn/ That kissed the maiden all forlorn.' Jack Walker watches Blackburn Rovers in the house that he built as they are relegated in 1999.

McCallister v Stam. Skill v Strength. Beauty v the Beast. Number one all over v Head wax.

Jones mistimes his tackle completely and makes contact with the ball while also leaving Paul Merson intact.

Former Anfield idol John Barnes refuses to get off the fence before the 2012 Liverpool–Everton FA Cup semi-final. The Everton mascot, Changi the Elephant, has just missed a penalty.

Dwight Yorke captured on the way to the mandatory full-on toothy grin in 1999, while rumours circulating that Andy 'Andrew' Cole was about to break into a half-smile remain unsubstantiated at this time.

Unfortunately, O'Neill was determined to 'Go Martin'; he scowled for 85 minutes, pretended to pull his hair out, jumped 36 feet in the air when Leicester scored and then proceeded to talk down to a variety of journalists.

scene at Highbury in the late 1990s when Ian Wright was injured. He partnered successfully with Dennis Bergkamp in the Arsenal Double-winning team in the 1997-98 season, scoring in the FA Cup final 2-0 win over Newcastle.

Inevitably, want-away rumours caused him to fall out with the Arsenal faithful, and he moved to Madrid for a gargantuan £23 million (and, as Kevin Keegan put it, 'They built a training ground on him'). Egos clashed at the Bernabeu and he was suspended by the club after he missed training, but he came back to score in both legs of the Champions League semi-final against Bayern Munich, and had a hand in two goals in the final 3-0 victory over Valencia.

He moved on straight away, first for an unsettled spell at his first club, Paris St Germain (where he fell out with coach Luis Fernandez), then to Manchester City after a patchy loan spell at Liverpool. He won no trophies there, but scored consistently, likewise at Bolton, before moving to Chelsea where he picked up another Premier League medal in 2009-10 (to go with other serious honours including a Euro 2000 winner's medal with France), and converted successfully to a wide position in support of Didier Drogba.

Although he claims that this was the happiest time of his career, there were still ructions. After missing a penalty in the shoot-out during the 2008 Champions League final loss in Moscow against Manchester United, Anelka blamed the miss on manager Avram Grant for sending him into the game without enough time to warm up. Easy to admire, but hard to like, Anelka left England for a lucrative move to China in early 2012 where he is now player-manager at Shanghai Shenhua.

IP

WHO IS JAMIE REDKNAPP? Ask today's teenagers and they'll talk of the tight-trousered son of 'Arry and cousin of Frank, whose grin leers out from their television screens every Sunday afternoon like that of an over-enthusiastic uncle. Half of these youthful cretins will even snigger dismissively when you begin to swoon at the memory of the lovely Louise and her seminal solo hit 'Naked' ...

> ### THE MOMENT HE BECAME A LEGEND
>
> When Roy Evans replaced Graeme Souness as manager, he promoted Redknapp from fringe performer to Liverpool's creative fulcrum.

Anyway, where were we? Ah yes, Jamie. The face of Thomas Cook, Marks and Spencer, Nintendo Wii and Sky Sports was once, as hard as it might be for you young ones to believe, a footballer of some repute. In fact, were it not for an appalling string of injuries, he could quite conceivably have become one of the most elegant performers England ever had.

An excellent passer of the ball with a wonderful appreciation of space and an unerring ability to 'smash it' from distance, Redknapp was a far better player than many might remember. Indeed, between 1995 and 1996, he was perhaps the Premier League's pre-eminent playmaker; a midfielder who dictated the tempo of an outrageously gifted Liverpool team and enabled the likes of Steve McManaman and Robbie Fowler to thrive.

That he has only a 1995 League Cup winner's medal to show for such talent is a scandal – badges for the 2001 Community Shield and European Super Cup were earned as an unused substitute – and attributable more to injuries and the dominance of Manchester United than the Spice Boys persona that was used to denigrate that youthful Anfield side with their cream suits, exotic lifestyles and advertising commitments.

Redknapp freely admits that the team underachieved, but his own failings lay more in the frailty of his body. 'Playing for England cost me three years,' he says, without bitterness, of an 18-cap career. 'Three times I left

> ### WELL I NEVER ...
>
> He was the last player signed by Kenny Dalglish at the end of his first spell as Liverpool manager in 1991.

58 JAMIE REDKNAPP

PREMIER LEAGUE DEBUT:
Liverpool v Leeds United, 29 August 1992

PREMIER LEAGUE CLUBS:
Liverpool, Tottenham Hotspur, Southampton

PREMIER LEAGUE APPEARANCES/GOALS:

Liverpool	231	29
Tottenham H	48	4
Southampton	16	0
Total	295	33

PREMIER LEAGUE HONOURS:
None

COUNTRY:
England (born Barton-on-Sea, 25 June 1973)

on a stretcher during games for them, with two broken ankles and a torn hamstring.' Latterly, though, it was his knees that forced his 2002 exit from Liverpool, then eventually his retirement after three years at Tottenham – the club he rejected as a youth in favour of Bournemouth – and a brief sojourn at Southampton with his father.

The pair remain close, and while it might seem silly to suggest the son might eclipse the father's successes, Jamie has a sharper football brain than his punditry persona would suggest. Indeed, Redknapp Snr was rumoured to have sneaked into a quiet corner of the White Hart Lane dressing room at half time to seek solutions for a tactical problem from the younger man in the gantry.   **RW**

QUOTE

'Jamie used to say to me, "Can I come training rather than school?" and I used to say, "Yeah, come on, but don't tell your mum."'

Harry Redknapp finally lets the cat out of the bag.

HOW DIFFICULT can it be, this managing lark? Stuart Pearce settled down with a pen and paper to select his first line-up as emergency Nottingham Forest player-boss, and he was quietly pleased with the side he'd put together – until his wife Liz pointed out that he hadn't included a goalkeeper in his starting eleven. He got better at it, and soon won the January 1997 Manager of the Month award.

By March, however, and with Forest heading out of the Premier League, he was relieved of his duties. After this false start to his managerial career, it would be eight years before he picked up the reins again, when Kevin Keegan left Manchester City and he took over, first as caretaker and then permanently after being one missed penalty away from UEFA Cup qualification. As he told Robbie Fowler, the man who missed the spot kick, 'Welcome to the club.'

But after a decent start at City, two seasons of decline saw Pearce leaving the club and able to concentrate on his post as England Under-21 coach, where he's still working with some success. He was also put in charge of the GB team for the 2012 London Olympics, but 'Psycho' will forever be remembered as the sort of aggressive left-back that you'd hate to meet down a dark alley, or on the right wing at any time of day or night.

The Hammersmith-born, punk rock-loving electrician had been turning out for non-league Wealdstone before he took the huge step up to the top flight with Coventry City. Two years later, having signed for Nottingham Forest, he was still so unsure of his place at the top table that he used the club programme to advertise his services as an electrician. He need not have worried.

During his time in Nottingham he became a cult hero, played in League and FA Cup finals, and contributed committed performances for a dozen years. He made the Forest number three

57 STUART PEARCE

PREMIER LEAGUE DEBUT (PLAYER):
Nottingham Forest v Liverpool, 16 August 1992

PREMIER LEAGUE DEBUT (MANAGER):
Nottingham Forest v Arsenal, 21 December 1996

PREMIER LEAGUE CLUBS (PLAYER):
Nottingham Forest, Newcastle United, West Ham United

PREMIER LEAGUE CLUBS (MANAGER):
Nottingham Forest, Manchester City

PREMIER LEAGUE APPEARANCES/GOALS:

Nottingham F	123	18
Newcastle U	37	0
West Ham U	42	2
Total	202	20

PREMIER LEAGUE APPEARANCES (MANAGER):

Nottingham F	9
Manchester C	85
Total	94

PREMIER LEAGUE HONOURS:
None

COUNTRY:
England (born Hammersmith, 24 April 1962)

shirt his own and launched an England career that saw him partake in England's two most successful campaigns in recent history – Italia 90 and Euro 96. He missed his penalty in the 1990 semi-final shoot-out against the Germans, but had the guts to take another against Spain in the Euro 96 quarter-finals – he scored, roared with relief and the whole of England roared with him.

Pearce stuck with Forest as a player after their first relegation from the Premier League in 1992-93, but left for Newcastle the second time it happened and enjoyed a couple of good seasons at St James' Park, before falling out with new boss Ruud Gullit. The Dutch maestro was subject to a 'Psycho Special' in training and had probably decided Pearce's fate before he landed. After brief spells at West Ham and Manchester City, he called a halt to his playing career in 2002.   GS

56 KEVIN PHILLIPS

PREMIER LEAGUE DEBUT:
Sunderland v Chelsea, 7 August 1999

PREMIER LEAGUE CLUBS:
Sunderland, Southampton, Aston Villa, Birmingham City

PREMIER LEAGUE APPEARANCES/GOALS:

Sunderland	139	61
Southampton	64	22
Aston Villa	23	4
Birmingham C	33	5
Total	259	92

PREMIER LEAGUE HONOURS:
None

COUNTRY:
England (born Hitchin, 25 July 1973)

THE GENRE OF footballers' home movies is probably one best avoided, given some of the exploits committed to camera by the Premier League's finest. Just ask former Aston Villa goalkeeper Stefan Postma. Yet as far as Kevin Phillips is concerned, watching himself in action was a wonderful way of arousing his scoring senses.

It was during his staggeringly successful stint at Sunderland that the diminutive striker began following a pre-match routine of watching videos of himself rippling the rigging, believing it boosted his confidence before stepping on to the pitch. And, judging by his impact at the Stadium of Light, it worked.

THE MOMENT HE BECAME A LEGEND

August 1999. Sunderland travel to Newcastle looking to end 20 years without a derby victory. The match, Phillips' fifth outing in the Premiership, was poised at 1-1 when the striker scrawled his signature all over the rain-lashed stage. After Tommy Wright saved his initial shot, Phillips spun adroitly to fetch the ball from behind him and spoon it over the goalkeeper and his retreating defenders in one smooth movement.

A goalscorer of note in the lower leagues, few thought he could replicate his ratio in the top flight. The sceptics were correct: he didn't. He improved upon it. At the end of his debut campaign in the Premier League, he had scored an astonishing 30 goals in 36 games to become the only Englishman ever to win the European Golden Boot, his partnership with Niall Quinn entering Wearside folklore as the club secured a seventh-place finish.

That Phillips was unable to post such outstanding numbers in subsequent seasons fails to appreciate the development in his game over the past decade or so. When he arrived in the Premier League, Phillips was a finisher: quick, perceptive and gifted, with a remarkable sleight of foot. But over the years he has metamorphosed into a more rounded player, capable of dropping deep to embroider play, yet still able to convert chances with practised ease – something he was still doing with Blackpool in the Championship aged 39.

Relegation with Sunderland, a fate he would subsequently suffer with Southampton and Birmingham, served only to unfairly dull his shine in the eyes of successive England managers, despite a goals-per-game ratio that hovered around one every two-and-a-half matches. Kevin Keegan took him to Euro 2000, but consigned him to the bench for the entirety of England's truncated campaign, while Sven-Goran Eriksson showed an equal mistrust for his undoubted gifts. 'I think I deserved more than eight caps, but I was competing with some top-quality strikers,' said Phillips. Perhaps showing Sven his videos might have made all the difference. **RW**

> ## WELL I NEVER ...
>
> Phillips agreed to sign for Sunderland while sitting in the car park at Portman Road, having just finished talking terms with Ipswich.

> ## QUOTE
>
> 'When [Blackpool] played Crystal Palace, we were walking down past the back of the kitchens and a chef shouted: "Oi, Phillips. Good player," and as I was walking away he said: "Got no pace, though." I have never had electric pace. I like to think I use my brain a bit more.'
>
> Phillips answers his critic(s).

IF LES FERDINAND missed out on the usual route to a professional career in football, the apprenticeship and the privileges and the warped perspective they can offer, he was left with a lifelong appreciation of his star status, and kept his feet firmly on the ground ... even when he was piloting his own helicopter.

By contrast, it was a delivery van that provided Les with a living when he was playing semi-pro for non-league Hayes and that's when he was first noticed by QPR scout Frank Sibley.

> ## THE MOMENT HE BECAME A LEGEND
>
> He went on an Easter rampage in 1993, scoring a hat-trick in QPR's 4-3 win at home to Forest before repeating the feat two days later in a 5-3 victory at Everton.

Although he was sent off that fated afternoon, Sibley liked what he saw and by April 1987 Les had made his Division One debut for Rangers, aged 20.

After a successful loan spell in Turkey, which saw him net 14 goals in 24 games for Besiktas, Ferdinand returned to Loftus Road and set about establishing himself in the first team. In the following six seasons for QPR, he scored 80 times in 160 league games in a remarkable (and easily calculated) goal-every-other-game ratio, which made him one of the Premier League's early stars.

In 1995, Ferdinand made the big move from his native West London to Newcastle for a (then) huge fee of £6 million. For their money, United had bought a supreme athlete, very strong in the air, quick on the ground with a lethal eye for goal and the elegance of a Rolls Royce. He was at the top of his game in his two seasons at St James' Park and his 41 goals helped Newcastle to two Premier League runners-up places.

Ferdinand returned to London in 1997, spending six seasons at Tottenham. Although a series of injuries disrupted his time at White Hart Lane, he won his first medal – when Spurs beat Leicester in the 1999 League Cup

> ## WELL I NEVER ...
>
> When Newcastle paid QPR £6 million for Ferdinand, Hayes FC received a £600,000 sell-on bonus that funded the 'Ferdinand Suite' corporate facility.

55 LES FERDINAND

PREMIER LEAGUE DEBUT:
Queens Park Rangers v Manchester City,
17 August 1992

PREMIER LEAGUE CLUBS:
Queens Park Rangers, Newcastle United,
Tottenham Hotspur, West Ham United,
Leicester City, Bolton Wanderers

PREMIER LEAGUE APPEARANCES/GOALS:

Club	Appearances	Goals
QPR	110	60
Newcastle U	68	41
Tottenham H	118	33
West Ham U	14	2
Leicester C	29	12
Bolton W	12	1
Total	351	149

PREMIER LEAGUE HONOURS:
None; PFA Player of the Year 1996

COUNTRY:
England (born Paddington, 8 December 1966)

final – and fittingly, as one of the competition's major figures, he notched the Premier League's 10,000th goal, against Fulham on 15 December 2001.

In the autumn of his career, Ferdinand spent a season each at West Ham, Leicester and Bolton (scoring for each and becoming the only player to do so for six Premier League clubs), before finally dropping out of the top flight for a dozen games with Reading. Having entered the game late he also left it late, retiring just short of his 40th birthday. He was subsequently awarded an official MBE to go with his unofficial nickname of 'Sir Les'. **GS**

> QUOTE
>
> 'At Besiktas they even sacrificed a lamb on the pitch. Its blood was then daubed on my forehead and boots to bring me good luck. They never used to do that at QPR.'
>
> Ferdinand wonders if the 'Rs' might have missed a trick.

54 DAVID JAMES

PREMIER LEAGUE DEBUT:
Liverpool v Nottingham Forest,
16 August 1992

PREMIER LEAGUE CLUBS:
Liverpool, Aston Villa, West Ham United,
Manchester City, Portsmouth

PREMIER LEAGUE APPEARANCES/GOALS:

Liverpool	214	0
Aston Villa	67	0
West Ham U	64	0
Manchester C	93	0
Portsmouth	134	0
Total	572	0

PREMIER LEAGUE HONOURS:
None

COUNTRY:
England (born Welwyn, 1 August 1970)

IT IS HARD to believe that it is 20 years since David James first walked through the doors at Anfield to eventually replace his boyhood hero Bruce Grobbelaar, all 6ft 5in of wide-eyed wonder and burgeoning promise. Harder still to recall that, at that time, Liverpool had won six of their 18 league titles in the previous decade.

It was an unforgiving environment. Hitherto cosseted from criticism at Watford, James soon appreciated that a higher profile brought its own problems and scathing scrutiny was one of them. He was a 'Spice Boy', his

THE MOMENT HE BECAME A LEGEND

22 April 2007. Aston Villa's failure to breach Portsmouth's goal in a dreary encounter at Villa Park gave James a 142nd Premier League clean sheet, beating the record held by David Seaman.

critics pointed out, more interested in modelling for Armani than making saves; his performances were apparently compromised further by an addiction to computer games. And don't even start on his attempts to claim crosses.

Such slurs have stuck despite a continued career of astonishing resolve. In hindsight, they perhaps spoke as much about the changing face of the game in a shifting society as much as his footballing frailties, because James' goalkeeping abilities remain cherished by a succession of managers. Imposing, agile and brave, he proved a commanding figure for Aston Villa, West Ham, Manchester City and Portsmouth after leaving Liverpool, his consistency such that only Ryan Giggs has made more Premier League appearances.

Granted, James was prone to the odd glaring error, but more often than not those were balanced out by a save that few other goalkeepers could even contemplate. How many of his record 173 clean sheets were preserved by such a stop? He might not be able to offer an answer, but the question will appeal to him, given an obsession with statistics that has survived his travails. 'Liverpool sort of spoilt the illusion I could break records, but I still keep my eye on things, like the clean sheets record,' he has said.

He will, then, be aware that only four goalkeepers have won more caps for England, despite the turbulence that has characterised his international career. Indeed, his belated summons to the starting XI for South Africa 2010 (becoming the oldest-ever World Cup debutant at 39 years and 321 days) not only brought two clean sheets but also stability – albeit briefly – to a ragged defence. That impact may have been overlooked, but the one-time future of English goalkeeping, still playing for Bristol City in the Championship, can glance at the numbers and be satisfied with a job well done.

RW

53 | SOL CAMPBELL

PREMIER LEAGUE DEBUT:
Tottenham Hotspur v Chelsea,
5 December 1992

PREMIER LEAGUE CLUBS:
Tottenham Hotspur, Arsenal, Portsmouth,
Arsenal, Newcastle United

PREMIER LEAGUE APPEARANCES/GOALS:

Tottenham H	255	10
Arsenal	146	8
Portsmouth	95	2
Newcastle U	7	0
Total	503	20

PREMIER LEAGUE HONOURS:
2 (2001-02, 2003-04)

COUNTRY:
England (born Plaistow, 18 September 1974)

FANS ARE patriotic volunteers, footballers are mercenaries. That's how it works. True, there is the occasional example of a player who remains loyal – Matt le Tissier, beyond reproach in matters of both skill and virtue – but most are often seen as badge-kissing seditious money-chasers and still move, even between rivals, with only the minimum of resentment – the late Gary Ablett, for example, transferred from Liverpool to Everton with barely a Scouse sneer.

THE MOMENT HE BECAME A LEGEND

Campbell's marshalling of the defence in 2003-04 ensured that Arsenal went the season unbeaten – 'The Invincibles'. The title is won at Spurs.

Certainly, there was nothing in English football to compare with Luis Figo's hounding by fans on his relocation from Barcelona to Real Madrid. Until, that is, Sulzeer ('Sol') Jeremiah Campbell went from Spurs to Arsenal in 2001.

Campbell had been the best Spurs player since Hoddle, the youngest England captain since Bobby Moore. He was quick, powerful, aerially imperious, a marvellous tackler (one sliding effort was estimated to be 23 feet in execution), unflappable as an Easter Island statue. He said he'd never play for Arsenal. He'd been at Tottenham for years, a refreshing example of the one-club local lad. But no, he crossed to the other side.

At Highbury, he continued to perform brilliantly, as essential to Arsenal's success as Pires and Henry, but something must give when you can't step outside your Georgian townhouse without being compared to the Bible's least appealing character, Satan included, by a thousand hate-filled, bacon-faced strangers. His one-time girlfriend, interior designer Kelly Hoppen, is said to have described him as 'a tortured soul'.

WELL I NEVER ...

Campbell played every minute of every game in four consecutive major international tournaments for England and was selected in the 'Best XI' for three of them, the 1998 and 2002 World Cups and the European Championships in 2004.

The implosion of his brilliant career makes strange reading. It started in February 2006, when, at fault for West Ham's first two goals in Arsenal's 3-2 defeat, Campbell asked to be substituted at half time and then disappeared. Pires said Sol had a 'big worry' in his private life. Perhaps this is what caused him to remain incommunicado over the next few days. He left Arsenal for Portsmouth five months later.

He lasted three years, but the weirdest chapter was imminent. In September 2009, he signed a five-year contract for League Two Notts County, who had apparently been taken over by a Middle Eastern consortium and employed Sven-Goran Eriksson as director of football. Satisfyingly enigmatic, Campbell said it was best for 'where I am at the moment in my life'. He was wrong, and his contract was cancelled by mutual consent after one game (a 2-1 defeat away at Morecambe).

There were another 11 games for Arsenal and seven for Newcastle, but the limelight was extinguished – a splendidly unusual coda to his brilliant career.

FC

QUOTE

'I became insular because at home there was no space to grow or to evolve, everything was tight and there was no room to breathe. People don't realise how that affects you as a kid. I wasn't allowed to speak, so my expression was football.'

Campbell reflects upon life as one of 12 children growing up in a terraced house in East London.

THERE ARE usually two ways for centre forwards to use their head – one is to physically score goals, the other is to mentally work out the best way to beat a defender. Former Everton and Scotland striker Duncan Ferguson, however, devised a third way. Apparently, you can use it to deck an opponent.

> ## THE MOMENT HE BECAME A LEGEND
>
> When he threw Liverpool's Paul Ince to the ground during a 1998 Merseyside derby at Anfield, despite the fact he was about to serve a three-game suspension for a previous sending off. Referee Peter Jones kindly let it pass.

A classic case of unfulfilled Tartan potential, 'Duncan Disorderly' (surely the best nickname this side of 'One Size' Fitz Hall) came to Merseyside from Glasgow Rangers with a prison term looming for head-butting Raith Rovers' John McStay at Ibrox, an offence that hadn't even warranted a yellow card because the match officials had somehow missed it. But, by way of some kind of reciprocal arrangement, trouble loved Duncan and he'd already been up on three assault charges for off-field incidents, so off he went to the Barlinnie clinker for 44 days.

His goals were punctuated with frequent red cards. In 11 seasons at Goodison Park between 1994 and 2006 – sandwiching two years at Newcastle – he was ordered off no less than eight times. Ferguson was combative, as every striker has to be, and he was no doubt subject to more provocation than most due to his reputation. Yet he never seemed to lose his temper, as such. He just dealt with the situation with maximum determination and the minimum amount of fuss and walked away.

The Scot played only seven times for his country before falling out with the Scottish FA – he resented the 12-match ban levied on top of the three-month

> ## WELL I NEVER ...
>
> Finnish composer Osmo Tapio Räihälä wrote an opera about Ferguson's time in prison called *Barlinnie Nine*, which premiered in Helsinki on 20 April 2005, the same night Ferguson scored the winner in a 1-0 victory over Manchester United.

52 DUNCAN FERGUSON

PREMIER LEAGUE DEBUT:
Everton v Coventry City, 15 October 1994

PREMIER LEAGUE CLUBS:
Everton, Newcastle United, Everton

PREMIER LEAGUE APPEARANCES/GOALS:

Everton	239	60
Newcastle U	30	8
Total	269	68

PREMIER LEAGUE HONOURS:
None

COUNTRY:
Scotland (born Stirling, 27 December 1971)

prison sentence he'd already received for the McStay assault. He was also plagued by injury at both Everton and Newcastle, but retained the support of many fans who viewed with affection his persistent brushes with referees, opponents, and authority in general.

On top of that, he had a knack for scoring against Manchester United (six times, including one for Newcastle), his left-footed drive on the turn into the top corner at Old Trafford in August 1996 being a reminder that he wasn't just good in the air. And then he scored a second – with his head, of course – to earn the Toffees a 2-2 draw.

His only winners' medal (other than one with Rangers for the Scottish Premier League) also came against United in the 1995 FA Cup final. To further endear him to the blue side of the city, he also scored in four Merseyside derbies. Improbably perhaps, he's now planning to become a coach. IP

> QUOTE
>
> 'He could have been the best striker this country's ever seen.'
>
> Former Everton manager Joe Royle.

TEN THOUSAND pounds. That was the prize on offer by the *Sun* newspaper at the start of the 2005-06 season for the first player to beat Petr Cech, the South-west London club's goalkeeping colossus. But then that's the problem with being so consistently brilliant: people want you to slip up. Eventually, Aston Villa's Luke Moore penetrated the Blues' defence in September 2005, more than a month after the 2005-06 season began, with the reward duly donated to charity.

> ## THE MOMENT HE BECAME A LEGEND
>
> Between 18 December 2004 and 12 February 2005, Cech kept ten consecutive clean sheets and Chelsea went 1,025 minutes without conceding a goal.

Signed by Claudio Ranieri from French side Rennes for £7 million (more than all the previous Chelsea goalkeepers combined), Cech, who was named player of the tournament at the 2000 European U21 Championship, was initially brought in as Carlo Cudicini's understudy. But with a new manager – Jose Mourinho – came a new dawn. Cech became a key figure under the new multi-cultural regime; no hindrance to a man able to swear at his defenders in English, Portuguese and Spanish, as well as his native tongue.

Two and a half seasons into his Chelsea career, however, with just over a minute on the clock at Reading's Madejski Stadium on 14 October 2006 and racing to collect a loose ball, with Steve Hunt closing in, Cech plunged at the winger's feet. Hunt's knee collided with the keeper's head, he was knocked unconscious, stretchered from the pitch and subsequently required surgery to attach two steel plates to a depressed fracture in his skull.

He was lucky to survive the injury and the 30-minute wait for an ambulance (since then, stricter rules on medical attention have been introduced by the Premier League), and many thought he would never play again, but he defied the odds and came back against Liverpool on 20 January 2007, complete with the

> ## WELL I NEVER ...
>
> Growing up in a communist regime, his father worked at the local Skoda factory and Cech played ice hockey – as a goalie – while on the football field he began his school career as a striker.

51 PETR CECH

PREMIER LEAGUE DEBUT:
Chelsea v Manchester United,
15 August 2004

PREMIER LEAGUE CLUB:
Chelsea

PREMIER LEAGUE APPEARANCES/GOALS:
Chelsea   256   0
Total   256   0

PREMIER LEAGUE HONOURS:
3 (2004-05, 2005-06, 2009-10)

COUNTRY:
Czech Republic (born Plzen, 20 May 1982)

protective headgear that has become something of a trademark. Perhaps the greatest save of Cech's life did not occur on a football pitch.

Despite his first game back in club colours ending in a 2-0 defeat, Chelsea won the following six games in all competitions without any reply from their opposition. In fact, the Blues didn't lose again until 1 May when Liverpool progressed to the Champions League final at their expense.

Doubters will have been appeased and Chelsea fans will have rejoiced in the knowledge they had their number one back for the League and FA Cup finals, where they saw off the challenges of Arsenal and Manchester United. A further Premier League winner's medal, to add to the two he won in 2005 and 2006, followed in 2010, his post-injury agility, bravery and shot-stopping ability never called into question.   DM

QUOTE

'Cech is more than special. He is the best goalkeeper in the world, everybody knows that.'

Jose Mourinho in unusually
accommodating mood.

50 TONY YEBOAH

PREMIER LEAGUE DEBUT:
Leeds United v Queens Park Rangers,
24 January 1995

PREMIER LEAGUE CLUB:
Leeds United

PREMIER LEAGUE APPEARANCES/GOALS:

Leeds U	47	24
Total	47	24

PREMIER LEAGUE HONOURS:
None

COUNTRY:
Ghana (born Kumasi, 6 June 1966)

THE AFFAIR was short, torrid, spectacular and passionate, but doomed to end in tears because something this good couldn't possibly last. Yet even if Leeds United fans were left crushed and weeping as he left, they still had some enduring memories from the 1995-96 season, when Yeboah won both the BBC Goal of the Season and the Leeds United Player of the Year awards.

In late 1995, the magazine *When Saturday Comes* put Yeboah on its front cover, bug-eyed as he was about to strike the ball, and with the speech bubble, 'Let's see ... right foot in off the post ... or left foot into the top corner ...' He could score tap-ins but preferred not to if he could help it.

His sequence of astonishing goals that golden autumn included a volley from 25 yards out that won the game against Liverpool, a hat-trick away at

THE MOMENT HE BECAME A LEGEND

He scored the winner at Elland Road versus Liverpool on 21 August 1995 with a dipping killer shot that went in off the underside of the crossbar.

Monaco in the UEFA Cup (including a bicycle kick and a strike from outside the area) and another hat-trick away at Wimbledon, which included the above-mentioned goal of the season – a ball controlled on the chest, touched past a defender with his favoured left foot, then smashed into the top corner from 20 yards with his right. A volley against West Ham also made the season's top ten.

His goals almost always came from open play, such as the hat-trick he'd scored against Ipswich the previous season – a trio of perfectly executed finishes as stamped with quality as his forthcoming smashes from outside the box, often with an assist from Gary McAllister. And to think none of this would have happened if he hadn't fallen out with Jupp Heynckes, his manager at Eintracht Frankfurt, where he'd twice been the Bundesliga's top scorer.

Heynckes, a strict disciplinarian, made Yeboah, Jay-Jay Okocha and future Manchester City player Maurizio Gaudino do extra running because they weren't training hard enough, but when the three declared themselves 'too tired' to play for Eintracht the next day, they were immediately put on the transfer list. Yeboah was first loaned and then sold to Leeds.

And it was another spat with a manager that ushered in Yeboah's return to Germany and SV Hamburg. George Graham came to Leeds in the summer of 1996 after a poor end to the previous season, with Leeds having lost to Aston Villa in the League Cup final (Yeboah scored in both legs of the semi-final against Birmingham, including another bicycle kick). The new manager reportedly had issues with Yeboah's weight and fitness. When Graham subbed Yeboah off the field at Tottenham, the striker threw his shirt at the manager, and that was that.   IP

WELL I NEVER ...

His birthday – the sixth day of the sixth month of 1966 – was chosen by his mother as Yeboah was two weeks overdue and delivered by Caesarean section.

QUOTE

'Sometimes when I score, I can't even explain to myself how I did it.'

So that'll be Yeboah and the rest of us, then.

49 | CESC FABREGAS

PREMIER LEAGUE DEBUT:
Arsenal v Everton, 15 August 2004

PREMIER LEAGUE CLUB:
Arsenal

PREMIER LEAGUE APPEARANCES/GOALS:
Arsenal   212   35
Total   212   35

PREMIER LEAGUE HONOURS:
None

COUNTRY:
Spain (born Vilessoc de Mar, 4 May 1987)

WHAT MUST surely go down as one of football's greatest-ever alleged crimes took place in 2003, when Arsenal manager Arsène Wenger physically kidnapped an under-age Spanish player, bringing to an end 16-year-old Cesc Fabregas's happy childhood in the Barcelona youth set-up and forcing him to join a small army of French children being similarly held captive in North London.

At first, back in 2004, it seemed almost absurd when Wenger elected to replace the injured midfield powerhouse Patrick Vieira with such a non-combative lightweight, a 17-year-old veteran of only a few League Cup games. And yet when Vieira moved on to Juve in 2005, the club's youngest-ever goalscorer's ball skills, incredible awareness and finely tuned art of arriving at just the right time made him a natural choice to step into the playmaker's boots.

Ironically, Cesc won his only

THE MOMENT HE BECAME A LEGEND

As Arsenal captain in 2009-10, Fabregas played only 27 Premier League games due to injury, but still weighed in with 15 goals (set against 20 spread over his other six seasons) and 15 (his second highest total) assists.

major honour with Arsenal that season, when the Gunners defeated Manchester United on penalties to lift the FA Cup. Growing almost weekly in stature and status, he was central to the side that reached the 2006 Champions League final – only to be beaten by Barcelona, whose subsequent capture of Thierry Henry in 2007 signalled the definitive end of Arsenal's 'Invincible' era.

Weighed down by stadium debt and unable to spend with abandon, Wenger made Fabregas captain in 2008, both in recognition of his ability to keep the club in European contention almost single-handedly and to spur him on to yet greater efforts. Long suspicious of the empty bunk in the club dorm, Barcelona's interest in their lost prospect was, however, inevitably highlighted by his pivotal role in Spain's Euro 2008 and 2010 World Cup victories.

Domestically, the BBC reported in 2011 that 'Fabregas has created 466 chances since 2006-07, more than any other player in Europe's top five divisions [England's Premier League, Spain's La Liga, Italy's Serie A, France's Ligue 1 and Germany's Bundesliga].'

Only then did Estanislau Fors i Garcia, first citizen of Frabregas' tiny Catalan home town of Arenys de Mar, finally open his mouth to echo the righteous pleas of his red-faced local superclub. 'We want him to come right away, he is experiencing a kidnapping,' claimed the civic dignitary. 'If the English are so honourable they should behave properly. Wenger has to stop clowning around because it's disorienting for all of us.'

Eventually, a ransom of around £34 million – pure profit for the evil Wenger – proved sufficient to restore the 24-year-old to the bosom of his family club.   DH/RA

WELL I NEVER ...

According to Fabregas, after a reception for the team at Buckingham Palace, '[The Queen] told us she was an Arsenal fan. She appeared to definitely know who I was and we exchanged a few special words.'

QUOTE

'It is one of my biggest regrets, not to be able to lift a trophy as an Arsenal captain ... I wish them all the best and I will be watching them tomorrow, I will be watching them every weekend.'

Fabregas, possibly suffering from Stockholm Syndrome, makes his excuses and leaves.

APPARENTLY ALLERGIC to playing for teams not called 'United' – keep an eye out, Southend, he's lost a bit of pace but he could probably still do a job for you at the back – Rio Ferdinand has twice been the world's most expensive defender. The first time was when he moved from West Ham to Leeds for £18 million in 2000 and then, as the Elland Road club faced financial meltdown in 2002, to Manchester United for £30 million. He is held to have justified the fee on both occasions.

> ## THE MOMENT HE BECAME A LEGEND
>
> He scored a last-minute bullet header against Liverpool from a Giggs free-kick at Old Trafford in 2006. 'Oh goodness me!' gasped Martin Tyler. 'Rio Ferdinand rises to the occasion.'

At his best, he is a player with poise and elegance married to speed and power, while having a long-term and passionate affair with vision and intelligence. This *ménage à trois* will no doubt have helped him in the acquisition of more medals than the Duke of Edinburgh, with the added bonus that he has actually earned them – five Premier League titles, one FA Cup, two League Cups and the 2008 Champions League standing out among other less important baubles. He is also in possession of 81 England caps and has captained his country.

The fact he is chiefly remembered in certain circles as a hapless loon who forgot a drugs test in 2003 because he wanted to spend the afternoon choosing lampshades in Harvey Nicks is unfair. In football terms, Ferdinand is a Renaissance man – as he has said, 'I'm a person that is a free spirit, and I don't like to be put into a box and kept to one thing.'

To that end, he has fronted a TV programme (*Rio's World Cup Wind-Ups* – a prank show that provoked David Beckham to jump out of a car at the lights in Moss Side and run down the street because he was late for a meeting), and has his own clothing line and music label. He also has an executive producer's credit for the 2008 film *Dead Man Running* starring 50 Cent, runs a restaurant in Manchester (Rosso, on King Street), owns his own digital magazine called *#5*, his shirt number at United, and has plans to make a documentary about

> ## WELL I NEVER …
>
> Ferdinand studied ballet at the Central School of Ballet in Clerkenwell three days a week as a youngster. 'I remember Rio having particularly long and perfect ballet legs,' recalls his teacher. 'He really loved it.'

48 RIO FERDINAND

PREMIER LEAGUE DEBUT:
West Ham United v Sheffield Wednesday,
5 May 1996

PREMIER LEAGUE CLUBS:
West Ham United, Leeds United,
Manchester United

PREMIER LEAGUE APPEARANCES/GOALS:

West Ham U	127	2
Leeds U	54	2
Manchester U	270	6
Total	451	10

PREMIER LEAGUE HONOURS:
5 (2002-03, 2006-07, 2007-08, 2008-09,
2010-11)

COUNTRY:
England (born Peckham, 7 November 1978)

Peckham, an area of South-east London notorious for its problems with gangs and gun culture.

This latter project is the key to the man. He transcended his start in life and knows about Peckham because he grew up on the Friary estate and was a few years below murder victim Stephen Lawrence at the Blackheath Bluecoat School, a young man killed because of the colour of his skin. He remembers 'messing around with him and his mates', and the headmaster explaining to the school what had happened. Is it any wonder he is such a tireless and vehement anti-racism campaigner? **RA**

QUOTE

'I feel stupid for thinking that football was taking a leading role against racism. It seems it was just on mute for a while,' Ferdinand wrote on his Twitter account after [FIFA president] Sepp Blatter had argued that any racism on the pitch could be resolved with a simple handshake afterwards. He then contacted Blatter directly: 'Your comments on racism are so condescending it's almost laughable.'

47 ANDREW COLE

PREMIER LEAGUE DEBUT:
Newcastle United v Tottenham Hotspur, 14 August 1993

PREMIER LEAGUE CLUBS:
Newcastle United, Manchester United, Blackburn Rovers, Fulham, Manchester City, Portsmouth, Sunderland

PREMIER LEAGUE APPEARANCES/GOALS:

Newcastle U	58	43
Manchester U	195	93
Blackburn R	83	27
Fulham	31	12
Manchester C	22	9
Portsmouth	18	3
Sunderland	7	0
Total	414	187

PREMIER LEAGUE HONOURS:
5 (1995-96, 1996-97, 1998-99, 1999-00, 2000-01)

COUNTRY:
England (born Nottingham, 15 October 1971)

COLE GREW UP in Nottingham when Forest were in their pomp and headed by the most charismatic manager to ever patronise an interviewer or build an English European Cup-winning team. No doubt the young Andrew raced home after another comfortable home victory as the winter gloaming thickened, kicking cans into the Trent, feinting past brambles, dreaming: 'And it's Burns to Robertson, Robertson looks up, in to Cole, and Cole scores again. Hat-trick for Cole!'

Hardly. Cole never went to see Forest play. You have to take his

> ### THE MOMENT HE BECAME A LEGEND
>
> He hit 34 goals in 40 games in Newcastle United's first Premier League era season.

explanation seriously – racism made him fearful of the reception he would receive, so he played rather than watched. There might be a secondary reason, though. Andy Cole doesn't get on with many people. Even the superlatively taciturn Paul Scholes called him 'miserable'. Sheringham, Hoddle, Souness – Cole fell out with them all, and is happy (maybe the wrong word) to say so. Perhaps in a crowd of twenty-odd thousand Cloughites, there would simply have been too many punters who might have got on his easily frayed nerves.

He was made for Old Trafford. When Nicky Butt is considered the life and soul of the party, you have a footballing equivalent of The Smiths. The team consisted mainly of skilful but brand-bland youngsters (Beckham, Giggs), scowling dements (Keane, Ince) and the unlovably poker-faced

Nevilles and Scholes, the latter the most gifted player never to successfully negotiate a smile.

How strange, then, that Cole's great partnership should have been with the preposterously joyful Dwight Yorke, a man who seemed to be permanently reliving a rum-soaked Trinidadian beach-party. The Caribbean Dr Jekyll and the East Midlands Mr Hyde really did seem to be one person on occasion. They developed an intuitive understanding of each other's positioning and movement that was often breathtaking, their lightning interchanges anticipating the tiki-taki Barcelona style of recent years; they demonstrated the potency of small, speedy strikers.

Cole flourished. Average players can be excellent goalscorers, as with Cole at Newcastle. At United he also became an excellent footballer, linking play, scoring, crossing, always seeking obscure one-twos and unexpected reverse-passes. On scoring he would even occasionally attempt a simulacrum of Dwight's daft grin but never quite got there – after all, for Cole, there's more to life than being heftily remunerated for having fun.

When he left United, he joined a bewildering succession of clubs for increasingly brief periods. People kept disappointing him. He has a season ticket at Old Trafford – but does he go?

FC

FLASHBACK TO the ecstasy of France 98 – to the big screen in your local juicer – and the gates to the Promised Land swinging open courtesy of tiny, turbo-charged Michael Owen. 'Beckham to Owen, and here's another Owen run,' warbled Brian Moore. 'He's going to worry them again, and he might finish it off ... Oh! It's a wonderful goal to make it two-one for England.'

THE MOMENT HE BECAME A LEGEND

It has to be *that* goal against Argentina. As Brian Moore went on to say, 'His nerve and courage are not in doubt. His finishing reminds me of Jimmy Greaves – similar build, same icy nerve and nimble brain ... he has a forty-eight-year-old head on an eighteen-year-old frame.'

Recall the winning aura of the new wonderkid off the blocks, his scampering run from deep past two hapless Argentine defenders, and that dipping strike remembered in slow motion. Now the world apparently lay at England's feet. It lasted all of 15 minutes, of course, until the intervention of the petulantly flicked boot of 'Golden Bollocks'.

And yet, despite the short-term disappointment and the expectation heaped on to his slim shoulders, Michael Owen's own spectacular rise continued unabated. Having just won the Golden Boot as the Premier League's top scorer in his first full season in the Liverpool side, the well-spoken, modest BBC Sports Personality and PFA Young Player of the Year proceeded to repeat his scoring feat in 1998-99.

And, after his first ominous injury scare, he came back to enjoy his best season of all in 2000-01, single-handedly winning the FA Cup (you know you've arrived when you lend your name to a final, see also Sir Stanley Matthews) and helping to lift both the League Cup and the UEFA Cup. Oh, and becoming European Footballer of the Year. It's testimony to the Owen legend that there's still a sense that he, like the England side of that Golden Era, might have achieved so much more.

But success is relative, memory fickle. Despite recurrent hamstring problems, he finished every season at Liverpool as their top scorer. Even as an £8 million

WELL I NEVER ...

Owen is a big darts fan. In 2012 he tweeted, 'Darts is the best TV ever,' and was upset to miss a bevvy of oche legends who dropped by the Manchester United training ground. 'Gutted!' he continued. 'Was desperate to see who had the biggest belly!!!'

46 MICHAEL OWEN

PREMIER LEAGUE DEBUT:
Liverpool v Wimbledon, 6 May 1997

PREMIER LEAGUE CLUBS:
Liverpool, Newcastle United, Manchester United

PREMIER LEAGUE APPEARANCES/GOALS:

Liverpool	216	118
Newcastle U	71	26
Manchester U	31	5
Total	318	149

PREMIER LEAGUE HONOURS:
1 (2010-11)

COUNTRY:
England (born Chester, 14 December 1979)

'flop' at Real Madrid, he scored 18 goals in 15 starts. As the wear and tear of supersonic travel hit early, Newcastle United's £16 million man still notched 30 in 65 starts.

And then Sir Alex Ferguson's clear recollections of Owen's prodigious talent took him to Manchester United on a free transfer for perhaps one final fling. He finally won a league title in 2010-11, but by then was a bit-part player. His time at Old Trafford was perhaps best summed up by his performance in the 2010 Carling Cup final, when he scored an accomplished equaliser, but was substituted before half time after picking up a hamstring injury. His United contract was not renewed in the summer of 2012. **DH**

QUOTE

'He's a born goalscorer, a killer. A clean killer. It's an odd and potent combination. Owen is invariably polite, never pops off in the press, and says he doesn't drink beer, tea or coffee.'

Praise indeed from former England coach Sven-Goran Eriksson, a man not unfamiliar with the ice-cold demeanour.

45 PAUL INCE

PREMIER LEAGUE DEBUT (PLAYER):
Manchester United v Sheffield United,
15 August 1992

PREMIER LEAGUE DEBUT (MANAGER):
Blackburn Rovers v Everton, 16 August 2008

PREMIER LEAGUE CLUBS (PLAYER):
Manchester United, Liverpool,
Middlesbrough, Wolverhampton Wanderers

PREMIER LEAGUE CLUB (MANAGER):
Blackburn Rovers

PREMIER LEAGUE APPEARANCES/GOALS:

Manchester U	116	18
Liverpool	65	14
Middlesbrough	93	7
Wolves	32	2
Total	306	41

PREMIER LEAGUE APPEARANCES (MANAGER):

Blackburn R	17
Total	17

PREMIER LEAGUE HONOURS:
2 (1992-93, 1993-94)

COUNTRY:
England (born Ilford, 21 October 1967)

'TACKLING IS BETTER than sex,' said Paul Ince at the peak of his career in 1998. The fact that he picked up 71 yellow cards in just over 300 Premier League games proves that he wasn't shy about indulging in his favourite pleasure. Ince, though, was much more than just a dirty midfield ball-winner. Like his Manchester United team-mate Roy Keane, he could not only scrap for the ball, he also knew what to do when he got it.

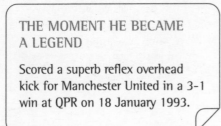

THE MOMENT HE BECAME
A LEGEND

Scored a superb reflex overhead kick for Manchester United in a 3-1 win at QPR on 18 January 1993.

A key player in Alex Ferguson's smooth-passing line-up of the early 1990s, he won two Premier League titles, two FA Cups, a League Cup, and the European Cup-Winners' Cup while at Old Trafford, although his move to United cost him the affection of the West Ham fans. Photographed in a United shirt while still a West Ham player, he was booed as a 'Judas' every time he returned to Upton Park. It didn't seem to bother him, however, and in early 1994, he unsentimentally netted the goal for United at his old stomping ground that made the score 2-2 with three minutes left.

Ince was one of the few English players to prosper in Serie A, enjoying two successful seasons with Inter Milan after leaving United, before returning to England to play for Liverpool in 1997. That inevitably made him unpopular at another former club, and in a strange repeat of history, he scored a late leveller for the Merseysiders at home to United in another 2-2 game, making a big show of kissing the club badge as he celebrated in front of the Kop. So it wasn't just tackling that turned him on – taunting his exes seemed to be a bit of a thrill too.

Ince then cut his ties with Liverpool after Phil Thomson became Gerard Houllier's assistant manager. 'They are two-faced and treat people like dirt,' he said of the pair, claiming that Thomson's idea of coaching was to swear constantly at the players. He then spent three years at Middlesbrough, before helping Wolves out of the second tier for one final season at the top level. He won over 50 caps for England, was the first black player to captain the side, and missed a penalty in the shoot-out against Argentina at the 1998 World Cup.

He liked to be known as 'The Guv'nor' and lived up to his self-styled nickname when he moved into management, and became the first black English manager of a top-flight club when appointed at Blackburn in 2008. He was also the first to be sacked, just six months later. IP

> **WELL I NEVER ...**
>
> Ince is the cousin of former world middeweight and super middleweight boxer Nigel Benn, and also the uncle of The Saturdays singer Rochelle Wiseman.

> **QUOTE**
>
> '[It's] not because we were nasty people. It was because we were winners and we wanted to win.'
>
> Ince offers an explanation for the on–pitch behaviour of himself and Roy Keane.

IN LATE 1959, a young woman named Betty McGrath travelled over from Ireland to Ealing, London, to give birth to a son without the knowledge of her father. She was petrified of his reaction to her having an illegitimate baby, let alone one of mixed race – the Nigerian father having disappeared soon after conception. The baby was given up for adoption, and spent much of his childhood in a bleak Dublin orphanage with only tyres in the yard and Christmas cast-offs for toys.

> ## THE MOMENT HE BECAME A LEGEND
>
> McGrath won PFA Player of the Year in 1993.

Fortunately, Paul McGrath was one hell of a footballer. It offered him a way out but, unfortunately, his would be a life of two halves – on-field glory and private despair running concurrently.

Having signed professional terms with St Patrick's Athletic in 1981, he picked up the PFAI Player of the Year Award in his first season. This led the imperturbable ball-winning prodigy inexorably to Manchester United, where he spent seven years and became a firm fans' favourite for Man of the Match performances, such as the 1985 FA Cup final win against Everton.

When Alex Ferguson took over from the more convivial Ron Atkinson, however, time was called on the club's drinking culture, and McGrath – already battling with alcohol problems in his mid-20s – and Norman Whiteside were earmarked for departure. Although Manchester United were keen that he retire rather than move on, Aston Villa bought McGrath for £400,000 in August 1989. Despite his fragile state of mind, persistent knee injuries and drink problems – he wore sweatbands when he played to hide the wrist injuries caused by his first suicide attempt – 'Ooh Aah' Paul McGrath somehow grew in stature as a player in the Premier League era.

Brought back into a defensive role for club and country, his magnificent reading of the game led Ireland manager Jack Charlton to compare him with Bobby Moore after a superb performance against Italy in the

> ## WELL I NEVER ...
>
> In the late 1980s, while on holiday, a delegation from Napoli held extensive talks with McGrath, with view to a possible move to Serie A. He would have been in the same side as Maradona.

44 PAUL McGRATH

1994 World Cup. The Holte End called him 'God', that much is unsurprising, but as former manager John Gregory put it, 'He was also known as "God" in the dressing-room.' His cumulative career transfer total of £560,000 represents an astonishingly small outlay for a man generally regarded as the best centre-half of his generation.

But, however brilliant on the pitch, McGrath's personal life was still a train crash, with arrests, two failed marriages and three more suicide attempts. McGrath retired in 1997, after short spells at Derby and Sheffield United, and is still engaged in his battle with the booze. His memoir, *Back from the Brink*, is a painfully honest read. He is adored by United, Villa and Ireland fans, but has never, it seems, quite learned to love himself.   GS/BB

QUOTE

'I had wonderful children, a wonderful career, the supporters seemed to genuinely love me, I got on well with my team-mates and opponents, I couldn't have asked for more in life. And yet ... there was still something in there telling me I was a piece of shit, basically.'

Paul McGrath reveals the mental turmoil from which he suffered.

AT THE TURN of the millennium, when Arsenal won the Premier League title three times in seven seasons, they had a defence of solid English oak. The foreign flair players and fancy-dans ran the midfield and the attack, but at the back it was Dixon, Winterburn, Bould or Keown, Adams ... about as much fun for an opposing striker as having his head repeatedly slammed in a door. And, as if that wasn't enough, the last line of defence was genial 6ft 4in Yorkshireman David Seaman – England's number one.

The Rotherham-born youngster had been forced to endure the early disappointment of being rejected by his boyhood team, Leeds United, but worked his way back into the big time via Peterborough, Birmingham and QPR. By the time he moved to Arsenal in 1990, George Graham had to part with £1.3 million, a British record for a goalkeeper and, in retrospect, a steal at just £100,000 per season for 13 years of outstanding service and reliability.

This was the dawn of a golden age for Arsenal – Seaman soon accumulated league title, FA Cup, League Cup and European Cup-Winners' Cup medals ... and with the arrival of Arsène Wenger things got even better. Wenger's Arsenal matched the legendary 1971 Double winners, landing the league and FA Cup in 1997-98 and then surpassed them by repeating the feat in 2001-02.

Despite playing for the Gunners, wearing a very dodgy England kit (not his fault) and latterly sporting a long ponytail (very much his fault), Seaman was a popular figure – penalty saves against Scotland and Spain in Euro 96 cementing his place in the heart of the nation's fans. But he also had his critics who tried to define him by his mistakes; he famously conceded two speculative, long-

---

THE MOMENT HE BECAME A LEGEND

Having played every game of the 1990-91 league championship-winning season, conceding just 18 goals in the process, the Arsenal defence went one better in 1998-99, conceding just 17 times, though Seaman did miss six games.

WELL I NEVER ...

Although Seaman was left-handed, he took kicks with his right foot and threw the ball out with his right arm.

43 DAVID SEAMAN

PREMIER LEAGUE DEBUT:
Arsenal v Norwich City, 15 August 1992

PREMIER LEAGUE CLUBS:
Arsenal, Manchester City

PREMIER LEAGUE APPEARANCES/GOALS:

Arsenal	325	0
Manchester C	19	0
Total	344	0

PREMIER LEAGUE HONOURS:
2 (1997-98, 2001-02)

COUNTRY:
England (born Rotherham, 19 September 1963)

range efforts from Nayim in the 1995 Cup-Winners' Cup final and then Ronaldinho in the 2002 World Cup quarter-final in Japan.

But the growing clamour that Seaman was no longer up to it was silenced when he saved the best until last in 2003. In the dying minutes of an FA Cup semi-final against Sheffield United at Old Trafford, Paul Peschisolido directed a header towards the goal from six yards out. Seaman looked to have no chance, but dived backwards across his goalmouth to claw the ball out from under the bar for a world-class save that was favourably compared to Gordon Banks' Mexico 1970 effort against Pelé.

The score remained 1-0, Seaman setting up a perfect finish to his Arsenal career – subsequently lifting the FA Cup as captain, having beaten Southampton at the Millennium Stadium.

GS

QUOTE

'I know where I come from. I've had tea with the Queen, but I keep everything in perspective.'

Seaman proves that while you can take the boy out of Yorkshire ...

42 ASHLEY COLE

PREMIER LEAGUE DEBUT:
Arsenal v Newcastle United, 14 May 2000

PREMIER LEAGUE CLUBS:
Arsenal, Chelsea

PREMIER LEAGUE APPEARANCES/GOALS:
Arsenal 156 8
Chelsea 181 6
Total 337 14

PREMIER LEAGUE HONOURS:
3 (2001-02, 2003-04, 2009-10)

COUNTRY:
England (born Stepney, 20 December 1980)

CAST AS THE Premier League's ultimate pantomime villain, Ashley Cole has hardly endeared himself to the public with scandalous acts of behaviour that have included verbally abusing policemen, exceeding speed limits, shooting a work experience trainee and, of course, allegedly mounting anything that moved (sometimes only pausing to be sick) while still married to national treasure Cheryl Cole.

These discrepancies in his private life, however, should not be allowed to detract from his unerring dedication and dependability as a truly world-class player. Able to seamlessly balance defensive durability with attacking verve, he is rarely beaten for pace (as even

THE MOMENT HE BECAME A LEGEND

Cole's youthful enthusiasm and unbridled celebrations while holding aloft a plastic Premier League trophy after winning the title as an 'Invincible' in 2004 showed Arsenal fans what the club meant to him ... little did they know.

Cristiano Ronaldo can confirm) and is always dangerous in an opponent's half – while his undying athleticism allows him to cover his marauding tracks.

Cole rose to prominence while still a teenager at Arsenal, the club he had supported since childhood. Arsène Wenger groomed the fleet-footed former striker towards becoming a model of consistency as an exciting defender – winning three FA Cups and two Premier League titles (one of them as part of the 'Invincibles' side who went an entire season unbeaten in 2003-04) along the way.

> **WELL I NEVER ...**
>
> Soul diva Mariah Carey found out that she was a distant cousin of Ashley Cole after researching if she was related to jazz legend Nat 'King' Cole.

Typically perhaps, he will be remembered without fondness by counterfeit note-waving Arsenal fans as 'Cashley' – for his clandestine meeting with Jose Mourinho who eventually gave him 90,000 reasons (a week) to leave for Chelsea. But, loyalty has become an obsolete word in the 21st-century game and, with Arsenal failing to win any silverware since his acrimonious departure, Cole's decision has benefited more than just his bank balance.

The move to Stamford Bridge has brought him another league title and four more FA Cups – making Cole the only player ever to win the competition seven times – as well as being named Chelsea's Player of the Year on two occasions. On 19 May 2012, he helped the Blues to become the first London side to win the Champions League title, scoring one of the penalties in their successful shoot-out against Bayern Munich.

He has represented England at three World Cups and subsequently come to be recognised the 'best left-back in the world', renowned for his reliably flawless displays on the field (if you ignore the petulant back-turning reaction to receiving a caution from referee Mike Riley against Tottenham).

> **QUOTE**
>
> 'I nearly swerved off the road. "He is taking the piss, Jonathan [Cole's agent]!" I yelled down the phone. I was so incensed. I was trembling with anger. I couldn't believe what I'd heard.'
>
> Ashley Cole recalls the moment he was offered a trifling £55,000 a week by Arsenal.

You don't have to love him as a person, but football is not a popularity contest and, if judged purely as a player, Ashley Cole is the finest full-back in the history of the English game.   RA

41 | KEVIN KEEGAN

PREMIER LEAGUE DEBUT (MANAGER):
Newcastle United v Tottenham Hotspur,
14 August 1993

PREMIER LEAGUE CLUBS (MANAGER):
Newcastle United, Manchester City,
Newcastle United

PREMIER LEAGUE APPEARANCES (MANAGER):
Newcastle U   162
Manchester C   105
Total   267

PREMIER LEAGUE HONOURS:
None

COUNTRY:
England (born Doncaster, 14 February 1951)

AS A PLAYER, 'Mighty Mouse' (the nickname given to Keegan at Hamburg) made up for a lack of technical ability with a huge amount of spirit, endeavour and determination. The same positive and motivational approach to management worked too, but only up to a point. At Newcastle, where he was already revered for having taken the team up to the old First Division at the end of his playing career in the 1980s, he achieved promotion in 1993 with the attacking philosophy and swashbuckling approach to the game that would become his hallmark as a manager.

His teams were often thrilling to watch, if susceptible at the back. Perhaps unusually attuned to the one thing he had always lacked as a player, he was a sucker for flair and signed Faustino Asprilla, Peter Beardsley,

THE MOMENT HE BECAME A LEGEND

In a TV interview as Newcastle United manager during the 1995-96 season, when asked if he thought his team could finish ahead of Manchester United, he burst out that he'd 'love it if we beat them. Love it!' They didn't.

Andy Cole and David Ginola. He was rewarded with a third-place finish in 1994, but the following season he sold the prolific Cole to Manchester United in exchange for cash and winger Keith Gillespie. He explained his actions to the fans directly outside St James' Park, but the die was cast. Newcastle finished sixth.

In 1995-96, his team blew a ten-point lead at the top and once again Alex Ferguson took the title. A 4-3 defeat in a thrilling match at Liverpool (often cited as the best Premier League game of all time) typified the Keegan approach. A goal ahead with just over 20 minutes to go, he lacked the tactical nous, and possibly the will, to defend a slender lead. The image of him slumped over a hoarding is an enduring one.

Keegan resigned halfway through the following season, later citing the expression on defeated Tottenham manager Gerry Francis's face when Newcastle had whacked Spurs 7-1 the month before – he felt so sorry for him that it eclipsed his joy at winning. Keegan later left Fulham to manage England, and left England after falling at Wembley to Germany in a World Cup qualifier and admitting to his own tactical shortcomings at that level.

During four years at Manchester City between 2001 and 2005, Keegan again proved good at bringing a team up from the second tier, but failed to land any honours in the Premier League – though once again he collected attacking players like a kleptomaniac in a riot. He came out of retirement in 2008 to manage Newcastle a second time, and Geordies hailed the return of 'King Kev', but he left the following September claiming he did not have full control over transfers. The club denied this, but Keegan sued them and won.

IP

> ### WELL I NEVER ...
>
> If he hadn't played football, Keegan would have been a tap maker.

> ### QUOTE
>
> 'Some parts of the job I did very well, but not the key part of getting players to win football matches.'
>
> Keegan reflects upon his time as England manager with a certain rueful charm.

THERE IS little unusual about our hero outside the confines of a football pitch. Married with two children, he now works for an international development charity. Clean-cut to the point of perfection, he never even seemed to dirty his shorts. It's true he was involved in a training-ground tiff with Cristiano Ronaldo (understandable) and some disappointingly brief argy-bargy with Arsenal's Martin Keown, but overall there is little entertainingly strange about the man from Oss.

Mind you, the same was true of Clark Kent and once RvN had changed into his red Superman kit, he became an exceptional goalscorer in terms of both quantity and quality.

THE MOMENT HE BECAME A LEGEND

In 2001-02, his first season at United, and recently recovered from ruptured cruciate knee ligaments, van Nistelrooy scored 23 Premiership goals in 32 appearances, including goals in eight consecutive games.

He started in the Netherlands as a central midfielder for Den Bosch and could have played anywhere, but he could poach, was adept in the air and had a special gift – he could score repeatedly from unpromising situations. Thinking inside the box you might say. The only kind of goal he didn't score was the long-range drive.

But why shoot from distance when you can dribble into the box at will? He was a striker, not a sniper. For fans of both United and their opponents – though for different reasons – the abiding memory of van Nistelrooy will be of him gaining possession 40 yards out with his back to goal, turning

WELL I NEVER ...

In five seasons for Manchester United, he did not score once from outside the penalty area.

smartly and racing goalwards, head down, before unleashing his special powers. In fact, there was a time in the early 2000s when the only time he looked up was to have a shave. And he even gave that up for a couple of years.

40 RUUD VAN NISTELROOY

PREMIER LEAGUE DEBUT:
Manchester United v Fulham, 19 August 2001

PREMIER LEAGUE CLUB:
Manchester United

PREMIER LEAGUE APPEARANCES/GOALS:

Manchester U	150	95
Total	150	95

PREMIER LEAGUE HONOURS:
1 (2002-03); PFA Player of the Year 2002

COUNTRY:
Netherlands (born Oss, 1 July 1976)

He could change direction sharply at speed, Messi-style, and was nimble for a man of 6ft 2in. His shooting was characterised by accuracy and deftness rather than outstanding power – as George Best said, 'It only has to cross the line.' A typical goal involved manoeuvring the ball in tight situations, where his quick feet created all the time he needed, given his short back-lift. And, on top of all these technical attributes, in typical superhero fashion, he never panicked at the crucial moment. The inevitable result, yet again: 'Ruuuuuuud!' The more he scored, the longer the name.

FC

QUOTE

'The life story of the footballer Ruud van Nistelrooy will not be a book filled with scandals. I haven't the need or desire to seek revenge or hang the dirty washing out to dry. Look at all the books written by footballers ... they've written the most awful things, slating and slagging their colleagues or managers – I'd be ashamed to be associated with that sort of publication.'

Van Nistelrooy demonstrates precisely why he will not be handling the pre-publicity for any future autobiography.

39 HARRY REDKNAPP

PREMIER LEAGUE DEBUT (MANAGER):
West Ham United v Leeds United,
20 August 1994

PREMIER LEAGUE CLUBS (MANAGER):
West Ham United, Portsmouth,
Southampton, Portsmouth, Tottenham
Hotspur

PREMIER LEAGUE APPEARANCES (MANAGER):

West Ham U	269
Portsmouth	158
Southampton	22
Tottenham H	144
Total	593

PREMIER LEAGUE HONOURS:
None; Manager of the Season 2010

COUNTRY:
England (born Poplar, 2 March 1947)

WHEN HARRY Redknapp was cleared in court of tax evasion in early 2012, the world at last knew for sure that Redknapp was a diamond geezer, not a dodgy one. Finally, we could all love and embrace the curmudgeonly old fella with the hangdog chops and maybe even hail him as the next England manager. After Roy calls it a day, that is.

'We get carried away with coaching and coaches,' Redknapp stated while manager at West Ham. 'I have my coaching badges, but they came out of a Cornflakes packet.' He is, then, part of the great English tradition of managing teams without any great need for tactical depth and planning. 'Pick up a few good lads, and get 'em motivated' is the simple way of looking at his preferred methodology. There's little evidence to suggest that, in Redknapp's case, this approach is any less successful than hiring a po-faced, technocrat armed with dossiers and a PowerPoint presentation on the virtues of 4-3-2-1.

A journeyman midfielder with West Ham and Bournemouth in the 1970s, Redknapp returned to the same clubs as manager and enjoyed some success, taking the latter up as champions of the old Third Division and the former to consecutive eighth- and fifth-place finishes in the Premier League, while bringing through young prospects such as Rio Ferdinand, Frank Lampard, Michael Carrick and Joe Cole – all future England internationals and eventually sold on for good money. In 2001, he moved to Portsmouth as director of football, then a year later began his first spell there as manager, taking the team up to the Premier League before falling out with club owner Milan Mandaric.

He moved to Southampton, much to the disgust of Pompey fans, and oversaw their relegation to the Championship before falling out with chairman Rupert Lowe. Back at Pompey, everything forgiven, he won the FA Cup in 2008 with a 1-0 win over Cardiff City, only to be lured to Spurs, who coughed up £5 million in compensation.

Though stalked by a stream of allegations related to his finances, Redknapp's teams play good football, and he gets results. He took Tottenham off the bottom of the Premier League to Champions League qualification in less than two years. Glorious European nights at White Hart Lane against Real Madrid, Inter and AC Milan soon followed, but in 2012, and despite having secured fourth spot in the Premier League, he was denied another tilt at the Champions League by Chelsea's victory over Bayern Munich in the final. Soon after he left the club after apparently failing to agree a new contract.   IP

THE MOMENT HE BECAME A LEGEND

Hit by a wayward shot from a player during a TV interview at the Portsmouth training ground, an extremely aggrieved Redknapp excoriated the anonymous player, turned back to the camera and opined, 'No wonder he's in the fakkin' reserves.'

WELL I NEVER ...

After injury finished his playing career, Redknapp was negotiating to buy a Bournemouth taxicab for £14,000 ... when he got a call from Seattle Sounders.

QUOTE

'I can't work a computer, I don't know what an email is, I've never sent a fax and I've never sent a text message. You talk to anybody at the football club – I couldn't even fill a team sheet in ... I write like a two-year-old and I can't spell.'

Redknapp's combined corruption defence/application for the England manager's job.

38 OLE GUNNAR SOLSKJAER

PREMIER LEAGUE DEBUT:
Manchester United v Blackburn Rovers,
25 August 1996

PREMIER LEAGUE CLUB:
Manchester United

PREMIER LEAGUE APPEARANCES/GOALS:
Manchester U   235   91
Total   235   91

PREMIER LEAGUE HONOURS:
6 (1996-97, 1998-99, 1999-00, 2000-01,
2002-03, 2006-07)

COUNTRY:
Norway (born Kristiansund,
26 February 1973)

IMAGINE IT'S May 1999, and you're that common breed of fan who dislikes Manchester United more than any other team. Someone forces you to choose the one United player you'd least mind scoring the injury-time winner in the Champions League final. Of all the players available, you'd have to concede, cherubic Norwegian striker Ole Gunnar Solskjaer would be the least objectionable choice.

Solskjaer, however, is not remembered just for that improbably late touch against Bayern Munich in the last Champions League final of the 20th century. He was a striker as reliable as he was unselfish – as well as racking up almost a century of league goals, he chipped in with 62 assists during his decade as a player at Old Trafford. Had it not been for the ravenous striking partnership of Dwight Yorke

THE MOMENT HE BECAME A LEGEND

Bringing the Champions League trophy back to Old Trafford after a 31-year wait.

and Andy Cole in the late 1990s, he would surely have played more often.

The forward was the opposite of a typical Norwegian striker. He was light and nimble, rather than the archetypal boulder of a target man usually expected of Nordic stock. He opted to stay where he felt at home, rather than moving to a lesser club where he would undoubtedly have been the first name on the team sheet. As a late option off the bench, he was of incalculable value to Alex Ferguson.

Solskjaer's goal against Bayern was no fluke – he had an incredible knack of turning up in the right place at the right time. His nickname was the 'baby-faced assassin', but it wasn't quite accurate. He may well have had skin like a baby's bottom, but he was more of a poacher than a killer, mopping up rebounds and loose balls between four and ten yards in front of the opposition goal, and darting into the narrowest of spaces to fire home with immaculate precision. He also used his time on the bench to spot where his opportunities might lie, if he came on to the pitch. The result was he scored a remarkable 28 goals as a substitute in all competitions for United.

> **WELL I NEVER ...**
>
> As manager of Manchester United reserves, he led the team to four honours. He's also been knighted by King Harald V of Norway.

> **QUOTE**
>
> 'When I was a player I could never be Giggs, Scholes, Beckham, Cantona or Keane. But I could still take bits from David's mentality or Eric's ability to improve myself.'
>
> The eminently reasonable and modest Solskjaer makes it even more difficult to hate him.

His most notable goalscoring achievement came as a substitute at the City Ground in early 1999. With United already leading 4-1, Solskjaer was sent on with instructions from Alex Ferguson's assistant Jim Ryan: 'We don't need any more goals – just keep the ball. Play nice and simple.' He clearly wasn't listening as he rattled in another four in the game's final 12 minutes to humiliate Nottingham Forest. As if to prove it was no fluke, he scored four against Everton in a 5-1 home victory the following season.   IP

'**NOW THEN,** Seamus, you know the rules. The smallest goes in nets and the rest of us belt the ball at you as hard as we can from six yards out. OK?' 'OK.' 'And then you stay in until we say you can come out. OK?' 'OK.' And so it came to pass that Seamus ('Shay') Given, born in Lifford, County Donegal and the youngest of four brothers, spent many long summer holidays between the sticks.

Duly trained and toughened, he debuted for his local junior (i.e. adult league) side, Lifford Celtic, at the tender age of 14. Fortunately, he recovered from the potentially damaging experience of picking the ball out of his net seven times on his debut and soon caught the eye of a Celtic scout with a series of mature and, soon-to-be his hallmark, consistent performances.

> ## THE MOMENT HE BECAME A LEGEND
>
> An inspirational Man of the Match display for Newcastle in a 1-1 draw with Sunderland at the Stadium of Light in 2001 that ultimately helped prevent the Black Cats from qualifying for the UEFA Cup.

Kenny Dalglish then brought him first to Premier League Blackburn Rovers, where he had loan periods at both Swindon and Sunderland (his 12 clean sheets in 17 appearances making a big contribution to Sunderland's Division One title and earning him a call-up to the Ireland team), and on to Newcastle in 1997, where he was installed as number one.

These were good times for the 'Magpies' and Given suddenly found himself playing against Barcelona in the Champions League and Arsenal in the FA Cup final rather than sitting on the bench.

The king of the parry stepped up well to this new level with his brave and agile style – as Thierry Henry put it, '[Shay Given] is a pretty amazing goalkeeper ... to put the ball in the back of the net

> ## WELL I NEVER ...
>
> Given's pre-match ritual of shaking hands with the opposition without wearing his gloves is because 'You always worry someone might still have Vaseline on their hands.'

takes something really special.' He also continued to add to his international caps and is now the record-holder at international level for

37 SHAY GIVEN

PREMIER LEAGUE DEBUT:
Blackburn Rovers v Wimbledon,
14 December 1996

PREMIER LEAGUE CLUBS:
Blackburn Rovers, Newcastle United,
Manchester City, Aston Villa

PREMIER LEAGUE APPEARANCES/GOALS:

Blackburn R	2	0
Newcastle U	354	0
Manchester C	50	0
Aston Villa	32	0
Total	438	0

PREMIER LEAGUE HONOURS:
None

COUNTRY:
Republic of Ireland (born Lifford, 20 April 1976)

the Republic of Ireland. After almost 12 years' dedicated service at club level, and as Newcastle slid towards relegation, his desire to remain in the Premier League led him to newly wealthy Manchester City for £7 million in February 2009.

Although Given had a superb opening spell to his City career, a dislocated shoulder suffered at the end of the 2009-10 season saw him displaced by the emerging Joe Hart. Even at the age of 35, Given wasn't satisfied with anything less than a first-team place and moved to Aston Villa, his £3.5 million fee testament to his enduring quality.   GS

QUOTE

'I must be the only Irishman who doesn't know where Dublin is.'

Given makes a joke at his own expense after throwing the ball down to kick it out of his area without noticing Coventry City striker Dion Dublin lurking behind him. Dublin nipped in and scored.

36 ROBIN VAN PERSIE

PREMIER LEAGUE DEBUT:
Arsenal v Manchester City,
25 September 2004

PREMIER LEAGUE CLUB:
Arsenal

PREMIER LEAGUE APPEARANCES/GOALS:
Arsenal   194   96
Total   194   96

PREMIER LEAGUE HONOURS:
None; FWA and PFA Player of the Year 2012

COUNTRY:
Netherlands (born Rotterdam,
6 August 1983)

IF LOOKS COULD kill, then Robin van Persie would not be alive ... The eyes belonged to Arsène Wenger, as the manager turned the air *bleu* in reaction to the young Dutchman's dismissal for a petulant challenge on Southampton's Graeme Le Saux. 'I do not support [him] today,' he said afterwards. One football writer described the striker as 'twenty-one going on nine'. But that was then.

Van Persie arrived in the Premier League with a bad reputation that he brought with him from childhood and led to an irreparable rift with his manager at Feyenoord. Many questioned

THE MOMENT HE BECAME A LEGEND

The Valley, 30 September 2006. Van Persie scored a brace in this game against Charlton, but only his second will be remembered – a mid-air volley from 20 yards that seared into the top corner. RvP was on his way to becoming Arsenal's MVP.

Wenger's judgement in spending £2.75 million on the fiery 20-year-old, nominally the replacement for his glacial compatriot Dennis Bergkamp, but the erudite Arsenal manager specialises in the French polishing of tainted talent.

Using mind tricks of mentorship worthy of a Jedi master, Wenger guided the arrogant rebel with a dark side towards becoming Arsenal's leading light. Born from artist parents, van Persie is blessed with innate creativity and a technical perfection that draws beauty from the game. He is an expressionist.

Like Thierry Henry before him, van Persie was a winger who was tutored to become a central striker. He also possesses a lethal left foot and graceful style that came to be described by his manager as like 'Bergkamp with goals'. He has struggled with injuries, but when away from the treatment table there were always glimpses of the greatness to come – including an airborne volley against Charlton in 2006 and his delicate cushioning of a long pass before unleashing an Exocet with his supposedly weaker right foot (his 'chocolate leg' as he calls it) against Liverpool two years later.

In the last two seasons, however, his evolution has become complete and the once erratic firebrand has assumed the responsibility of a leader to ultimately become Arsenal's captain. A player who was once pursued by opponents in search of an aggressive reaction is now calmness personified – even when former team-mate Emmanuel Adebayor attempted to use his face as a dance floor in 2009.

His manager's faith has been returned with interest, and van Persie set a new Premier League record in May 2011 by netting in nine consecutive away games – a vintage period that also witnessed him surpass Thierry Henry's Arsenal record of 35 goals in a calendar year. He finished the 2011-12 season as the Premier League's top scorer, with 30, and as a double winner of both the FWA and PFA Footballer of the Year awards.   RA

'**THERE WERE** tough times, growing up in "Fuerte Apache",' Tevez has said. 'When it was dark and you looked out of the window, what you saw would scare anyone. After a certain hour, you couldn't go into the street.' A set of tower blocks created to facilitate slum clearances in the 1970s, it was street football on glass- and rubble-strewn concrete pitches, often with a tennis ball. It taught Tevez to stay on his feet and neither expect nor give any quarter. Along with his ability, they remain his defining characteristics as a player.

> ## THE MOMENT HE BECAME A LEGEND
>
> The cheeky 'Welcome to Manchester' billboard that went up at the gateway to the city, but also next to the road that leads to the borough of Trafford, home of 'Manchester' United.

According to his biography *Welcome to Manchester*, 'Years later when questioned about the punishing tackles dished out in the Premier League, he thought of his early days in "Fort Apache", smiled and slowly shook his head.' Before the Premier League, he had starred for Boca Juniors and Corinthians of Brazil, won every trophy possible and been named South American Player of the Year three times in succession. His affairs were soon being looked after by a company called Media Sports Investment (MSI).

He did not part company with Corinthians on the best of terms (turning up for a press conference in a Manchester United shirt not being the least of it) and, determined to play in the Premier League, arrived with Javier Mascherano at West Ham United in 2006 for an 'undisclosed fee'. He settled in well and scored the goal that kept them up against Manchester United on the last day of the 2006-07 season. Sir Alex Ferguson had been keeping tabs on the player since a friendly between Boca and United at Old Trafford in 2002 – Tevez had been sent off for elbowing Paul Scholes.

West Ham attempted to block a move to United, but eventually he agreed a two-year loan deal at Old Trafford. In his time at the club, he won everything apart from the FA Cup but became agitated when not offered a permanent contract. United finally agreed to meet the option fee of £25.5 million with the promise of a five-year contract, but in July 2009,

> ## WELL I NEVER ...
>
> Scalded by a kettle of boiling water aged ten months, he has refused all offers of plastic surgery. 'It was a defining experience,' he argues. 'It marked me for life. You either take me as I am or you don't. The same goes for the [chipped] teeth. I won't change the way I am.'

Abi wears a daring Jasper Conran number that sees the playsuit perhaps replacing the LBD as the must-have item this summer. The strappy heels are an excellent accessory, however the clutch bag and the Premier League footballer are *so* 2010.

And this is 'Psycho' celebrating another Stan Collymore goal for Forest in 1995. An alarmed Steve Stone decides to leave him to it.

Elvis: 'Have I told you lately that I love you?'
Kevin Phillips: 'Don't think twice, it's all right.'

A late starter, 'Sir' Les Ferdinand never forgot his non-league roots and would often help them take down the nets – sometimes in the middle of a game, which was less than helpful.

David James: 'Doctor, I've got this unsightly lump on the back of my head.'
Doctor: 'Well, tell him to get off.'

'What have I done now?' asks a bemused Duncan Ferguson. 'I hardly touched him.'

'I've got him boss, grab a pen . . .' Alexander Hleb assists Arsène Wenger with the contractual arrangements for Cesc Fabregas. Unfortunately for Arsenal, he was able to escape.

Taking time off from his extensive portfolio of 'exciting' side projects, Rio Ferdinand drops by Old Trafford to score against Liverpool before leaving to work on a new space tourism idea with that miserable Scottish git from *Dragons' Den*.

Michael Owen does everything expected of him before the 1998 World Cup – that is to say, raise the hopes of all England fans to unrealistic levels just to make the inevitable disappointment harder to take.

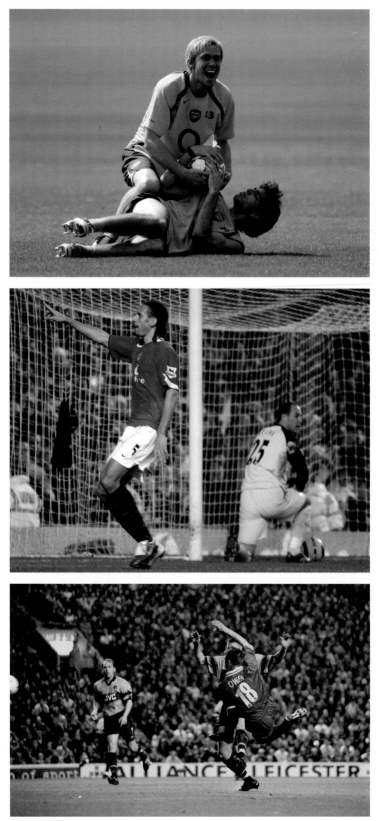

'Peschisolido shoots, and Seaman's all over the place!' Yes, it would have been better if it had been Julian Dicks, and it had not actually been a header and he was actually 'all over the place', but old 'Safe Hands' still . . . ahem . . . pulled off one of the all-time great saves in the 2003 FA Cup semi-final.

Sometimes after training, Sol and Ashley would just nip down the local for a game of cribbage. But on other occasions they would drop into the Royal Academy to check out the Giorgio Armani retrospective.

In all fairness, the challenge to find five bare-chested males in the Newcastle area was one of Banksy's less arduous challenges . . .

'Van Nistelrooy's clear, boss. He's definitely not wearing a wire.' Ole Gunnar 'The Smiling Assassin' Solskjaer was Ferguson's eyes and ears on the pitch.

'And point six, I can't count either.' Former Tottenham manager Harry Redknapp explains why the FA made a mistake appointing Roy Hodgson as England manager.

'Van Persie is captured here in the classic style of the late-eighteenth and early-nineteenth century silhouettist, John Miers. A study in pose and balletic grace befitting the son of two artists.' Having missed the ball entirely, he was allowed to retake the free-kick.

Carlos Tevez with dummy in mouth, pictured shortly before spitting it out. Again.

Gary Speed out-jumps Alex Rae to win the ball for Newcastle in November 2003. Determination was one of the characteristics of the late midfielder.

talkSPORT's Stanley Victor Collymore celebrates becoming only the third player in Aston Villa's history to score a hat-trick in Europe.

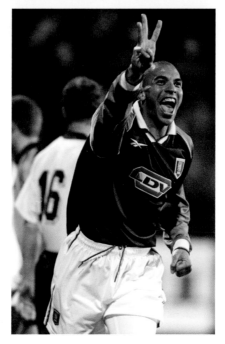

Just one of the many merchandising opportunities provided by the Premier League, this key ring has been left unopened – presumably by the Chelsea fan who bought it after he heard Hasselbaink was off to Middlesbrough, or perhaps by a Cardiff fan who has misplaced his keys.

Literally minutes after this picture was taken, Didier Drogba collapsed to the ground holding his throat until a paramedic pointed out that he was not in the penalty area and John Terry was, in fact, his team-mate and not an opposition defender.

'Why do birds suddenly appear/ Every time you are near?/Just like me/They long to be/Close to you . . .' As Gary Neville goes all Karen Carpenter, it is probably safe to say that this picture is not in a frame above the mantelpiece chez Scholes.

Tony Adams (to Arsène Wenger): 'I don't know what it is boss, I just feel like I'm carrying him.'
Ian Wright: 'Try putting me down and I'll break the Arsenal goalscoring record.'

It was the usual equation: Patrick + Vieira + Old + Trafford = Trouble.

With compassion dripping from his lips, Royston Keane commiserates with Alf-Inge Haaland . . . before walking straight down the tunnel and putting his feet up.

The complete perfectionist, Frank Lampard Jr is captured here gauging the wind direction and checking for moisture in the air before taking a free kick.

35 CARLOS TEVEZ

PREMIER LEAGUE DEBUT:
West Ham United v Aston Villa,
10 September 2006

PREMIER LEAGUE CLUBS:
West Ham United, Manchester United,
Manchester City

PREMIER LEAGUE APPEARANCES/GOALS:

West Ham U	26	7
Manchester U	63	19
Manchester C	79	48
Total	168	74

PREMIER LEAGUE HONOURS:
3 (2007-08, 2008-09, 2011-12)

COUNTRY:
Argentina (born Buenos Aires,
5 February 1984)

Manchester City stepped in with an offer estimated, but never confirmed, to be in the region of £45 million.

He hit the ground running and won both the fans' and players' Player of the Year awards. He was made club captain in August 2010 but, as at other clubs, it was never that simple – transfer request in, transfer request out, joint winner of the Premier League Golden Boot in 2010-11, FA Cup, never going back to Manchester, 'happy at City and not moving', suspended for refusing to come on as a substitute, AWOL for three months, apology, reacceptance, key role in club landing first title for 44 years.

What happens next? Watch this space. **BB**

> QUOTE
>
> 'Look, I liked the ideas of Kia [Joorbiachian – owner of MSI]. I really believed in the project. But you need to know I have only ever been transferred where I wanted to go; I have never been influenced otherwise. Not by anyone.'
>
> Tevez does his best to dispel rumours that he is just a multi-million pound money-making machine.

THE TERM 'model professional' could have been coined specifically for the late Gary Speed, as few would have any hesitation in bestowing that most suitable epithet on his lengthy and distinguished football career. Speed was an attacking left-sided midfield player, although he covered almost every outfield position at some time in his career.

He started out with Leeds United and won his only major honour with them in 1992, the old First Division title, when he starred as part of an illustrious midfield containing Gordon Strachan, David Batty and Gary McAllister. He had a short spell at Everton and a slightly longer stay at Bolton, either side of a long and relatively successful career at Newcastle, where he flourished under the tutelage of Bobby Robson and where he remembered being 'happiest over a period of time'. He finished playing at Sheffield United in 2010.

He remains, with 85 appearances, the most capped outfield player for Wales, playing nearly 40 of them as captain. It is perhaps also significant that he was made captain at Everton in his spell there and deputised as captain at Bramall Lane. On retirement, he was the boss at Sheffield United for just short of four months before being asked to take over the management of the Welsh national team, where he had a very promising start, with very little in the way of experience at even club level.

The tragic circumstances surrounding his death in November 2011 created a great sense of loss, confusion and lingering bewilderment both in and out of football. The *Guardian* recorded that he was 'a skilful, athletic and versatile left-sided

midfield player with exceptional heading ability and a healthy knack of scoring goals', and, it could be added, usually important ones.

He was supremely fit and paid attention to diet and hard work on the

34 GARY SPEED

PREMIER LEAGUE DEBUT:
Leeds United v Wimbledon, 15 August 1992

PREMIER LEAGUE CLUBS:
Leeds United, Everton, Newcastle United,
Bolton Wanderers

PREMIER LEAGUE APPEARANCES/GOALS:

Leeds U	143	22
Everton	58	16
Newcastle U	213	29
Bolton W	121	14
Total	535	81

PREMIER LEAGUE HONOURS:
None

COUNTRY:
Wales (born Deeside, 8 September 1969)

training pitch that enabled him to carry on playing until aged 39. The *Daily Telegraph* reinforced and added to these attributes by declaring that he was 'noted for his efficiency, intelligence and commitment to the team' and 'also showed himself to be a natural leader, a quality that later found its expression in his coaching role.'

He was popular and well-respected, a view echoed by Mark Hughes when endorsing his appointment as the new Welsh boss: 'He's got a strong personality, he's good with people, [the players] will relate better to Gary than they perhaps did with the previous manager.' Speed was awarded an MBE in 2010 for services to football.

GSt

QUOTE

'Three things that sum me up ... hardworking, honest, self-critical.'

Speed's self-assessment serves as a suitable epitaph.

33 JIMMY FLOYD HASSELBAINK

PREMIER LEAGUE DEBUT:
Leeds United v Arsenal, 9 August 1997

PREMIER LEAGUE CLUBS:
Leeds United, Chelsea, Middlesbrough, Charlton Athletic

PREMIER LEAGUE APPEARANCES/GOALS:

Leeds U	69	34
Chelsea	136	69
Middlesbrough	58	22
Charlton A	25	2
Total	288	127

PREMIER LEAGUE HONOURS:
None

COUNTRY:
Netherlands (born Paramaribo, Suriname, 27 March 1972)

THE MOMENT HE BECAME A LEGEND

His hat-trick against Tottenham on 13 March 2002. The first – he beats two defenders and curls it in with his right from 20 yards. The second – a fine leap and a firm header. The third – he collects the ball on the right touchline, beats two defenders, and bends the ball in from an angle with his left, this last goal particularly enjoyable as he causes two opponents to run into each other, the cherry on the cake of possibly the Premiership's finest hat-trick.

JIMMY FLOYD Hasselbaink (real name, Jerrel Hasselbaink) was born in the small South American country of Suriname, but plied his marvellous trade on the sodden western littoral of our chilly continent – first in the Netherlands, then in Portugal, and subsequently in England (with an interlude in Spain). Possibly as a result of his outrageous good fortune at travelling Europe kicking a ball about and getting paid handsomely for it, he acquired a permanently amazed expression, as though he had just opened Idi Amin's fridge.

He can be forgiven for the look of surprise. Growing up in a 14-storey tower block in a tough part of Zaandam, near Amsterdam, he ran with the wrong crowd as a youth and carried a knife; life as a multi-millionaire superstar did not seem an option. But football provided a way out and Hasselbaink spent his imperial period in the late 1990s and the early part of the 21st century continually re-enacting roadrunner-coyote cartoons with hapless defenders in pursuit, scoring at will, and ostentatiously refusing to celebrate splendid goals against former clubs.

The arrangement at Chelsea, where Hasselbaink was perhaps at his best (though his stay at Leeds is still fondly remembered), seemed to be that Jesper Gronkjaer, or another foreign minion, would give him the ball before he played an entirely predictable but seemingly unstoppable one-two with peerless career-stroller Eidur Gudjohnsen. On receiving the return pass, Hasselbaink would release the ball at the velocity of something propelled through the Hadron collider before acknowledging his goal in a mildly pleased manner. The only thing that didn't seem to surprise him was scoring again.

Hasselbaink was a complete centre-forward. He could shoot with both feet, and nobody from outside Brazil has ever hit the ball harder or in more goalie-unfriendly parabolas. His trademark was the curling shot millimetres inside the far post, usually from outside the penalty area – tap-ins really were beneath him; he was an inverse Lineker.

FC

> ## WELL I NEVER ...
>
> Arrested for handling stolen property as a youth, Hasselbaink was sent to a detention centre for three months. It was, he remembers, 'A big shock.'

> ## QUOTE
>
> 'Abramovich came into the dressing room [after the Champions League quarter-final victory at Highbury in April 2004]. We'd been promised £50,000 each if we made it to the semi-finals and [Adrian] Mutu jokes, "C'mon, man, double the bonus for fun!" ... He just said, "OK, why not?" I went on holiday with that bonus.'
>
> Presumably, Hasselbaink enjoyed his week at Butlins in Minehead.

WHEN A DAZED Gianluca Vialli staggered up the tunnel, the braying of the Southampton supporters crammed into The Dell ringing in his ears, he could have been forgiven for wondering why he had ever left Juventus.

This was not the place for an urbane Italian. There might have been familiar comfort in the exquisite execution of an acrobatic effort that cannoned against an upright, but the goalless draw that marked his Chelsea debut in 1996 was still an eye-opening introduction to a type of football the striker came to describe as 'like playing rugby'.

> ## THE MOMENT HE BECAME A LEGEND
>
> February 1997. Excluded from the Chelsea starting XI after a disagreement with Ruud Gullit, Vialli was spotted on the bench consoling himself with a cigarette.

A scorer of great goals, rather than a great goalscorer, the 1995 World Player of the Year was a powerful yet agile striker, and a wonderful foil to childhood friend Roberto Mancini in the successful Sampdoria side of the late 1980s and early 1990s. A world-record transfer fee of £12.5 million took Vialli to Juve in 1992, where he continued to accumulate trophies, becoming the only player in history to have winners and runners-up medals in all three main European club competitions.

When he came face to face with English football culture he was bemused by most of it, including the drinking habits – he claimed the half-dozen Marlboro he smoked each day were of less damage to his body – but quickly came to terms with the locker-room mentality. It takes a confident, not to mention naïvely brave, man to put itching powder in Graeme Souness' underwear and shaving foam in his shoes,

> ## WELL I NEVER ...
>
> His father was a self-made construction millionaire, and a chunk of Vialli's childhood was spent living in a castle.

and it has long been suspected that a similar stunt involving parmesan and a handkerchief was behind the dispute with Arrigo Sacchi that curtailed Vialli's international ambitions.

Indeed, falling out with people was a recurring theme during a stellar career. Having feuded with Ruud Gullit while a Chelsea player, he was made coach when the Dutchman departed, only to quarrel with his senior players

32 GIANLUCA VIALLI

PREMIER LEAGUE DEBUT (PLAYER):
Chelsea v Southampton, 18 August 1996

PREMIER LEAGUE DEBUT (MANAGER):
Chelsea v Leicester City, 21 February 1998

PREMIER LEAGUE CLUB (PLAYER):
Chelsea

PREMIER LEAGUE CLUB (MANAGER):
Chelsea

PREMIER LEAGUE APPEARANCES/GOALS:

Chelsea	58	21
Total	58	21

PREMIER LEAGUE APPEARANCES (MANAGER):

Chelsea	94
Total	94

PREMIER LEAGUE HONOURS:
None

COUNTRY:
Italy (born Cremona, 9 July 1964)

in the months before his sacking in 2000. By then, though, he had returned success to the club, winning the FA Cup and League Cup and, at 33, became the youngest manager to win the European Cup-Winners' Cup and UEFA Super Cup; a record which stood until André Villas-Boas' success with Porto.

He subsequently spent a depressing period as manager of Watford, leaving a trail of shattered expectations behind him, but the wonderful goals for Chelsea and his bracingly short but successful time in charge of the club ensure that his legacy is secure.   RW

> QUOTE
>
> 'English football strives for Utopia, while Italian football is rooted in realism – which is one step away from cynicism.'
>
> Vialli reflects on his life in English football, 2006.

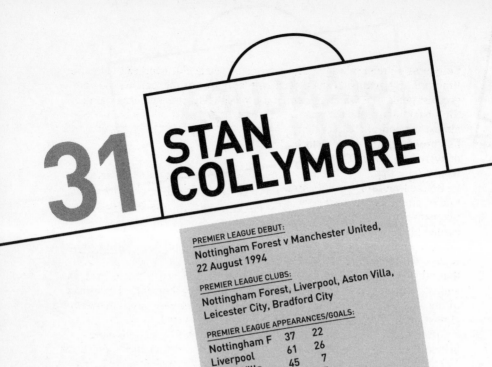

31 STAN COLLYMORE

PREMIER LEAGUE DEBUT:
Nottingham Forest v Manchester United,
22 August 1994

PREMIER LEAGUE CLUBS:
Nottingham Forest, Liverpool, Aston Villa,
Leicester City, Bradford City

PREMIER LEAGUE APPEARANCES/GOALS:

Nottingham F	37	22
Liverpool	61	26
Aston Villa	45	7
Leicester C	11	5
Bradford C	7	2
Total	161	62

PREMIER LEAGUE HONOURS:
None

COUNTRY:
England (born Cannock, 22 January 1971)

THE PRE-WAR Hollywood actress Lana Turner called it 'The Paragraph' – referring to the fact no interview or magazine profile was complete without reference to the story that her daughter stabbed Turner's abusive lover to death. Stan Collymore's 'Paragraph' is that he was caught dogging (having sex in public car parks with strangers – something he has described as: 'Actually quite amusing in a "Carry On" [film] sort of way') and that he also once hit former TV weathergirl, Ulrika Jonsson, his partner at the time, at a bar in Paris in 1998.

He has talked openly and frankly about both, so shall we move on to the football? That is why he is here, after all.

The penultimate goal of Stan

> ### THE MOMENT HE BECAME A LEGEND
>
> He scored the last-gasp winner in arguably the Premier League's greatest game, Liverpool's 4-3 win over Newcastle on 3 April 1996.

Collymore's Premier League lifetime was a spectacular overhead volley for Bradford City against Leeds United, arguably one of the league's all-time greatest goals – of which he scored a few. The Sky commentator claimed, 'He's back!' but in fact it was almost the end of a career that had promised way more than it delivered. Although Collymore would deny that.

Before Bradford, his high strike rate of more than a goal every two games for Nottingham Forest earned him a record £8.5 million move to Liverpool in 1995. But it wasn't just the volume of goals that attracted the Merseyside club, it was the way he scored them. With the ability to swivel on a sixpence, Collymore stung his shots into the corners of the goal with unforgiving accuracy. He could also ease past defenders almost before they realised they'd been done and busted.

After starting his career at Crystal Palace and Southend, Collymore helped Forest up to the Premier League, and then to a third-place finish in 1994-95. The following two seasons at Liverpool, in tandem with Robbie Fowler, brought a measure of success, but for a club with expectations as high as those at Anfield, third place in the Premier League and runners-up in the FA Cup weren't enough. Collymore was sold on to Aston Villa for £7 million.

At Villa, his boyhood team, and despite becoming only the third player in the club's history to score a hat-trick in Europe (in a 3-0 UEFA Cup win at Stromsgodset), Collymore struggled for form and suffered from clinical depression. After just seven league goals in three years, he was being passed on for free, and brief spells at Fulham (on loan), Leicester (where he broke his leg) and Bradford betrayed fleeting, heart-breaking signs of what might have been.

He scored just twice for Bradford before moving to Real Oviedo in Spain, but after only three games there he retired from professional football aged 30. In reality, his life was only just beginning and he recovered by publishing a candid autobiography, *Stan: Tackling My Demons*, acting in films (including *Basic Instinct 2* with Sharon Stone), recording music, and lately by making a career for himself as a TV commentator and, of course, as an intelligent no-nonsense presenter on talkSPORT Radio.

IP

QUOTE

'If you want to f*cking get it on, we'll go round the f*cking back, get our mics off and I'll cave your f*cking head in.'

Collymore has a word with rapper Vanilla Ice on Channel 5's reality TV show *The Farm*.

30 DIDIER DROGBA

PREMIER LEAGUE DEBUT:
Chelsea v Manchester United,
15 August 2004

PREMIER LEAGUE CLUB:
Chelsea

PREMIER LEAGUE APPEARANCES/GOALS:
Chelsea   226   100
Total   226   100

PREMIER LEAGUE HONOURS:
3 (2004-05, 2005-06, 2009-10)

COUNTRY:
Ivory Coast (born Abidjan, 11 March 1978)

NOWADAYS, IT can be hard to make sense of Didier Drogba's initial impact at Chelsea back in 2004-05, partially blinded as we are by both mythology and logic, secure in the knowledge of what was to come. Today, the £24 million club-record signing from Marseille is universally recognised for the contribution he made to claiming Roman Abramovich's precious first Premier League title, as well as the follow-up in 2005-06 and the Double season of 2009-10. Not to mention goals in four FA Cup finals and one in the Champions League final in 2012.

The stats alone show that he's obviously one of the greatest strikers of the Premier League era, as he became the first African to score 100 goals in the league. And yet it wasn't always so.

talkSPORT's own Andy Jacobs, a Blues lifer, was quick to describe Drogba as 'basically a very

THE MOMENT HE BECAME A LEGEND

At the end of the 2009-10 season, Drogba scored a hat-trick in an 8-0 thrashing of Wigan to secure both his third Premier League trophy with Chelsea, and his second Golden Boot, notching 29 league goals and 37 in all competitions. Chiefly remembered for the tantrum between himself and Lampard over who should take the first penalty.

expensive Ade Akinbiyi'. From the beginning, fans at the Bridge queried the direct style of the muscular Ivorian, querying whether he was too much of a blunt instrument for a Chelsea forward line. For perhaps the first time in football history, goals weren't considered good enough if they involved a barge, a thump, a boot into the net.

And then there was Drogba's habit of going to ground rather easily, and suspected handball incidents, which culminated in a shocking response at the final whistle against Manchester City at Stamford Bridge on 25 March 2006. 'Chelsea fans were whistling and jeering me, and I don't know many players who would like that – being booed by your own crowd.' This came despite having scored two goals, even if one did seem to come off his hand.

It's an experience that Drogba may have forgiven, but certainly hasn't forgotten. He later admitted: 'Now I'm really proud that, after my third season in England, I managed to change the way people in this country looked at me and saw me as a footballer.'

But even as his hugely impressive power, poise and insistent goal-banging won game after game, Chelsea hearts were again hardened by Drogba's talk of 'treachery' in the Chelsea dressing room at the time of Jose Mourinho's sacking. In 2007, the £100k-a-week 'wantaway' star claimed in *The Incredible Destiny of Didier Drogba* DVD that he had felt 'disgust' at re-signing for Chelsea. In 2011 he warned, 'The squad is exploding,' under André Villas-Boas. 'You sense total disorganisation at Chelsea right now. It is collectively falling apart.'

Outspoken, possibly arrogant, Drogba has never been the most popular Premier League legend with the fans of his own club. But, in time, they have grown to grudgingly accept his goals and the silver spoils he has brought them.   DH

> ## WELL I NEVER ...
>
> In 2010 *Time* magazine named Drogba one of the world's 100 most influential people after his impassioned pleas helped bring an end to five years of civil war in the Ivory Coast.

> ## QUOTE
>
> 'If I go to war and I could choose one person to go with me, I would choose Didier – because I know I would be with a fantastic man.'
>
> Jose Mourinho butters his star striker's parsnips.

'MANY GREAT players have worn the shirt of Manchester United,' said Sir Bobby Charlton in 2008. 'Players I worshipped, then lost with my youth in Munich. Players like Denis Law and George Best, who I enjoyed so much as team-mates and now, finally, players I have watched closely in the Alex Ferguson era. And in so many ways Paul Scholes is my favourite.' High praise indeed, but unlikely to merit more than an embarrassed shrug from the player himself.

Brought up an Oldham fan, Scholes played in the 'Latics' junior team, Boundary Park, along with Nicky Butt and Gary and Phil Neville, and they all went on to play for Manchester United and England. It was Brian Kidd who brought him to United, telling youth team coach Eric Harrison: 'He's only tiny; he's got ginger hair – you'll probably have a bit of a laugh. But he can't half play.'

THE MOMENT HE BECAME A LEGEND

In United's 1999 Treble-winning season, he was instrumental in guiding the team through the later rounds of the Champions League – before picking up a yellow card in the semi that made him ineligible for the final. He also sealed the Double with a crashing 20-yard strike in the FA Cup final win against Newcastle.

He wasn't wrong. Scholes went on to become the fourth player ever to rack up 600 appearances for the club, and one of only three to score 100 Premier League goals for them. And even outside Manchester (and the Home Counties), he's revered for his record of popping up just when England needed a goal, scoring 14 times in 66 international appearances.

But the 'Ginger Prince' never let any of the adulation go to his head. Over the years, he hardly passed comment, never mind an ill-tempered remark, even in the heat of the post-match arc lights. It was a different situation on the pitch, however, and, at the time of writing, he is the third most-booked player in Premier League history with 92 yellow cards, and out on his own in the Champions League. As Arsenal manager Arsène Wenger put it, 'There is a dark side to him.'

There has, however, never been any doubting his ability – he takes the ball first time, can hit volleys from 30 yards, pass the ball any distance with unerring accuracy (his nickname is 'Sat Nav'), he can (almost) tackle and times his runs to perfection. His commitment has never been called

WELL I NEVER …

Shock, horror! Scholes wasn't in the legendary 1992 FA Youth Cup-winning side along with Beckham, Butt, Gary Neville, Giggs, Robbie Savage and Keith Gillespie. But he was a losing finalist the following year.

29 PAUL SCHOLES

PREMIER LEAGUE DEBUT:
Manchester United v Ipswich Town,
24 September 1994

PREMIER LEAGUE CLUB:
Manchester United

PREMIER LEAGUE APPEARANCES/GOALS:

Manchester U	483	106
Total	483	106

PREMIER LEAGUE HONOURS:
10 (1995-96, 1996-97, 1998-99, 1999-00,
2000-01, 2002-03, 2006-07, 2007-08,
2008-09, 2010-11)

COUNTRY:
England (born Salford, 16 November 1974)

into question. The late, great Brazilian Socrates once commented, 'He could have played for Brazil.' In May 2011, seven years after he announced his retirement from England duty (to 'spend more time with my family'), he decided to quit for good.

Well, not exactly for good. Seven months later, as United's title-chasing team required a little experience, he returned for a final lap of honour at the age of 37 and scored in his first game back at Old Trafford against Bolton. 'Someone just asked me if he'd said anything about his goal,' smiled team-mate Michael Carrick after the game. 'I said: "You don't know Scholesy."' **DH**

> ## QUOTE
>
> 'My toughest opponent? Scholes of Manchester [United]. He is the complete midfielder. Scholes is undoubtedly the greatest midfielder of his generation.'
>
> French meastro Zinedine Zidane gives understatement a miss.

28 | TONY ADAMS

PREMIER LEAGUE DEBUT (PLAYER):
Arsenal v Norwich City, 15 August 1992

PREMIER LEAGUE DEBUT (MANAGER):
Portsmouth v Liverpool, 29 October 2008

PREMIER LEAGUE CLUB (PLAYER):
Arsenal

PREMIER LEAGUE CLUB (MANAGER):
Portsmouth

PREMIER LEAGUE APPEARANCES/GOALS:

Arsenal	255	12
Total	255	12

PREMIER LEAGUE APPEARANCES (MANAGER):

Portsmouth	15
Total	15

PREMIER LEAGUE HONOURS:
2 (1997-98, 2001-02)

COUNTRY:
England (born Romford, 10 October 1966)

'I DON'T actually like people,' Adams explained to a local newspaper reporter. 'I'm a loner and if I had my way I'd just walk my dogs every day, never talk to anyone and then die.' Which could explain why, having been sacked as Portsmouth manager in 2010, he decided to move to Azerbaijan to take over at Gabala FC. It is unreported whether he took his dogs.

He left after mixed success 18 months later, citing personal reasons. It was the same line he had used when leaving Wycombe Wanderers in November 2004, before a peripatetic coaching and scouting role in Europe led to the Portsmouth job. It is fair to say that his post-playing career has not been

THE MOMENT HE BECAME A LEGEND

After scoring against Everton in 1998, he held his arms up to the sky with an expression that said, 'Of course I can play like a seasoned striker' – a moment immortalised by his bronze statue outside the Emirates.

covered in the glory of his hugely successful career as Arsenal and England central defender and captain. But that was one hell of an act to follow.

All the more remarkable when you consider that he not only overcame addiction, but served two months in jail for drink-driving in 1990. His eventual recovery, and his honesty, endeared him to more than just the Arsenal fans, who revered their tough-tackling captain as the face beneath the numerous trophies the club lifted throughout the 1990s and the following decade – four titles (including two in the Premier League era), three FA Cups, two League Cups and one UEFA Cup.

He was a one-club man who signed for the Gunners at the age of 14, made his debut at 17 in 1983 and was captain of the team by 21. Very much 'Old Arsenal', he was the leader of an all-English defence that for most of the 1990s consisted of himself, Lee Dixon and Nigel Winterburn as full-backs, and either Steve Bould or Martin Keown by his side in the middle. This is the back line fondly recalled by a certain generation of Arsenal fan who finds it hard to relate to the stars three tiers below at the Emirates.

> ## WELL I NEVER ...
>
> In one pre-tournament team meeting, Adams was instructed by England manager Bobby Robson to play the ball out of defence, in order to avoid giving the ball to Maradona. Adams seemed utterly convinced that it was unlikely to be a problem. It was before the 1988 European Championships.

After successfully coming through rehab (England colleague Alan Shearer remarked, 'I was never too aware of his problems with booze, but he was still a hell of a player when he had them'), Adams had transformed himself from the nightclub-fighting, car-crashing, fire-extinguisher incident-prone 'Donkey' into a superb all-round player who was named in the Premier League 'Team of the Decade' in 2002. He

> ## QUOTE
>
> 'Dennis [Bergkamp] is such a nice man, such a tremendous gentleman with such a lovely family. It's going to be very hard for me to kick him.'
>
> Tony Adams experiences a moral dilemma before England v Netherlands at Euro 96.

was also an enlightened man who, based on his own experiences, set up the Sporting Chance clinic to provide a specialist addiction and recovery facility for sportsmen and women in 2000.   IP/BB

IT SEEMS preposterous to talk of Ian Wright as a nearly man; he was part of the Double-winning team in 1998, broke the Arsenal scoring record (since surpassed by Thierry Henry), made the PFA Premier League Team of the Year twice and was capped 33 times by his country. And all after coming into the game at the age of 21. He was spotted, when he wasn't working as a plasterer, playing for non-league Dulwich Hamlet. It is daunting to think what he might have accomplished had he made his professional debut three or four years earlier.

> ## THE MOMENT HE BECAME A LEGEND
>
> As well as being Arsenal's leading scorer in the first Premier League season in 1992-93, he also scored in the FA Cup final against Sheffield Wednesday and again in the replay.

It was not for the want of trying. He had numerous trials from the age of 12, but got nowhere. 'I can only put it down to the fact that I was quite small and skinny,' he has since reasoned. However, fortune made a rare appearance in Wright's career when Crystal Palace signed him in August 1985, and for six seasons he repaid their faith, scoring 117 goals in 253 starts and being named the club's Player of the Century in 2006. He was a peerless finisher with the boundless energy of an eight-year-old on a four-pack of Red Bull – witness his performance coming off the bench for Palace in the 1990 FA Cup final against Manchester United (two goals in 20 minutes).

He eventually made his England debut in February 1991, aged 27, before George Graham took him to Arsenal, then reigning champions, for a club record £2.5 million. Naturally, he scored on his debut (in the League Cup) and then followed that with a hat-trick in his first league game against Southampton. He started as he meant to go on and finished as the club's leading scorer for six seasons in a row – tap-ins, 30-yarders, showboaters, he had the whole lot going on.

As winner of the Golden Boot in the season before the Premier League began, he was expected to go to Sweden for Euro 92 but was left out of the squad – this combination of inexplicable managerial decision-making and rank misfortune would feature prominently in Wright's career.

He kept his end of the bargain, scoring goals (particularly in the '1-0 to the Arsenal' era), but was suspended for the Cup-Winners' Cup final in 1994, while England

> ## WELL I NEVER ...
>
> He starred in a film called *Gun of the Black Sun* (2011) – it features a mystical Luger handgun that belonged to the Nazis, some Romanian druid types, motorbikes, a Ferrari and, according to one reviewer, 'Ian Wright is the best thing in it.'

27 IAN WRIGHT

PREMIER LEAGUE DEBUT:
Arsenal v Norwich City, 15 August 1992

PREMIER LEAGUE CLUBS:
Arsenal, West Ham United

PREMIER LEAGUE APPEARANCES/GOALS:

Arsenal	191	104
West Ham U	22	9
Total	213	113

PREMIER LEAGUE HONOURS:
1 (1997-98)

COUNTRY:
England (born Woolwich, 3 November 1963)

also failed to qualify for the World Cup that year. Subsequently recalled to the national side, he was left out of the Euro 96 squad ('I know I would have scored the Golden Goal in the semi-final'), suffered a hamstring injury that ruled him out for the run-in to the 1998 Double and the World Cup squad that year, and was 36 by time Euro 2000 came around. After a brief period at West Ham, Nottingham Forest on loan and Burnley in the Championship, he retired.

To his eternal credit, however, Wright remains grateful for the years that he spent in the game and his infectious no-nonsense personality has guaranteed him a successful broadcasting career in radio – not least of course alongside Adrian Durham at talkSPORT – and television. His popularity with fans of all clubs (except, bizarrely perhaps, those of Southampton) ensures that he is regularly called upon as a pundit or to endorse products as various as Chicken Tonight and Nintendo Wii. Not bad for a nearly man.   BB

> QUOTE
>
> 'You've got to take the rough with the smooth. It's like love and hate, war and peace, all that bollocks.'
>
> Summing up his own career, Wright comes over all philosophical.

WEARING THE FACE of a hard man on the door of an East End gangster's favourite nightclub, John Terry has been loyally standing guard over the Chelsea and England defence for well over a decade. A one-club man since moving from West Ham aged 14, Terry is the kind of courageous and uncompromising player that every successful team needs as an anchor.

There are few fans or players who would not want a man like 'JT' at the core of its backline, wearing the captain's armband and fighting for every ball like a lion with legs of oak and the heart of John Bull. That, at least, would be the general public relations pitch on the plaque beneath any future statue of Terry erected outside Stamford Bridge.

But he's more complicated than that. There have been alleged unsavoury nightclub incidents, a fine of two weeks' wages for drunken behaviour at Heathrow Airport towards American tourists the day after the 2001 terror attacks in the US, and he was fined £10,000 by the FA for bringing the integrity of referee Graham Poll into question.

He lost the England captaincy for a year after unproven allegations that he slept with a former team-mate's former girlfriend, and then there was the charge that he racially abused QPR's Anton Ferdinand during a game in late 2011 – charges he denied, but which were due to go to court after this book went to press. During his career, his consistency and excellence at the highest level aside, he has lived his life in the spotlight like every professional footballer. Consequently, he is as used to controversies, both genuine and alleged, as he is dealing with dead-ball situations.

Yet there are few Chelsea fans who would do anything other than worship the last-ditch tackler who, as captain in more than 400 games since 2004, has led them to two League Cups, four FA Cups, three league titles and, at last and despite the fact he was suspended for the final, the 2012 Champions League title. He may have cried like a braying wean when he cost Chelsea its first

> ## THE MOMENT HE BECAME A LEGEND
>
> He leapt to score the decisive goal in a vibrant 4-2 Champions League win over Barcelona in 2005, making the aggregate score 5-4.

> ## WELL I NEVER ...
>
> He used to be a Manchester United fan as a child.

26 JOHN TERRY

PREMIER LEAGUE DEBUT:
Chelsea v Southampton, 26 December 1998

PREMIER LEAGUE CLUB:
Chelsea

PREMIER LEAGUE APPEARANCES/GOALS:
Chelsea   373   28
Total   373   28

PREMIER LEAGUE HONOURS:
3 (2004-05, 2005-06, 2009-10); PFA Player of the Year 2005

COUNTRY:
England (born Barking, 7 December 1980)

such title by missing a penalty in the shoot-out against Manchester United in Moscow in 2008, but he was forgiven and the banner complete with his picture at Stamford Bridge remains, 'CAPTAIN, LEADER, LEGEND.'

His personal honours are so extensive as to preclude a comprehensive listing in the space available, suffice to say that for five successive years he was voted by his peers on the international stage on to the FIFPro (from 2009 the FIFA FIFPro) World XI. Age and back problems have slowed him a little, but Chelsea somehow won't be quite the same team the day he steps down.   IP

> QUOTE
>
> 'I'm quite soft and gentle away from football. People who don't know me, old ladies in the supermarket, often say they thought I would be more aggressive. They're surprised if I'm nice. I don't know what they think I'm going to do. Hit them with a two-footed tackle in the fruit and veg aisle, maybe.'
>
> Terry explains away the public misconception of his off-the-field behaviour.

25 PATRICK VIEIRA

PREMIER LEAGUE DEBUT:
Arsenal v Sheffield Wednesday,
16 September 1996

PREMIER LEAGUE CLUBS:
Arsenal, Manchester City

PREMIER LEAGUE APPEARANCES/GOALS:
Arsenal   279   28
Manchester C   28   3
Total   307   31

PREMIER LEAGUE HONOURS:
3 (1997-98, 2001-02, 2003-04)

COUNTRY:
France (born Dakar, Senegal, 23 June 1976)

AROUND THE turn of the century, the competition between Arsenal midfielder Patrick Vieira and his combustible counterpart at Manchester United, Roy Keane, dominated the frequent title deciders at both Old Trafford and Highbury. If there is a thin line between love and hate, you have to think that if they ever stopped trying to kick lumps out of each other and their eyes met across a crowded midfield, they'd collapse into a passionate embrace.

The Senegalese-born Vieira was graceful and lanky compared with the terrier-like Keane, but their virtues as defensive-minded midfielders were not just confined to their aggression and ball-winning determination, but also their ability to gain possession and then race forward from a deep position to either build a counter-attack or score the occasional goal (an average of about one every ten games for Vieira – compared to Keane's one in eight). And, for a hard man, Vieira's footwork was remarkably adept.

He was signed at the insistence of Arsène Wenger even before the

Frenchman had taken up the manager's position at Arsenal in 1996. The hefty fee of £3.5 million for a player who had managed only two appearances for AC Milan – after signing from Cannes as a teenager – prompted Arsenal fans to raise a quizzical eyebrow at this incipient Gallic takeover. By the time Vieira and Wenger had helped Arsenal to a Premier League and FA Cup Double just over two years later at the end of the 1997-98 season, such doubts had long been replaced by fans wearing berets and travelling to games on bikes adorned with strings of onions.

During nine years with the club, Vieira won three league titles and three FA Cups (Arsenal actually lifted a fourth during this time, but Vieira was out injured and ineligible for a medal). Since he left for Juventus in 2005, Arsenal have won nothing – is it a coincidence that the trophies stopped coming when Arsenal lost a quality midfield enforcer to prop up its pretty play further down the field? No.

> ## THE MOMENT HE BECAME A LEGEND
>
> Smacked a cracker from the edge of the penalty into Peter Schmeichel's top corner at Highbury in a 3-2 win over Manchester United during the Double-winning 1997-98 season.

> ## WELL I NEVER ...
>
> It wasn't just Keane. Vieira also had a running feud with Internazionale's Marco Materazzi (the player on the wrong end of Zinedine Zidane's World Cup head-butt in the 2006 World Cup final). What made this more interesting is that they were actually team-mates at Inter ('the most idiotic' player he had ever played with, according to Vieira). In a pre-season game for Manchester City in 2011, he laid him flat with an elbow to the head and received the red card like he was being handed a receipt for his shopping.

Vieira's cutting-edge play did come with a price, however. He was ordered off a joint Premier League record eight times for Arsenal, including two successive red cards at the start of the 2000-01 season. Both he and Wenger pleaded victimisation, but the Arsenal–Manchester United rivalry of this era was the Premier League's main talking point, fuelled by Wenger's psychological verbal spats with Sir Alex Ferguson, and Vieira's robust encounters with Keane. 'When we got the fixture list, the first thing we looked for was that Manchester United game,' Vieira later confessed. They were tense and tough, but for players and fans alike, the high point of the season.

> QUOTE
>
> 'There are players who have no interest in playing the game properly ... they are just trying to upset Patrick. There are certain managers who encourage this.'
>
> Wenger underlines the importance of his player after successive red cards in 2000, while in no way attempting to influence referees.

Vieira played for France, his home after leaving Senegal aged eight, and boasted a massively successful international career, winning the 1998 World Cup when he came on as a sub and set up a goal for his Arsenal midfield partner Emmanuel Petit. He also won a Euro 2000 medal, and played in the 2006 World Cup final against Italy in Berlin, although he had to retire with an injury. In all, he racked up 107 French caps.

In North London, though, he'll always be remembered as the player that captained the team to its remarkable 2003-04 Premier League title when, over 38 games, they went the season unbeaten, 'The Invincibles' as they have become known. Before moving to Manchester City in 2010 (and gaining another FA Cup winner's medal in 2011), it is perhaps fitting that his final kick for the Gunners was to win the 2005 FA Cup final in the penalty shoot-out against Manchester United. Arsenal and Arsène have been missing him ever since.

IP

24 ROY KEANE

PREMIER LEAGUE DEBUT (PLAYER):
Nottingham Forest v Liverpool, 16 August 1992

PREMIER LEAGUE DEBUT (MANAGER):
Sunderland v Tottenham Hotspur, 11 August 2007

PREMIER LEAGUE CLUBS (PLAYER):
Nottingham Forest, Manchester United

PREMIER LEAGUE CLUB (MANAGER):
Sunderland

PREMIER LEAGUE APPEARANCES/GOALS:

Nottingham F	40	6
Manchester U	326	33
Total	366	39

PREMIER LEAGUE APPEARANCES (MANAGER):

Sunderland	53
Total	53

PREMIER LEAGUE HONOURS:
7 (1993-94, 1995-96, 1996-97, 1998-99, 1999-00, 2000-01, 2002-03); PFA and FWA Footballer of the Year 2000

COUNTRY:
Republic of Ireland (born Cork, 10 August 1971)

'HE'S MAD, BUT he's funny too,' Ryan Giggs once said of his team-mate Roy Keane, the devil-eyed midfield motivator who'd have eaten alive his beloved labrador Triggs rather than shirk a 40:60 challenge. Keane feared nothing – not opponents, not referees, not authority, and certainly not controversy. He was as much a maverick as Eric Cantona, and perhaps an all-round better player, too. As a young Steven Gerrard put it: 'I'm a great admirer of Roy Keane. He has been there, done it and still wants to do it. I don't like Manchester United, but to be mentioned in the same breath as him is great.'

For a dozen seasons after being signed from Nottingham Forest in 1993, Keane was the heartbeat of Britain's strongest club, surging backwards and forwards from box to box, serving late (sometimes very late) tackles, delivering superlative passes, scoring goals, and all the while exhorting his fellow players to do the same. If you weren't giving 100 per cent for the full 90 minutes, you'd be subject to Keane's glares and tirades. If purple-faced Fergie was the bad cop, Keane was the even badder cop. He racked up a total of 13 red cards in his club career.

THE MOMENT HE BECAME A LEGEND

When he condemned a generation of parasitic corporate football fans, leading to the phrase 'the prawn sandwich brigade'.

'You don't contest football matches in a reasonable state of mind,' Keane claimed in his autobiography. Too honest by half, the book brought him a five-match ban and a £150,000 fine for bringing the game into disrepute when it was interpreted as admitting that he'd deliberately set out to hurt Manchester City's Alf Inge Haaland in a Manchester derby. The reason? Four years earlier, while playing for Leeds, Haaland had leant over a badly injured Keane and accused him of faking it. Keane didn't forget. Or acknowledge the fact that he had hurt himself in making the challenge.

Keane, though, raised a cheer from fans who felt the Premier League era meant too many soulless all-seater stadiums and corporate guests concealed behind smoked glass. He praised United's away support as 'hardcore', but said that at Old

WELL I NEVER ...

A comedy musical play, parodying the fracas between Mick McCarthy and Roy Keane, called *I, Keano*, ran in Dublin from 2005 to 2008. It generated over £7 million in ticket sales.

Trafford there were too many people sitting around who didn't understand football, and who weren't paying attention in any case. Then again, it was partly thanks to such fans that Keane became one of the first players to earn more than £50,000 a week.

Keane's international career was just as fractious. He played for Ireland in the 1994 World Cup, but didn't think they'd achieved much, even though they beat Italy and reached the final 16. After playing a major role in the qualifying campaign, he walked out on the 2002 squad after complaining about the training facilities in Japan, and telling manager Mick McCarthy that he was a wanker and exactly where he could temporarily house his World Cup. But after retiring as a player following a brief spell with Celtic, he discovered that management wasn't as easy as it looked when he parted company with both Sunderland and Ipswich.

QUOTE

'Stick it up your bollocks!'

Roy Keane's anatomically improbable suggestion to then Republic of Ireland manager Mick McCarthy, shortly before walking out on the national team before the 2002 World Cup in Japan and South Korea.

Seven Premiership titles and four FA Cups during his time at Manchester United tell their own success story, as well as a 2000 Footballer of the Year award, and five spots on the PFA Team of the Year. But it's his 1999 Champions League winner's medal that perhaps best illustrates the turbulent brilliance of Keane's career. Without him, United would never have lifted the European title in Barcelona, yet that night he wasn't even in the team.

In the semi-final second leg at Juventus, Keane had led the team from 2-0 down to a magnificent 3-2 victory, scoring in the process and playing like a man possessed. But he had also picked up a yellow card, meaning suspension from the final. Swedish midfielder Jesper Blomqvist played Keane a terrible pass that went to Zinedine Zidane in a dangerous position. Keane knew what he had to do – foul Zidane, knowing that it would mean a yellow, but he took it for the team. As compensation, he turned around and bawled out the useless Blomqvist.

Keane was later honest enough to admit that, despite United's victory, the 2-1 win over Bayern Munich was one of the most difficult nights of his career. He wanted to be out there where he belonged – shouting, competing and winning.

IP

23 FRANK LAMPARD

PREMIER LEAGUE DEBUT:
West Ham United v Coventry City,
31 January 1996

PREMIER LEAGUE CLUBS:
West Ham United, Chelsea

PREMIER LEAGUE APPEARANCES/GOALS:
West Ham U   148   24
Chelsea   374   126
Total   522   150

PREMIER LEAGUE HONOURS:
3 (2004-05, 2005-06, 2009-10);
FWA Footballer of the Year 2005

COUNTRY:
England (born Romford, 20 June 1978)

AS THE BALL hit the net he wheeled away in celebration, removed the black band that had adorned his left arm, held it in both hands and kissed it repeatedly until sinking to his knees in front of thousands of screaming fans, before being mobbed by jubilant team-mates. That one was special for Lampard. It was extra time at Stamford Bridge, the Blues were playing Liverpool for a place in the 2008 Champions League final, and Lampard was appearing for his club just six days after his mother, Pat, had died. They won 4-3 on aggregate.

Contrary to popular belief, Frank James Lampard's rise to the top had been far from easy. The path to greatness was initially dogged by accusations of nepotism at boyhood club West Ham. There, he'd come through the ranks and he was managed by his uncle, Harry Redknapp, who was assisted by his father, Frank Snr, themselves former Hammers players.

Match days at Upton Park often brought with them jeers and boos from sections of West Ham fans unhappy at his inclusion in the squad. Some held the opinion that the midfielder did not possess the talent required to be included so frequently. The love Lampard once held for the club he had spent every moment dreaming of playing for had been drained from him, and he moved to Chelsea for a fee of £11.1 million in 2001. It is safe to say that time has proved his critics wrong.

An inner determination, though, would soon see him become the heartbeat of the Chelsea midfield, while also racking up countless individual awards. In the Abramovich era from 2003, he quickly realised that he would have a fight on his hands to keep his place in the side, as midfield talent was brought in from around the world. Not one to shirk a challenge, Lampard set about proving his worth and, under Jose Mourinho in 2004-05, formed the backbone of the title-chasing side.

His brace in the 2-0 win against Bolton at the Reebok Stadium helped seal the crown in late April. Party time – until Liverpool spoiled the celebration days later, when Luis Garcia's controversial goal sent them into the Champions League final at the Blues' expense. Chelsea were still the best team in England and, according to the Football Writers' Association, Lampard was the best player. Naturally, he was also voted the club's Player of the Year, for a second time (he won it again in 2009 – the only player to win it on three occasions).

In December 2005, he was also runner-up to Ronaldinho, during the Brazilian's period of dominance in Europe, in both the Ballon d'Or and the FIFA World Player of the Year awards. Those 'fans' had been answered.

He added another Premier League winner's medal in 2006, topping Chelsea's goalscoring charts for the second successive season, with 16. Winning the FA Cup for the first time followed in 2007 and then again in 2009; his third triumph in 2010 culminated in another Premier League win when, under Carlo Ancelotti, the Blues won the Double. FA Cup number four arrived in 2012, before memories of Moscow heartache in 2008 were put to one side in a dramatic Champions League final success in 2012.

The midfielder is fourth on the list of leading appearance-makers in the Premier League, and fifth in the Premier League's all-time scoring charts, closing fast on Robbie Fowler's 163 goals. For nine consecutive seasons to the end of 2011-12, he scored at least ten goals a campaign, a feat unmatched by any striker, let alone a midfielder.

Frank Lampard has already taken his place among the pantheon of football greats and an insatiable appetite to be the best has made him an immovable object at Stamford Bridge. And he is not ready to stop just yet.

DM

22 KENNY DALGLISH

PREMIER LEAGUE DEBUT (MANAGER):
Blackburn Rovers v Crystal Palace,
15 August 1992

PREMIER LEAGUE CLUBS (MANAGER):
Blackburn Rovers, Newcastle United,
Liverpool

PREMIER LEAGUE APPEARANCES (MANAGER):

Blackburn R	126
Newcastle U	56
Liverpool	56
Total	238

PREMIER LEAGUE HONOURS:
1 (1994-95); Manager of the Season 1995

COUNTRY:
Scotland (born Glasgow, 4 March 1951)

IF YOU WANT to know the source of Kenny Dalglish's steel, the resolution that made him supremely successful as both player and manager, consider his roots – the informal, working-class football academy that was post-war Glasgow. King Kenny was born into the Lanark nobility – the labour aristocracy, his father an engineer from the East End.

The family finally fetched up in Govan, the same area that nurtured the young Alex Ferguson. Typically for the time, he worked as an apprentice joiner when on loan from Celtic to Cumbernauld United. In a horrible foreshadowing of his experiences at Heysel and Hillsborough, he was in the stands during the Ibrox disaster of 1971.

Everything seemed to conspire to toughen him up, and this manifested itself on the field of play. A slight striker in an age when skilful forwards were afforded little protection (shinpads and liniment usually), Dalglish was formidably courageous – and gloriously gifted:

George Best, no less, likened him to his childhood hero, the great Alfredo di Stefano. Kenny's career was a slideshow of countless trophies, beautiful goals and weeping defenders. How could his managerial years fail to be an anti-climax?

Well, we now know that Dalglish is the only man in the English game to be equally successful as player and manager. His pre-Premiership stewardship of Liverpool was outstanding – three league titles and two FA Cups in five seasons – but perhaps not altogether astonishing, given the club's recent achievements.

What he did at Blackburn, though, was truly remarkable. Although Dalglish didn't arrive at Second Division Rovers until October 1991, he managed to lead them to victory in the play-offs and hence their first season in the top flight since 1966. In 1992, he signed Alan Shearer. They finished fourth. The squad was strengthened by the acquisition of England internationals Tim Flowers and David Batty, and finished second.

At the start of the 1994-95 campaign, Dalglish bought Chris Sutton to operate alongside Shearer, the final piece of the jigsaw. Blackburn pipped Manchester United to the title on the last day of the season – and Dalglish became only the third manager ever to lead two different clubs to top-flight titles. When you're in the same bracket as Herbert Chapman and Brian Clough, 'King' is not hyperbole.

It's true that chairman Jack Walker's tendency to regularly tip wheelbarrows full of cash onto Kenny's desk made his job easier, but, actually, Dalglish's team, though costly, was not star-packed, Shearer being their

only true all-time great. The fact that Batty played for England says more about England than it does about Batty. Instead, Rovers' success was built on teamwork and industry, precisely the qualities Dalglish would have acquired in his artisanal youth.

No sooner had he won the title than he stepped away from the limelight, moving upstairs to become director of football, making way for Ray Harford. Dalglish left Blackburn a year later, but was soon back in action – this time at Newcastle, where (as in 1977) he followed Kevin Keegan. Dalglish's footballing philosophy didn't fit naturally with the all-out attacking approach the Geordies had become used to under Keegan, and soon he was on his way. A brief spell back at Celtic came to an end, and for more than a decade he was more often to be found on the golf course.

When he came back, it was with an irresistible groundswell of support. Liverpool fans had seen their idol waiting in the wings, and believed he was the man for the job – not Roy Hodgson. They soon got their way as the club's new American owners bowed to the inevitable. Sitting in 12th position when he took charge in January 2011, Dalglish lifted his side to sixth by the end of the campaign.

A Champions League spot was the next target, but despite a Carling Cup victory and an FA Cup final, Liverpool ended the season in eighth after a campaign that had also featured several PR disasters for the club. After the season was over, so was Dalglish's second reign.

Dalglish's world remains a stark contrast to the demented hall of mirrors of the modern footballer – that non-haircut, the Man At C&A outfits, the quietly spoken thoughtfulness. Charisma is often just a projection of the observer's delusions, but Dalglish is the real thing. Having authentic character, he has no need to develop a 'personality'.

Most importantly, after the Hillsborough Disaster Dalglish attended many of the funerals, including four in one day, and was the driving force behind the club's immaculate response to the tragedy. The highest praise you can bestow on Dalglish is that he is a worthy successor to giants such as Bill Shankly and Bob Paisley.

FC

21 | PETER SCHMEICHEL

PREMIER LEAGUE DEBUT:
Manchester United v Sheffield United,
15 August 1992

PREMIER LEAGUE CLUBS:
Manchester United, Aston Villa,
Manchester City

PREMIER LEAGUE APPEARANCES/GOALS:

Manchester U	252	0
Aston Villa	29	1
Manchester C	29	0
Total	310	1

PREMIER LEAGUE HONOURS:
5 (1992-93, 1993-94, 1995-96, 1996-97,
1998-99)

COUNTRY:
Denmark (born Gladsaxe,
18 November 1963)

IT'S DIFFICULT to imagine a more perfect ending to Peter Schmeichel's career at Manchester United than when, in May 1999, he held the Champions League trophy up to the night sky in the Nou Camp, after United had pulled off the biggest smash-and-grab in the history of the competition.

Bayern Munich had led from the sixth minute right up until the 90th. Thirty seconds into injury time, the Great Dane charged up field for a corner and caused confusion in the German defence, leading to Teddy Sheringham's equaliser. Moments later, Ole Gunnar Solskjaer prodded home to snatch a dramatic, impossible victory.

And so it came to pass that Schmeichel, in his last game for United and captain for the night, ushered Alex Ferguson over to help him with the trophy-lifting duties. Not only was it the ultimate accolade in European club football, but it completed a historic Treble along with the Premier League title and FA Cup.

And yet it could all have been so different.

In January 1994, Schmeichel and Ferguson had a spectacular falling-out in the Anfield dressing rooms following a 3-3 draw against Liverpool, which United had once led 3-0. The 6ft 4in Schmeichel was no shrinking violet and objected to being singled out by his manager for the famous 'hairdryer' treatment – which he returned with interest.

On Monday, the Dane was called into the manager's office to be told: 'I have to sack you. I can't tolerate my players speaking to me like that. It goes against my authority.' Fortunately for both parties, Schmeichel apologised and Ferguson relented, perhaps realising the folly of letting such a huge talent go.

When Schmeichel had arrived at Old Trafford from Brøndby in 1991, United hadn't won the league title for 24 years. And yet during his eight seasons with the club, they won the Premier League five times. It was no coincidence.

THE MOMENT HE BECAME A LEGEND

In Alex Ferguson's mind, it was probably when he juggled his foreign players for a Champions League match against Barcelona in 1994-95, preferring Gary Walsh over Schmeichel. In the 43 games he actually played that season, he kept 26 clean sheets, including an unbeaten run of 1,135 minutes. United were thrashed 4-0 by the Spaniards. Never again.

WELL I NEVER ...

His dad Tolek was a popular jazz pianist in Denmark, and Peter also plays piano and drums. He wrote, played most of the instruments and rapped on a Danish hit single for Euro 96 – 'We Can Do It' (Yes! Sådan! Såmænd!). The Danes, reigning champions, crashed out in the first round.

If strikers are judged by their goals then goalkeepers live and die by clean sheets, and Schmeichel can boast a Premier League record of conceding no goals in an incredible 42 per cent of his games. On the way to United's first league title in 26 years, the inaugural Premier League competition in 1992-93, the opposition drew a blank against Schmeichel on 18 occasions.

All those other legends running around in red, viewed from the standpoint of the impassable United goal-line, well, their job was relatively easy.

Difficult as it was to penetrate United's midfield and back four in that glorious decade, success in getting that far led only to an opponent forward coming face to face with a platinum-haired man mountain – a Bond villain's sidekick of a goalie. Not only was Schmeichel big, he was agile, so even a shot heading right for the top corner would be palmed away. In a one-on-one situation, Schmeichel was unsurpassable, spreading himself to such great effect that there seemed no way round him.

Named UEFA Goalkeeper of the Year in 1992, 1993, 1997 and 1998, he's regarded by many as the greatest keeper in the history of the game, and has the polls to prove it.

He even has a remarkable 11 goals to his name, mostly scored for his first Danish club Hvidovre, but also for Brøndby, United, Denmark and Aston Villa, where he became the first keeper to score in the Premier League during a brief stay at Villa Park in 2001-02. Finally, after picking up yet another league title with Sporting Lisbon – the club he left for Old Trafford – Schmeichel ended his career with a season at Manchester City, pulling off some horribly familiar tricks in front of his old master, helping the Blues to a 3-1 win over the Reds.

GS

> ## QUOTE
>
> 'He was towering over me and the other players were almost covering their eyes. I'm looking up and thinking "If he does hit me, I'm dead."'
>
> Sir Alex Ferguson remembers his confrontation with Schmeichel.

20 TEDDY SHERINGHAM

PREMIER LEAGUE DEBUT:
Nottingham Forest v Liverpool,
16 August 1992

PREMIER LEAGUE CLUBS:
Nottingham Forest, Tottenham Hotspur,
Manchester United, Tottenham Hotspur,
Portsmouth, West Ham United

PREMIER LEAGUE APPEARANCES/GOALS:

Nottingham F	3	1
Tottenham H	236	97
Manchester U	104	31
Portsmouth	32	9
West Ham U	43	8
Total	418	146

PREMIER LEAGUE HONOURS:
3 (1998-99, 1999-00, 2000-01); FWA and
PFA Footballer of the Year 2001

COUNTRY:
England (born Highams Park, 2 April 1966)

IN THE SOPHISTICATED, cosmopolitan Premier League of the 21st century, it takes more than a forward dropping off the front line to play 'in the hole' to befuddle an opposition back line; and yet only 20 years ago, such a tactic was popularly regarded as a novelty, as a devilish display of tactical lateral thinking.

In this country, you can trace the confusion wrought by the deep-lying forward back to 1953 and the 'surprise' 6-3 thrashing handed out to England by Ferenc Puskas and the Hungarian world number ones. Nándor Hidegkuti was the spanner in the works that day, dropping deep to act as a versatile link-man and playmaker. Such foreign trickery didn't catch on in the home of football; however, Manchester City reached consecutive FA Cup finals in 1955 and 1956, with string-puller Don Revie befuddling domestic centre-halves with the so-called 'Revie Plan' tactic of dropping into midfield to engineer play.

In the modern era, Forest's Nigel Clough stands out as the first centre-forward to pull off the shock tactic, under the astute guidance of Ol' Big 'Ead (or, as he knew him, 'Dad'). It was so easy to dumbfound even well-drilled defences by leaving a centre-half with no one to mark, and no spare midfielder to pick up the newly arrived playmaker. All you needed was a player smart enough to fulfil the role ...

> ## THE MOMENT HE BECAME A LEGEND
>
> He scored in injury time and then set up fellow sub Solskjaer to melodramatically nick the 1999 Champions League – and the historic Treble – for United. 'Eleven great days which I wouldn't change for anything.'

Enter Teddy Sheringham to the Forest fray, a free-scoring forward for top-tier Millwall but, at the age of 27, hardly a name being touted for international recognition or multiple Player of the Year awards, never mind celebrity playboy poker star status, or as the potential suitor to Miss Great Britain. Clough hadn't even bought Sheringham as his deep-lying option, but as a more traditional attacking partner for Nigel, the quick-witted, leisurely paced playmaker; but something surely rubbed off.

'Teddy Sheringham tells of how he was dropped by Clough at Forest,' says Jonathan Wilson, the nation's tactical tutor, 'and watched the next match with him from the bench. Listening to Clough during the game, he realised the importance of a centre-forward holding the ball up to relieve the pressure on his

> ## WELL I NEVER ...
>
> Girlfriend Danielle Lloyd was stripped of her Miss GB title after letting slip that she'd been dating Sheringham, who was one of the judges.

defence, rather than attempting flicks that might break through the opposition, but might equally surrender possession.'

Keep the ball. Use the ball. Go fetch the ball ...

Within scant seasons, our late starter had arrayed all the aforementioned feathers in his cap, and had become England's undisputed ace in the hole. Transferred to Spurs early in the inaugural Carling Premiership season, he scored 29 goals in all competitions and won the first-ever Golden Boot. He proved the ideal strike partner first for Jürgen Klinsmann and then Chris Armstrong, holding up the ball, picking a killer pass, laying the ball off unselfishly, bringing the best out of others, popping up in (yes, still) unexpected positions – quite literally thinking outside the box.

Having made his international debut aged 27 in 1993, it was a trick he was able to repeat for England in tandem with the complementary blunt instrument of Alan Shearer in a second, no less successful 'SAS' partnership, with Teddy going on to win an incredible 51 caps.

And to think they imagined Sheringham was past his best when he exited Tottenham in 1997. But, of course, Alex Ferguson had different plans for the only domestic player who could roam and rove between midfield and attack, successfully filling the void left by the genius Cantona.

Previously without a major honour in his career, by the time he returned in 2001 for another spell at Spurs, 'Sweet Sherry' had been instrumental in securing three Prem titles, the FA Cup and Champions League for United – his special vision and bespoke role even enabling him to further extend his career at Pompey and West Ham, where aged 40 in 2006 he became the oldest outfield player in Premier League history.

DH

19 DAVID GINOLA

PREMIER LEAGUE DEBUT:
Newcastle United v Coventry City,
19 August 1995

PREMIER LEAGUE CLUBS:
Newcastle United, Tottenham Hotspur,
Aston Villa, Everton

PREMIER LEAGUE APPEARANCES/GOALS:

Newcastle U	58	6
Tottenham H	100	12
Aston Villa	32	3
Everton	5	0
Total	195	21

PREMIER LEAGUE HONOURS:
None; FWA and PFA Footballer of the Year
1999

COUNTRY:
France (born Gassin, 25 January 1967)

HIS SIX-PACK rippled and his biceps bulged, while his eyes fixed on John Gregory, his Aston Villa manager. Who ate all the pies? Certainly not David Ginola, as his boss suggested.

'He's carrying a bit of timber,' Gregory claimed, in reference to the Frenchman's fitness in the lead up to Villa's clash with Manchester City in December 2000. However, as his dramatic equaliser flew past Nicky Weaver with minutes to spare, he ripped off his shirt and revealed his cut, honed physique. Enough said. He was anything but fat.

There were, of course, happier times in England for Ginola. Vilified in his home country for losing possession in a crucial game against Bulgaria that denied *Les Bleus* a place at the 1994 World Cup, the Frenchman was feted in the Premier League and was something of a deity among the Newcastle and Tottenham faithful.

His flowing locks, model looks and flamboyance on the pitch had Magpies fans flocking to St James' Park to pay homage to the enigmatic winger, after Kevin Keegan successfully lured him from Paris St Germain in the summer of 1995. In Keegan's free-flowing, attacking side, Ginola was given the stage on which to display his splendour and scintillating pieces of skill. And boy, did he love to show it off. It seemed the two were destined for one another.

At Newcastle, he came desperately close to clinching the 1995-96 Premier League trophy, so it was no surprise that a club of Barcelona's stature should come calling. Were it not for Keegan's resoluteness when the late Sir Bobby Robson, then manager of Barcelona, enquired about securing Ginola's services in 1996, those that regularly packed White Hart Lane to admire his wing wizardry may never have had the privilege.

But his manager left shortly after rebutting Robson and under Kenny Dalglish, Keegan's successor, Ginola wanted out. That fall-out on Tyneside was to Tottenham's advantage, and chairman Alan Sugar swooped in the summer of 1997. It was

THE MOMENT HE BECAME A LEGEND

We couldn't switch on the TV in the late 1990s without seeing his shiny, flowing barnet glowing from our screen. Before the rise of brand Beckham, Ginola starred in a series of TV adverts for L'Oreal. Funnily enough, in those days it was unusual to see footballers promoting such mainstream brands.

WELL I NEVER ...

His fondness for the odd cigarette almost got him kicked out of his first club, Toulon, when making his way as a teenager. Before going to sleep at the club's lodgings one night, he lit up and stubbed the butt out in his shaving foam cap, putting the can back in his locker. It wasn't long before the room was engulfed in smoke and his team-mates all evacuated to wait for the fire brigade.

hoped that the new £2 million signing could restore some glamour to a team previously renowned for its attractive style of football.

It didn't quite go to plan in the first season, and by December 1997 the club was in the relegation zone, with Gerry Francis leaving his position as manager a month earlier. Under Christian Gross, Spurs narrowly avoided relegation, but Ginola's panache, even in a struggling team, was evident.

Gross did not last long into the 1998-99 season, and the winger was soon playing under his fourth Tottenham manager in George Graham, after David Pleat's stint as caretaker boss. It was a season that brought a host of plaudits and some very special goals. Newcastle fans had been treated to this sort of genius previously, as his strike against Ferencvaros in 1996 attests. Flicking the ball from his right foot to his left on the edge of the area, his shot nearly burst a hole in the net.

Similarly, Tottenham fans are unlikely to forget his dazzling run against Barnsley in the 1999 FA Cup quarter-final where he danced his way through the defence at Oakwell before slotting the ball into the bottom corner. Neither will they forget his 20-yard thunderbolt against Chelsea in 1999, or his tendency to celebrate the goals he made possible, taking in the acclaim of the crowd as if he had scored himself.

Manchester United won their famous Treble in 1999, yet it was Ginola, star of mid-table Tottenham, that reaped the game's individual rewards, taking the Football Writers' and Players' Player of the Year awards home. Tottenham also won the League Cup after defeating Leicester 1-0. It was a shame, then, that his time in North London was cut short, with the Frenchman claiming George Graham forced him out in 2000. He believed that White Hart Lane was where his career would end.

He made just 32 starts in two seasons at Aston Villa before retiring in 2002, shortly after making a handful of appearances for Everton. David Ginola is the very personification of French flair, his website reads. Certainly the thousands that were lucky enough to witness his elegance at first hand would not disagree. He was well and truly worth it.

DM

18 JOSE MOURINHO

PREMIER LEAGUE DEBUT (MANAGER):
Chelsea v Manchester United,
15 August 2004

PREMIER LEAGUE CLUB (MANAGER):
Chelsea

PREMIER LEAGUE APPEARANCES (MANAGER):

Chelsea	120
Total	120

PREMIER LEAGUE HONOURS:
2 (2004-05, 2005-06); Manager of the
Season 2005, 2006

COUNTRY:
Portugal (born Setubal, 26 January 1963)

'PLEASE DON'T call me arrogant, because what I'm saying is true,' declared 41-year-old Jose Mourinho, before announcing, scanning a packed media room for the first time as Chelsea manager undaunted: 'I'm a European champion. I'm not one from the bottle, I think I'm a special one.' And so English football sat up and took notice. 'THE EGO HAS LANDED,' claimed one tabloid of the game's most self-assured character since Brian Clough.

Everton's David Moyes, a manager cut from very different cloth, remembers doubting how '[Mourinho] could display that kind of arrogance in this country and get away with it ... There were a few [managers] queuing up, waiting to have a crack at him ... but his team became so good, so soon that you had to admire him.' Just over three years after joining Chelsea in June 2004, the Portuguese departed as the club's most successful ever manager, boasting six trophies including successive Premier League titles in his first two seasons.

On the training ground, a unique blend of charisma and tactical aptitude instilled new-found resolve into Chelsea's players, who finished the 2004-05 campaign with 95 points, a Premier League record. Away from the lush training fields of Cobham, the forensic examination of forthcoming opponents kept his backroom staff away from their families.

'If I'm marking someone,' revealed club captain John Terry in October 2005, 'I know where he's going to run. I know he might have beaten me in the air, but I know where he's going to run to. I've got half a yard on him as a result.'

Meanwhile, a love affair was blossoming with the British press. There was the occasional complaint about a perceived caution in big matches, but they hung onto his every word; headlines, more often than not, were published about Mourinho's compelling, controversial performances in press conferences or post-match interviews. He memorably described Arsenal manager Arsène Wenger as 'one of these people who is a voyeur ... who, when they are at home, have a big telescope to see what happens in other families. He speaks, speaks, speaks about Chelsea.' And he accused Sir Alex Ferguson of having too much power over referees.

Good looking, well presented, confident and witty, Jose became the shining beacon of a sport brimming with comparatively mundane personalities. He won best-dressed awards from glossy men's magazines and women fancied him, while many of those offended by his comments admired the sheer

THE MOMENT HE BECAME A LEGEND

Stamford Bridge, 29 April 2006. Following a 3-0 victory over Manchester United to seal his second Premier League title, Mourinho threw his medal into the Matthew Harding Lower Stand (it subsequently went for £21,600 at auction) along with his jacket and, when provided with a second one, Mourinho gave that away as well. 'I have a Premiership medal from last season,' he later explained. 'And it's the same medal. I only need one. I can't keep everything I have.'

WELL I NEVER ...

Mourinho never shaves with a razor on the day of a match – part-superstition and part-vanity. He is fearful of meeting the press with a shaving cut on his face.

audacity with which they were delivered. 'When I face the media before or after the game,' he said with a smile, 'I feel it as part of the game.'

Selflessly perhaps, Mourinho attributed Chelsea's unprecedented trophy haul to his own 'hard work', yet no one appreciated his presence more than those he trusted with delivering results. Following the abrupt sacking of 'the Special One' in September 2007, amid rumours of disagreements with owner Roman Abramovich, the usually cool and detached Frank Lampard explained that, although he didn't usually 'get emotionally involved in these matters ... in this case it was more than a manager who was going, it was a friend.' While Terry admitted: 'We [the players] spoke with the club, and told them clearly that we did not want Jose to go.'

> ### QUOTE
>
> 'I made a point of walking on alone, before the team ... it was fantastic, an amazing feeling ... upon hearing the whistles and jeers, I felt as if I were the most important person in the world.'
>
> Mourinho reminisces about a return to Benfica as Porto manager. Enough about me. What do you think about me?

Never had a Premier League manager earned so much loyalty and respect from a group of players in such a brief period. Indeed, even five years on, the shadow of Mourinho still looms large over the club, despite the fact that they have won many more trophies since his departure.

Looking back at the moment Mourinho sat Chelsea's players down to explain his departure, Didier Drogba 'wept like a child' and described hearing the news as, 'unreal, as though it was a movie.' But there was never any doubt as to who had star-billing in this £225 million blockbuster.

CM

17 ROBBIE FOWLER

PREMIER LEAGUE DEBUT:
Liverpool v Chelsea, 25 September 1993

PREMIER LEAGUE CLUBS:
Liverpool, Leeds United, Manchester City,
Liverpool, Blackburn Rovers

PREMIER LEAGUE APPEARANCES/GOALS:

Liverpool	266	128
Leeds U	30	14
Manchester C	80	21
Blackburn R	3	0
Total	379	163

PREMIER LEAGUE HONOURS:
None

COUNTRY:
England (born Liverpool, 9 April 1975)

'I WAS A cheeky little lad who played football every night, pissed around with his mates, and overnight, literally overnight, came fame,' recalled Robert Bernard Fowler in his 2005 autobiography. 'Nothing had changed in my routine, except that when I went down the chippy and got me special fried rice, it would be wrapped in a newspaper that had my picture all over it. It's no wonder I struggled to come to terms with it all ...'

For a handful of goal-soaked seasons during the mid-1990s, Liverpool striker Robbie Fowler rivalled Alan Shearer as the most dangerous front man in the Premier League, a prodigious teenage talent who scored goals by any means necessary and terrified the top flight. The only downside to such an explosive start would be the ensuing years of injury and ill-discipline that gradually eroded fine memories of a prodigy in his prime. But what a prime.

Fowler could score goals with both feet and, despite a relative lack of height, was also a threat in the air. He had speed and agility and no offside trap was safe. As David O'Leary, the man who would later buy him for Leeds United, put it: 'You could run a university course on how to score goals, based on his finishing.' Graeme Souness, the man who gave him his debut at Anfield, ranked him alongside Ian Rush as one of the all-time greatest goalscorers.

At Liverpool, where it all began (and some might say finished), Fowler announced himself to the world with a five-goal haul against Fulham in the League Cup at the age of 18 on 5 October 1993, and then set about battering bigger fish. In just his second season, he scored 25 league goals, second behind Shearer. He made his England debut in 1996, shortly before his 21st birthday, and won the 1995 and 1996 PFA Young Player of the Year Awards.

Was it all too much too soon? In 1995, he got into a fight with team-mate Neil 'Razor' Ruddock after supposedly vandalising the latter's £300 Gucci boots on a flight back from Russia. He was also fined and/or banned by the FA for hitching up his shorts at Leicester; for pretending to snort coke off the touch-line after scoring against Everton at Anfield, where away fans had taunted him about entirely false allegations of drug-taking; and for on-field homophobic taunts aimed at Blackburn's (heterosexual) defender Graeme Le Saux.

> ## THE MOMENT HE BECAME A LEGEND
>
> Scoring a hat-trick against Arsenal at Anfield in a record four minutes, 33 seconds. He was 19 at the time and it is still a Premier League record.

> ## WELL I NEVER ...
>
> A regular in the *Sunday Times* Sports Rich List for several years, the footballer has supplemented his career earnings with an impressive portfolio of almost 100 properties and other interests. Most recently he was estimated to be worth £31 million.

Fowler hates the image some may have of him as a dumb scally and, although perhaps he didn't help himself at times, there is another side to him.

In 1997 he was fined by UEFA for displaying a t-shirt under his jersey that expressed his support for striking Liverpool dockers, but he also won a UEFA Fair Play Award that same season for trying to persuade referee Gerald Ashby that he had made a mistake in giving Liverpool a penalty when he'd been 'brought down' by Arsenal's David Seaman. He is still known as 'God' on the Kop, but it was episodes like these that endeared him to fans everywhere outside Goodison Park and Old Trafford.

> ### QUOTE
>
> 'Would I play in League One or League Two? Without a shadow of a doubt ... I don't need the money but I love the game. I love being around people who are involved in the game, I love the day-to-day things and I love the match day. I want to play for as long as I can. You are a long time retired.'
>
> Robbie Fowler confirms his ongoing love affair with the game to the *Daily Mirror* in 2010.

Fowler was out injured for the 1998 World Cup, and a young team-mate called Michael Owen took the plaudits instead. By the time Fowler was fit, Owen and Emile Heskey were the first-choice Liverpool front line. Although Fowler played a part in Liverpool's three-trophy 2000-01 season, even coming off the bench to score in the UEFA Cup final win over Alaves, he left the club after being persistently passed over for selection by boss Gerard Houllier.

Less successful spells followed at Leeds, Manchester City (during which he and Steve McManaman failed to re-ignite their partnership), Liverpool a second time, and then briefly Cardiff and Blackburn. He deserved a better return for his talent. Now in his late 30s, he is still banging in the goals on a seemingly peripatetic world tour that has so far taken in Australia, Thailand and India and, cushioned by his enormous wealth, can afford to indulge his first love – playing 'footie'.

IP

16 CRISTIANO RONALDO

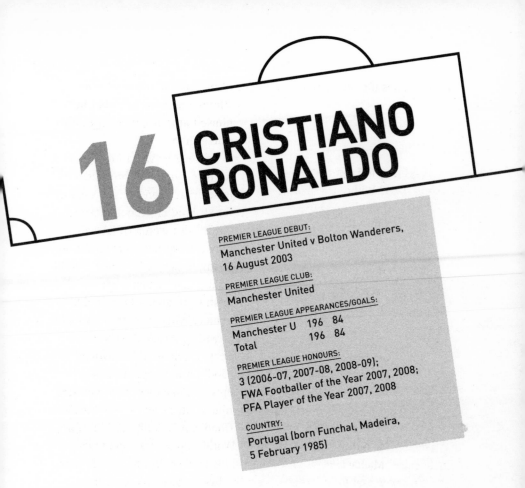

PREMIER LEAGUE DEBUT:
Manchester United v Bolton Wanderers,
16 August 2003

PREMIER LEAGUE CLUB:
Manchester United

PREMIER LEAGUE APPEARANCES/GOALS:
Manchester U   196   84
Total   196   84

PREMIER LEAGUE HONOURS:
3 (2006-07, 2007-08, 2008-09);
FWA Footballer of the Year 2007, 2008;
PFA Player of the Year 2007, 2008

COUNTRY:
Portugal (born Funchal, Madeira,
5 February 1985)

WHEN SIR ALEX Ferguson signed Cristiano Ronaldo from Sporting Lisbon for an estimated £12.5 million in 2003, after the striker had scored just three goals in 25 games for the Portuguese club, there were some who unwisely questioned the Scot's judgement. For although Ronaldo could clearly do clever things with his feet, it seemed that Manchester United had a one-trick pony(tail) with a skin problem and a failed hairstyle on its books.

It took a couple of years to silence the cynics (and clear up the acne), but by the time Ronaldo had won both the FIFA Player of the Year and the Ballon D'Or in 2008, the year he helped Manchester United become European champions for the third time, there were few who doubted his gargantuan talent, even if most failed to warm to him as a human being.

'Your love makes me strong, your hate makes me unstoppable,'

Ronaldo once said. He didn't care. And neither did the Manchester United fans who enjoyed his incredible last three years at the club, when he scored a series of memorable goals in the same effortlessly spectacular way as George Best over 40 years earlier. His partnership with Wayne Rooney brought United championships while playing the team's best football since they dominated the league in the mid-1990s.

He initially turned down the number seven shirt because he thought he wasn't worthy of its tradition, but the canny Ferguson insisted. Once he'd found his game, he used freestyle footwork to outfox bemused full-backs, often toying with two or three at the same time. His free-kicks dipped and swerved like something out of the pages of *Tiger* comic. He shot with despicable power, from all angles. His penalties were mostly as sure as death. His speed made him a counter-attacking dervish that few defenders were equipped to chase. As if that wasn't enough, he was one of the most accomplished headers of the ball in the Premier League.

For football fans beyond Old Trafford, Ronaldo was problematic. He could destroy your team, and looked thoroughly smug as he did it. Ronaldo was much, much better than anyone at your club, and he knew it. You wanted him to slip on his backside when he tried that stupid stepover, and how you cheered when he did. But when he carried it off (and he usually did), you couldn't help but gasp. If the fan next to you gave you a long, hard look, you just pretended that you were choking on a lozenge, then cheered extra hard when your titanium-thighed central defender took him out waist-high and left him in a heap.

Yet until Manchester City make Lionel Messi an offer he can't refuse, Ronaldo remains the purest footballing talent ever to appear in the

THE MOMENT HE BECAME A LEGEND

He totalled his £200,000 Ferrari in early 2009 on the way to training and walked away without a scratch. In fact, he still made it to training and later that week was named World Player of the Year. Easy.

WELL I NEVER . . .

He has slept with more than 300 women. At least that's what he told German teen magazine *Bravo* in 2009. It's probably more by now.

The Kop appeared uncertain about the return of Kenny Dalglish as caretaker manager in January 2011.

'You see,' explains Schmeichel to his back four, 'if I make myself "small" first, then when I make myself "big" I will look even bigger. Simple.'

Momentarily surprised, Sheringham didn't know whether to wear him or tackle him.

'Airbrush? No, no, I just let it dry naturally when I step out of ze shower.' David Ginola reveals one of his beauty secrets.

'Moisturiser, moisturiser, moisturiser . . . how could I be so stupid? I must be losing it, I never forget to moisturise.' Jose Mourinho begins to feel the pressure during the 2007 Premier League title race.

This was Robbie Fowler being ironic and NOT moronic, as some ill-informed members of the press casually observed.

'I have here a World Cup winner, described as the "driving force" of the Brazil team by his manager, and also managed to pick up this spotty Portuguese kid as well.' Alex Ferguson reveals his star signing Kleberson and Cristiano something or other in August 2003.

Everybody knew Le Tissier could make the ball talk, fewer knew that he actually listened to it.

Commentator: ". . . to Sinclair and he's looking for Di Canio. What a strike! [Pause] . . . he was airborne." Di Canio is seen here having just returned to Earth after scoring the volley rated by many to be the best goal in Premier League history.

On this occasion, Arsène Wenger could justifiably claim not to have seen the sending-off as he had his eyes closed, with his head tilted towards the heavens and was shouting something extremely rude in French.

And dramatic new evidence has just emerged that Jürgen Klinsmann *actually* came into contact with another player in November 1994 that caused a genuine loss of balance and resulted in him falling over.

Somewhere in there is Gianfranco Zola, who presumably regretted accidentally parking in one of the most notorious dogging hotspots in West London.

An under-par Dennis Bergkamp dispatches the last of his routine world-class goals in a hat-trick against Leicester in 1997.

An overhead kick executed with such precision and elan that it will always be, 'THAT Rooney goal'. Put said phrase it into YouTube if you are in any doubt. Over one million views should serve to reassure you.

fergie time *noun:*

The amount of extra time added on to a game that Manchester United need to win to be determined solely by Sir Alex Ferguson and his incontrovertible chronometer.

'This is your owner speaking. Please go to the club shop on your way out. It's on your right, just past the Marco Pierre White franchise . . . John Terry lampshades and Frank Lampard terry nappies are now at half price.'

Warning: This photograph contains flash photography. Occasional professional footballer David 'Brand' Beckham promotes his aftershave in Sydney. Is this the very essence of the man?

This is what they meant when they said that Shearer was head and shoulders above the rest. And it had nothing to do with dandruff.

'It's no good mate, it's stuck.' Selfless as ever, Liverpool captain Steven Gerrard takes time out from celebrating his side's second goal against Manchester United in 2010 to help a cameramen with an out-of-focus lens.

Ryan Giggs, the Premier League's original poster boy, is still holding up after 20 years and over 900 appearances . . .

'Second? I came second in the *talkSPORT Book of Premier League Legends*? Me? Thierry Henry, the greatest Frenchman to ever play in the Premier Lea . . . What do you mean, "Second again?"'

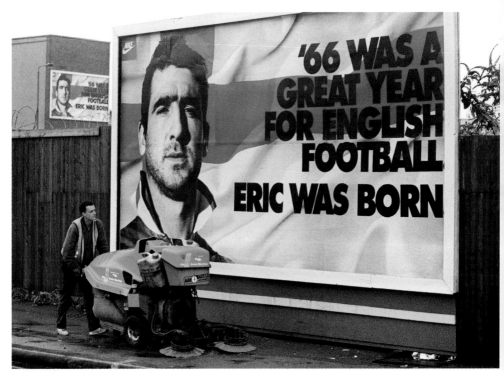

The moment the Premier League came of age and Cantona, simultaneously, the symbol of its global significance and street-level appeal. The thoughts of the dust-cart operative are unrecorded.

'And yet they did reach out to touch him and gaze upon him.' (Cantona 7:1)

Premier League. He dared to risk injury and ridicule by taunting the league's leaden extras with flicks, tricks, shimmies and backheels that for too long had been absent from football's repertoire. His flair for the unexpected brightened even those tedious maulings when Manchester United hosted an opponent barely capable of leaving its own half. His subsequent achievements at Real Madrid serve only to stress what we've been missing since his £80 million transfer in 2009.

> **QUOTE**
>
> 'Some fans keep booing and whistling at me because I'm handsome, rich and a great player. They envy me.'
>
> Cristiano Ronaldo tells it as he sees it.
> He probably didn't win round
> many doubters with his insight.

The one goal that sums up the unshakeable certainty of Ronaldo's gifts was scored away at Reading shortly after the start of the 2006-07 season. Still being booed by the crowd for his perceived part in getting Rooney sent off at the previous summer's World Cup in Germany, Ronaldo killed a long pass with one touch, set off for the Reading area with the jeers of the home crowd sending him on his way, then barely acknowledged the defender backing off him before he clipped a keen and accurate shot past Reading keeper Marcus Hahnemann. It was the birth of the league's three-year Rooney–Ronaldo dominance.

The following season, he was almost unstoppable. He scored 31 goals in the Premier League, one short of the club record (set back in 1959-60 by Dennis Viollet), and 42 in total, despite playing on the wing. It all left George Best to comment: 'There have been a few players described as the new George Best over the years. But this is the first time it's been a compliment to me.'

IP

15 MATT LE TISSIER

PREMIER LEAGUE DEBUT:
Southampton v Tottenham Hotspur,
15 August 1992

PREMIER LEAGUE CLUB:
Southampton

PREMIER LEAGUE APPEARANCES/GOALS:
Southampton   270   101
Total   270   101

PREMIER LEAGUE HONOURS:
None

COUNTRY:
England (born Guernsey, 14 October 1968)

IT'S NOT HARD to see why Guernsey-born Matthew Le Tissier will always be known to Southampton fans as 'Le God'. Belonging to an era that long preceded the riches of the Premier League, the goal-toting midfielder was blessed with the kind of dreamy, effortless skill most thought had been put to death towards the end of the 1970s. Easing past players without breaking sweat, he unleashed enough shots into opposing top corners to fill a highlight reel so hot it could almost be classified as football porn.

'You're never sure you want him playing for you, but you're sure you don't want him playing against you,' Crewe manager Dario Gradi once said, perfectly summing up the Le Tiss conundrum. Everyone knew he was brilliant, it was just a case of when he would be brilliant. Opposing teams could be caught out by that flash of genius when they least expected it. Yet for Southampton managers trying to grind out a tough away point against durable opposition, a slow night from Le Tissier was of debatable benefit.

'The one thing I'd like to rid myself of is the word "but". You know, "He's a great player, but ..." or "So much skill, but ...",' Le Tissier said at the height of his career in 1997. Yet English football has always been wary of too much flair, and so Le Tissier's England experience was limited to six caps. Ironically it was Glenn Hoddle – whose own international career was similarly stunted by suspicions that he was too good by half – who left Le Tissier out of the 1998 England World Cup squad, despite the fact he had recently scored a hat-trick in a B international against Russia. 'Brazil would pick Le Tiss,' noted a Southampton fans' banner at the time. The player has said his form never recovered.

Apart from being too bloody good, Le Tissier's other problem may have been his loyalty. He wanted to play only for Southampton, so spurning early interest from Tottenham (because his fiancée didn't want to live in London) and later Chelsea, prompting charges that he lacked ambition. Indeed, the goals he scored against teams like Arsenal, Liverpool and Manchester United leave you wondering what he might have achieved alongside more quality team-mates. Would he have flourished, or been pushed into the shadows?

There's no point in pondering that question now when we can just sit back and enjoy the serially stunning goals. Like the one against Newcastle in 1993, two

> ## THE MOMENT HE BECAME A LEGEND
>
> 25 February 1994. From a free-kick just outside the area, he dared to flick the ball up before casually smacking it into the Wimbledon net on the volley with the same foot.

> ## WELL 1 NEVER ...
>
> In his 2009 autobiography, he confessed to an abortive spread-bet scam on the timing of the first throw-in during a 1995 game against Wimbledon. Police declined to follow up on the confession.

tricks better than Paul Gascoigne's similar goal for England against Scotland at Euro 96 – Le Tissier actually controls the ball as it's played behind him with a back heel that brings it into his path, then lobs it over two defenders before finishing in the corner on a half-volley. His second, 25 minutes later, wasn't bad either: controlled on the thigh, then volleyed into the same corner.

His own personal favourite, however, came against Blackburn in December 1994. 'Only Matthew Le Tissier could score a goal like that,' raved the commentator after his 35-yard dipper, preceded by a double shimmy that took him past the same opponent twice. 'Only Matthew Le Tissier would even think about trying to score a goal like that.' Indeed. Le Tissier looked as excited as a man about to embark upon the school run – spectacular goals were food and drink to him.

A chip over Peter Schmeichel at home to Manchester United illustrated another artistic speciality from his remarkable palette, but there were countless other goals that resulted from weaving, lanky dribbles past static back-liners wondering exactly how they were fooled by something so ordinary – an awkward, gangly player with a mundane, mid-table team and a reputation for being unfit. 'Le Tiss' was as unique and hard to fathom as the quirky, individualistic Dell where he scored so many of his goals.

He also boasts the remarkable record of having scored 47 out of 48 penalties he took for Southampton. That killer coolness goes a long way to explaining the genius behind this likeable, apparently lackadaisical, fantasy goalscoring phenomenon. If Le Tissier was a luxury, he's the kind of luxury the game can ill afford to live without.

IP

14 PAOLO DI CANIO

PREMIER LEAGUE DEBUT:
Sheffield Wednesday v Newcastle United,
9 August 1997

PREMIER LEAGUE CLUBS:
Sheffield Wednesday, West Ham United,
Charlton Athletic

PREMIER LEAGUE APPEARANCES/GOALS:

Sheffield W	41	15
West Ham U	118	46
Charlton A	31	4
Total	190	65

PREMIER LEAGUE HONOURS:
None

COUNTRY:
Italy (born Rome, 9 July 1968)

DESPITE THE trail of defenders and destruction left in his wake – despite the goals, the rows, the controversies, the endless contradictions – few English fans were prepared for the impact that Paolo Di Canio would make on an unsuspecting Premier League.

He was 29 when he made his debut for Sheffield Wednesday at the start of the 1997-98 season, and there was some sense that the slender, balding, once-notorious striker might have been past his best. Yes, he'd scored some goals for Celtic, but only in the SPL. It wasn't as if Di Canio had ever even come up to international standard.

Within the game, it's safe to assume that the flesh traders and power brokers were aware of Di Canio's potential – both for feats of footballing genius, and for his honesty to himself, however self-destructive. Why had Paolo quit Celtic in a huff? 'I'd been voted Player of the Year, but the chairman said I didn't deserve it. Well, I go, "It's that easy; I don't play for liars and traitors."'

His time at Inter had ended in a training-ground fight with Fabio Capello after Di Canio had challenged his decisions ('I pushed him and he lost his balance'). After another shouting match, Juventus boss Giovanni Trapattoni declared, 'There will have to be a bubonic plague for me to pick Di Canio.' And back at the beginning, at Lazio, Di Canio was banned and fined for twice returning neo-Nazi salutes to the Irriducibili Ultras. For the record, he equates Mussolini with loyalty and working-class solidarity, not fascism.

Luckily for us all, Ron Atkinson was willing to take a record £4.2 million punt on harnessing the whirlwind, and he was repaid with 14 goals from his top scorer. Setting the Premier League alight at Wednesday, we quickly learned that the audacious pullbacks, the swivels, the volleys and the dream goals weren't separable from Di Canio's volatile temperament, but, rather, derived their impetus from it. Of course, it all ended with a dressing-room fight with Big Ron.

Enter Harry. 'Paolo,' says Redknapp, 'did things with the ball that made you gasp. Other footballers would pay to watch him train.' And it was at West Ham that Di Canio blossomed. You could watch his collected moments of magnificence for hours, just noting down all the different ways he could beat a defender, starting with the bouncing-backward dribble. But, as ever, the storyline is heightened by crazy contradictions.

At Wednesday, Di Canio's career had come under threat after he'd reacted to his sending off against Arsenal by infamously pushing over referee Paul Alcock. He escaped with an apology – 'Even now, when I

THE MOMENT HE BECAME A LEGEND

His BBC Goal of the Season 1999-00, a sublime volley against Wimbledon, was later named the Premier League Goal of the Decade.

WELL I NEVER ...

When Di Canio was being interviewed for the post of Swindon manager, he became so animated that one of his shirt buttons popped off. He got the job.

---

watch it, I can't believe the way he went down, like a drunken clown' – an 11-match ban and a £10,000 fine. Then, in 2001, he balanced the ledger with a FIFA Fair Play Award, having caught the ball from a cross, turning down a strike on Everton's empty goal because keeper Paul Gerrard had twisted his knee and lay injured out on the edge of his box.

A code of honour. Loyalty. Individuality. Honesty. All precious rarities. Fans love Di Canio precisely because of his contradictions, not despite them.

He took it as a compliment when David Pleat described him as a 'gypsy'; he studies the way of the Samurai warrior, and observes pagan rituals. He turned down a move to Manchester United out of loyalty to West Ham fans, with whom his bond was as close as that with the Lazio Ultras – hence the tattoos. Meanwhile, he'd fight team-mate Frank Lampard for the right to take a penalty: 'I've always accepted orders because I'm a comrade, but if I think that by doing something different a better result can be achieved, I'll do it.'

After a swansong at Charlton Athletic, before returning to play in Italy, Di Canio came back to England to manage Swindon Town. Having just been relegated to the bottom tier, Di Canio led them to promotion in his first season in charge. The Premier League may not have seen the last of him after all.

DH

13 ARSÈNE WENGER

PREMIER LEAGUE DEBUT (MANAGER):
Arsenal v Blackburn Rovers, 12 October 1996

PREMIER LEAGUE CLUB (MANAGER):
Arsenal

PREMIER LEAGUE APPEARANCES (MANAGER):
Arsenal   600
Total   600

PREMIER LEAGUE HONOURS:
3 (1997-98, 2001-02, 2003-04); Manager of
the Season 1998, 2002, 2004

COUNTRY:
France (born Strasbourg, 29 October 1949)

THE NUMBERS carry such weight as to lose any sense of meaning: three Premier League titles, four FA Cups, another four Charity Shields, a Champions League final appearance, 49 games unbeaten and all done with a net transfer spend just shy of £4 million. That it is difficult to derive perspective, though, hardly matters, since Arsène Wenger's legendary status is forged not from prizes but from his influence on the English game.

Stories about the restaurateur's son forbidding his Arsenal players their traditional pre-match Mars Bars and curtailing their legendary boozing have become tired in the telling, but that in itself is a measure of how much the game has developed over the past 16 years. What is now commonplace was anathema to the average English footballer in the mid-1990s, but without the Frenchman's influence would that have happened?

Probably. But that Wenger was the catalyst is indicative of a man whose timing has always been impeccable. Take the Arsenal team he inherited from Bruce Rioch, or rather the back five bequeathed by his Scottish predecessors. There is a danger of repetition here, but for those who have skipped a few pages: Seaman, Dixon, Adams, Keown and Winterburn were the foundation on which he built his early successes, without which his tenure would have faltered. Let us put it another way: could you imagine a Premier League without Arsène Wenger? No 'Invincibles', no Francophone influx, no Emirates, perhaps? It would be a different league, certainly, but not as interesting.

> ### THE MOMENT HE BECAME A LEGEND
>
> 16 October 2004. Arsenal v Aston Villa at Highbury: a 49th consecutive Premier League game unbeaten, stretching from May 2003. 'The Invincibles.'

So, what can be said about Wenger the man that has not been said already? As obsessed with detail as Jose Mourinho and as protective of his players as Sir Alex Ferguson (famously, the Frenchman seems never to have seen a single Arsenal player transgress the rules of association football), he is more like his two most notable rivals than he would be keen to confess. Possessed of a quick temper and outspoken nature, it is easy to imagine either of those other managerial dons rallying against the same injustices as 'Le Professeur', but less straightforward to picture them offering to replay an FA Cup tie, as Wenger did against Sheffield United in 1999, because the winning goal had been scored in controversial circumstances.

> ### WELL I NEVER ...
>
> Despite his apparent distrust of English players, two of Wenger's earliest signings for AS Monaco were Glenn Hoddle and Mark Hateley.

It is almost impossible, too, to believe that either Mourinho or Ferguson would so readily sacrifice their transfer funds to build a stadium, focusing instead on developing their own players as Wenger did after the move from Highbury in 2006. 'I believed it would be the best way to create an identity with the way we play football, to get players integrated into our culture, with our beliefs, our values,' he said at the time. 'I felt it would be an interesting experiment to see players grow together with these qualities, and with a love for the club. It was an idealistic vision of the world of football.'

Idealism is Wenger's credo. Aiming for perfection in whatever he does is something that has driven him since his youth, be it earning a masters degree in economics, playing for Strasbourg, or coaching Nancy, Monaco, Nagoya Grampus Eight or Arsenal. That belief has been transposed to his teams, too, in the demand that they play in an aesthetically pleasing manner and assume moral responsibility for their actions, even if that is increasingly at odds with the chances of success.

His grasp of economics has certainly helped him in the transfer market, in which he has had few rivals. Many players have come to Arsenal for relatively small fees only to be sold on for much larger amounts – Anelka, Overmars, Petit, Adebayor among them. His belief in his methods and his team was rarely better highlighted than during the club's disastrous start to the 2011-12 campaign, when an 8-2 thrashing by Manchester United saw the Gunners languishing near the bottom of the table. Yet he remained steadfast in the view that Arsenal would again qualify for the Champions League. And so it proved.

It might be dogmatic and it might compromise his legacy, but Wenger's work has earned him the right to enforce his views.

RW

12 JÜRGEN KLINSMANN

PREMIER LEAGUE DEBUT:
Tottenham Hotspur v Sheffield Wednesday,
20 August 1994

PREMIER LEAGUE CLUB:
Tottenham Hotspur

PREMIER LEAGUE APPEARANCES/GOALS:

Tottenham H	56	29
Total	56	29

PREMIER LEAGUE HONOURS:
None; FWA Footballer of the Year 1995

COUNTRY:
Germany (born Göppingen, 30 July 1964)

'I HAVE A question for you ... is there a diving school in London?' pre-empted Jürgen Klinsmann to a scoop of journalists at White Hart Lane in August 1994. Leaden perhaps, and delivered with all the comic timing one might expect from a German, but a good line designed to disarm his critics in the press. And, like most things he attempted, it came off.

Tottenham chairman Alan Sugar's decision to bring the World Cup-winning ace to England in a £2 million deal was a coup. He convinced the striker to sign for him on board his yacht in Monte Carlo, and the deal paved the way for a mass influx of global superstars to come and join the Premier League.

But the deal was controversial, too. Playing for Arsène Wenger's Monaco in a European Cup semi-final shortly before moving to London, his fall under the 'challenge' of Alessandro Costacurta saw the Milan defender receive a red card and forfeit a place in the final. Similarly, an over-the-top reaction to Pedro Monzon's tackle in the 1990 World Cup final led to the Argentine becoming the first player in a World Cup final to get his marching orders.

By the time he made his Premier League debut at Hillsborough on the opening day of the 1994-95 season, Klinsmann had already established a reputation that went far beyond his formidable feats as a goalscorer. Spurs were 3-2 ahead against Sheffield Wednesday when Klinsmann rose to head in the club's fourth goal.

If you close your eyes you can still picture his next move – he celebrated opening his account with a mocking dive, full length and seemingly suspended in mid-air, an idea Teddy Sheringham is believed to have concocted before the game. The newspaper headlines such as 'Dive Bomber' were suddenly superseded by tabloid collectors' items along the lines of 'Jur-ger-king'.

From his beginnings at hometown club TB Gingen, where a ten-year-old Klinsmann once put 16 goals past the opposition, hitting the back of the net was never a problem. The road to N17 had taken in Stuttgart, Internazionale and Monaco, while at the 1994 World Cup he bagged five for his country. At Tottenham, he scored seven in his first six league appearances, including a spectacular overhead kick against Everton in front of the East Stand.

But he was much more than just a goalscoring international footballer; he had a life outside the game and was often seen driving around the capital in his 1967 Volkswagen Beetle. Traffic in London was so heavy, he reasoned, that it didn't matter whether he drove the prerequisite Italian sports car or his beloved Beetle, because he wasn't going anywhere fast.

WELL I NEVER ...

Under advice from his dad, who suggested his son should get a profession before taking up football full time and who also ran a bakery with his wife, the young Klinsmann trained as an apprentice baker. In an interview, he claimed his speciality was Swabian pretzels, a roll named after the region in which he grew up.

London's busy streets did not stop its newest resident hopping on an open-top bus tour and taking in all it had to offer as soon as he arrived, mind. The capital's cosmopolitan nature appealed to the cultured and well-travelled German.

However, the love affair with the capital ended almost before it had begun and shortly before the season reached its conclusion, Klinsmann announced his intention to join Bayern Munich. It was a move that later prompted Alan Sugar to angrily claim that he would not wash his car with the striker's shirt.

When he left for Germany in 1995, he took with him the Football Writers' Footballer of the Year award and 20 Premier League goals. When he returned, albeit in different circumstances, on loan in December 1997, his goals were again invaluable to Tottenham. Spurs were now battling relegation, but his nine strikes in 15 games, including four away at Wimbledon on the penultimate day of the season, helped the club beat the dreaded drop by four points. It was his last year as a footballer, too, with Klinsmann retiring after playing for his country in a third World Cup in 1998.

His final game in a Spurs shirt saw him sign off in true Jürgen Klinsmann style. Once his rocket had flown past Southampton goalie Paul Jones, he was mobbed by team-mates, who joined him in treating the fans to a celebratory dive just as he had done four years earlier.

DM

11 | GIANFRANCO ZOLA

PREMIER LEAGUE DEBUT (PLAYER):
Chelsea v Blackburn Rovers,
16 November 1996

PREMIER LEAGUE DEBUT (MANAGER):
West Ham United v West Bromwich Albion,
13 September 2008

PREMIER LEAGUE CLUB (PLAYER):
Chelsea

PREMIER LEAGUE CLUB (MANAGER):
West Ham United

PREMIER LEAGUE APPEARANCES/GOALS:

Chelsea	229	59
Total	229	59

PREMIER LEAGUE APPEARANCES (MANAGER):

West Ham U	73
Total	73

PREMIER LEAGUE HONOURS:
None; FWA Footballer of the Year 1997

COUNTRY:
Italy (born Oliena, 5 July 1966)

THIS DIMINUTIVE stocky striker with quads like a couple of coke cans end-on-end has been variously described as a 'wizard' (Claudio Ranieri), 'Magic Box' (Chelsea supporters) and, somewhat begrudgingly, as 'a clever little so-and-so' (Alex Ferguson). His specialties included curling free-kicks from just outside the box, delicate chips and lobs over the goalkeeper's head and, not least, audacious and extravagant back-heels that naturally delighted the Chelsea fans, but also made any neutral observer feel good to be alive and watching him play.

However, at Parma, he was described by Carlo Ancellotti as a 'square peg', seemingly because he did not fit into the coach's rigid system, but to any lover of the beautiful game he looked well-rounded enough.

Whatever you want to call his talent – wizardry, magic, technical ability, flair or another as-yet uncoined adjective – he had it in abundance, and Chelsea and English football were the beneficiaries of his being squeezed out at the Stadio Ennio Tardini.

The secret of some of his success must be traced back a little further, as his spell at Parma was preceded by a four-year stay at Napoli where he was initially understudy to Napoli's most famous adopted son, Diego Maradona. Zola is unstinting in his praise for the impact the Argentine had on his game: 'I learnt everything from Diego ... I used to spy on him every time he trained and learned how to curl a free-kick just like him. After one year I had completely changed.'

> ### THE MOMENT HE BECAME A LEGEND
>
> With his second touch, and within 30 seconds of coming on as substitute in the European Cup-Winners' Cup final against Stuttgart in 1998, he hit the roof of the net – the only goal of the game.

He joined Chelsea in November 1996 and was instrumental in his new club's resurgence that season, culminating in the winning of the 1997 FA Cup (against Middlesbrough). Previously he had helped to overturn a 2-0 deficit into a 4-2 win against Liverpool in the fourth round and scored in the semi-final against Wimbledon, aided by one of those audacious back-heels. Football writers were so taken with him that he was made their Footballer of the Year, despite playing only just over half a season.

> ### WELL I NEVER ...
>
> At Napoli he used to have a competition with Maradona after training when each would take penalties with their 'wrong' foot. 'All I can say is that he didn't enjoy it when he lost,' says Zola.

The following year saw him help Chelsea to the League Cup and the European Cup-Winners' Cup, with another FA Cup triumph in 2000 (this time against Aston

Villa). His most successful season from a goalscoring point of view was his last, 2002-03, in which he scored 16 goals in all competitions and at the end of which he left for Cagliari.

In the last match of that season, against Liverpool, he came on for 20 minutes and received rapturous applause from both sets of fans for a mazy dribble during which, tucked into the corner, he beat three players (including Jamie Carragher four times). He was subsequently voted Chelsea's Player of the Year.

There is an unconfirmed rumour that Roman Abramovich wanted him to come back after he acquired the club in 2003 and he was voted into Chelsea's Centenary XI in 2005. Even more impressively, Ken Bates, former chairman and a man not necessarily given to praise of any kind, has also acknowledged that Zola was one of the club's greatest players: 'He's been a joy to watch and a great influence both on and off the field, particularly because of his great interest with young fans. We owe him a hell of a lot of thanks.'

He received an honorary OBE in 2004 from the British Ambassador in Rome and has received a prestigious award from the island of Sardinia, where he is seen to be an ambassador for his compatriots.

He returned to the English game to manage West Ham in 2008. After a run of poor results, he departed two years later when his contract was terminated by the club's new owners. Even despite his brief sojourn at fierce rivals West Ham, he has remained amazingly popular among the Chelsea faithful and in a frequently tarnished profession has been described as a 'breath of fresh air' with a 'wholesome, enthusiastic and sportsman's attitude'.

GSt

10 DENNIS BERGKAMP

PREMIER LEAGUE DEBUT:
Arsenal v Middlesbrough, 20 August 1995

PREMIER LEAGUE CLUB:
Arsenal

PREMIER LEAGUE APPEARANCES/GOALS:
Arsenal   315   87
Total   315   87

PREMIER LEAGUE HONOURS:
3 (1997-98, 2001-02, 2003-04); FWA and
PFA Footballer of the Year 1998

COUNTRY:
Netherlands (born Amsterdam, 18 May
1969)

DENNIS BERGKAMP allowed the ball chipped forward by David Platt to fall over his shoulder and, while somehow balanced in mid-air, killed its momentum with a flick of his right foot. Without letting it touch the ground, a deft touch with his left boot then left Leicester defender Matt Elliott hurtling out of the equation before the Dutch maestro opened his stance and curled a low shot round Kasey Keller into the net.

Not only was it a world-class finish and one of the best goals ever seen at Filbert Street, it was also his third of the night. Added to a precision 20-yard stunner into the top angle and a break from deep, it was a genuine contender for the best hat-trick ever scored in the Premier League.

This game was early in 1997-98, which ended in Double glory for both Arsenal and Bergkamp, who lifted both the PFA and FWA Player of the Season awards to cap his greatest Premier League season. And so to

France 98, where the same gifts of speed, coolness, vision and poetic control contributed to an almost identical wonder-goal to win the World Cup quarter-final against Argentina. No fluke, then.

Again, Bergkamp made the near-impossible look easy. And this is how he'll be remembered for his 11 years at Arsenal, over which period he brought an entirely fresh, clinical level of close control and technical excellence to the English game.

THE MOMENT HE BECAME A LEGEND

A surging run through the midfield and 22-yard rocket against Southampton at Highbury saw the Dutch Master 'arrive' in the Premier League in September 1995.

Bergkamp arrived at Highbury from Internazionale in the summer of 1995 – Bruce Rioch's first signing, and a lasting legacy of his brief reign – but he was not an immediate hit and soon had the British press on his back.

'I didn't exactly hit the ground running in England and it took me a while to get going. There was a lot of pressure on me and I remember the newspapers running "Bergkamp Watch" features, asking how many hours it would take me to score. In the end, I scored against Southampton and I remember running away from the goal with all the pressure coming off my shoulders.'

He never looked back, and soon became one of the jewels in the Premier League's crown, benefiting from Arsène Wenger's visionary tactical awareness, which allowed him to play behind the front two, where he awaited his chance and swooped in to devastating effect. Bergkamp netted 51 goals in his first four Premier League seasons for 'The Gunners', before injuries and a change of role reduced his strike rate – but never his analytical, slide-rule effectiveness.

WELL I NEVER …

Dennis was named after his father's hero Denis Law, but they had to add to extra 'N' as 'Denis' means 'Denise' in Dutch.

'The pleasure of scoring goals is known, but for me the pleasure of the assist came close,' says the aptly monickered 'Iceman'. 'It's like solving a puzzle. I always had a picture in my head of how things would look two or three seconds later. I could calculate it. There's a tremendous pleasure in doing something that someone else couldn't see.'

After three frustrating years finishing runners-up to Manchester United, Arsenal regained the title in 2001–02, repeating their Double-winning feat, as Bergkamp formed a potent partnership with Freddie Ljungberg. During the run-in to this silverware haul, Bergkamp added another incredible goal to his portfolio at St James' Park. With his back to goal and closely marked by Nikos Dabizas on the edge of the penalty area, Bergkamp was picked out by a Robert Pires pass.

> ## QUOTE
>
> 'I am considering psychiatric help. I can't fly. I just freeze. I get panicky. It starts the day before, when I can't sleep.'
>
> The Non-Flying Dutchman describes his aircraft phobia.

With a poetic flick and turn, he was round his marker and clear on goal for an easy finish past Shay Given.

Having considered a move, it came as some relief to club and player that Bergkamp signed up for another year and contributed 28 games to Arsenal's historic unbeaten championship season of 2003-04.

Arsenal's final season at Highbury, 2005-06, was also Bergkamp's last and such was his standing at the club that a game against West Brom was declared 'Bergkamp Day'. Sticking to a script he'd apparently been planning for weeks, Dennis came on as sub and scored in the 89th minute.

GS

9 WAYNE ROONEY

PREMIER LEAGUE DEBUT:
Everton v Tottenham Hotspur,
17 August 2002

PREMIER LEAGUE CLUBS:
Everton, Manchester United

PREMIER LEAGUE APPEARANCES/GOALS:

Everton	67	15
Arsenal	251	129
Total	318	144

PREMIER LEAGUE HONOURS:
4 (2006-07, 2007-08, 2008-09, 2010-11);
FWA and PFA Footballer of the Year 2010

COUNTRY:
England (born Liverpool, 24 October 1985)

REMEMBER ENGLAND'S 2010 World Cup match against Algeria? Remarkably, it bears re-watching. Having played with all the cohesion and animation of a Subbuteo team, with Rooney himself performing like a hung-over parks player, England's number ten addresses the camera: 'Nice to see your home fans booing you. That's loyal supporters.' As you savour the anguished self-pity of the persecuted millionaire, it is hard not to wonder what David Moyes and Colleen made of Wayne's resourceful use of the 'L word' as he left the pitch that evening.

Rooney is two people. To the readers of the *Daily Telegraph*, he is a prole from a stranded sprawl of northern estateland, a bad loser, a worse winner, a serial swearer and spitter, simultaneously vain and plain, grasping and vulgar beyond parody. They would perhaps fail to recognise that he also embodies the best of the working class – brave, hard-working, tenacious, a team-player, prodigiously talented in a derided trade; he is, with Paul Gascoigne, the most comprehensively gifted player Britain has produced since George Best.

It was inevitable Rooney would join United. The club have a history of producing the outstanding type of their time: in the age of austerity, it was Duncan Edwards, the versatile genius on the maximum wage; then came Bobby Charlton, a transitional figure, a TV star but not a celebrity, unfashionable, culturally conservative; next it was George Best, the 1960s dream of itself, hedonistic, witty, cool, self-invented; later it was David Beckham, the Tony Blair of soccer, talented, superficial, as slick, shiny and empty as a toy balloon, an advertiser's notion of football's airbrushed future.

Like his predecessors, Rooney comes from a non-metropolitan, working-class family, but it's the differences that count. Edwards was paid the wage of a skilled working man; Rooney is estimated to earn about £15 million annually, enough to keep Duncan in mushy peas and roll-ups for eternity. Charlton was the archetypal loyalist, even now an ever-present at Old Trafford; on scoring for Everton in the 2002 FA Youth Cup final Rooney revealed a T-shirt proclaiming 'Once a Blue, Always a Blue' – two years later he joined United for £25.6 million.

Best, even in a decade of handsome dandies preening 24/7

> ### THE MOMENT HE BECAME A LEGEND
>
> 19 October 2002, aged 16, he scores from 30 yards against reigning Double-winners Arsenal and beats England keeper David Seaman.

> ### WELL I NEVER ...
>
> His favourite film of all time is *Grease*. 'It's a bit weird but I love *Grease*. It's a great film ... I think it's one of those films you can watch again and again.' He also admits to liking *Dreamgirls* and *Hairspray*. 'I love watching musicals.' Admit it, you didn't see that one coming.

for Cockney lensmen, stood out as a paparazzo's passport to a retainer with the *Daily Mirror*. Pop stars wanted to hang out with him, not the reverse. Rooney has the nickname 'Shrek' and has had a hair transplant. His favourite band are the risibly tedious Stereophonics.

Beckham headed the Sports Department of Cool Britannia. He wore sarongs, he was the subject of a video installation (*David Beckham Sleeping*) at the V&A; his was the smooth, plausible face and improbable torso of the false boom of the early years of the 21st century. Wayne Rooney has a profile and body for a double-dip recession; that of a sweaty, stocky artisan. The only video anyone would want to watch of Rooney is of him playing football, and that is where he eclipses even the sublimely skilful Beckham.

Beckham's passes were as pretty as he was, but Rooney can do everything. Take his goal against Manchester City in February 2011 at Old Trafford. Involved early in the move with an uncharacteristic miscue, he makes it into the box to receive Nani's cross in mid-air and with his back to goal. Top corner. His celebration was to run to the corner and look up to the sky with his arms outstretched. Christ-like. On the bench, Sir Alex Ferguson, a man who has witnessed a few remarkable goals in his time, seems to exclaim 'F*cking hell'. It is, at that moment, as precise a response as anything the commentators can come up with.

And, in that moment, when the two people who make up Wayne Rooney become one, the opinions of *Daily Telegraph* readers, or anyone else for that matter, are rendered meaningless. At his best, which is formidably often, he is the most effective player in English football and our only possible outfield candidate for inclusion in a world XI.

FC

8 ALEX FERGUSON

PREMIER LEAGUE DEBUT (MANAGER):
Manchester United v Sheffield United,
15 August 1992

PREMIER LEAGUE CLUB (MANAGER):
Manchester United

PREMIER LEAGUE APPEARANCES (MANAGER):
Manchester U   772
Total   772

PREMIER LEAGUE HONOURS:
12 (1992-93, 1993-94, 1995-96, 1996-97,
1998-99, 1999-00, 2000-01, 2002-03, 2006-
07, 2007-08, 2008-09, 2010-11); Manager of
the Season 1994, 1996, 1997, 1999, 2000,
2003, 2007, 2008, 2009, 2011

COUNTRY:
Scotland (born Glasgow, 31 December 1941)

IT'S LONG BEEN tempting for football fans and pundits alike to wax philosophical about Sir Alex Ferguson's career at United, and ask, 'What if?' What if Fergie had been sacked from United in 1990 following defeat against Forest in the third round of the FA Cup – his shaky hold on the job loosening from the moment fans had unfurled a banner that read, 'THREE YEARS OF EXCUSES AND IT'S STILL CRAP ... TA-RA FERGIE?'

What if, with his last throw of the dice, Mark Robins, had failed to nick that late goal – providing his boss with precious time to turn his team around and give them a chance to go on and win the Cup? What if he had ended up running a pub in Cheshire serving Paul 'I'll have a double' McGrath and George 'Make mine a treble' Best? You can see him with a glass of red in hand, looking down a long tunnel of intense regret to that excruciating afternoon. If only ...

Ferguson was born the son of a shipyard worker in working-class Govan. He came from the culture that produced the Lisbon Lions, Jock

Stein and Kenny Dalglish – an area that, in terms of talent per square mile, was for many years the football capital of Europe. The tenement in which he spent his childhood has since been demolished. When he worked as an apprentice on the Clyde, he was a shop steward at an age when his more privileged peers were still being tucked in at night.

These are the roots of Ferguson's toughness. Keane, Rooney, Hughes, Ince, Bruce – just some of the players he has bawled out. There is a steel cable at United of rivet-hard working-class brawlers, bruisers and spoilers upon which Ferguson has strung successive teams. It is not a coincidence that Steve Bruce was an apprentice at the Swan Hunter dockyard. They could all play a bit too, but without them the pretty players would not have stood a chance.

United teams are built to be mentally and physically invulnerable; they score an outrageous number of injury-time goals ('Fergie Time' is a statistical fact at Old Trafford) and that's because his players don't clock off early. They don't panic under pressure; in Ferguson's collectivist philosophy, the team is everything and optimism of the will prevails. This is why his talisman, Roy Keane, was allowed to leave in November 2005 – only the head of a one-party state is allowed to voice criticism of the Party.

It is because of his socialist credentials and outlook that the demolition of Kevin Keegan was so amusingly instructive. By Christmas 1995, Keegan's flamboyant, reckless attacking Newcastle side were ten points clear of United. However, Ferguson detected a hysterical, panicky streak in the over-excitable character of his rival for the title. Sure enough, and with a little prompting from United boss, Keegan provoked the ever-vengeful football gods in a foolish televised outburst in April the following year (familiarly known as the 'I would

> ## THE MOMENT HE BECAME A LEGEND
>
> If there was ever any doubt that he was already a legend, it was erased in 1998-99 when he claimed the Premier League title, FA Cup and Champions League in one incredible season.

> ## WELL I NEVER ...
>
> Ferguson worked in Kenny Dalglish's uncle's restaurant and used to give the young Kenny a lift to Rangers games.

love it if we beat them' suicide declaration) and the Red Devils won at the finishing-post.

As well as repeatedly demonstrating his Lanark war-baby determination, Ferguson has succeeded by dint of trusting in young players. At one time his 1970s St Mirren team had an average age of 19; its captain was 20 (had Alan Hansen been paying attention, he might have avoided his epically daft 'you can't win anything with kids' blunder). At United, the first thing Ferguson did was to revamp the youth team arrangements, and so began the production line of world-class teenagers that sold a billion replica tops to distant global punters who think that David Beckham played for 'Manchester'.

> **QUOTE**
>
> 'At the end of this game, the European Cup will be only six feet away from you and you'll not even able to touch it if we lose. And for many of you that will be the closest you will ever get. Don't you dare come back in here without giving your all.'
>
> Ferguson was not immune to using mind games on his own players.

Other managers may have been more tactically astute, or have done better in the transfer market, but surely none has matched him in his undying commitment to winning and to always finding ways of doing things better. Recently asked about the success of the famous Class of '92 that formed the core of so much that United have achieved since then, he didn't bask in their triumphs, instead he said: 'It's not a one-off. It's going to happen again. If the Academy system changes to what it should be, then we are capable of doing it.' In other words, he always expects more – of himself and everyone around him.

He is now fashioning another young team, with Jones, Welbeck, Smalling, De Gea and Cleverley among them. United may have finished second last season on goal difference and Manchester City might be poised to knock the septuagenarian off his 'f*cking perch' (as Ferguson famously promised and succeeded to do to Liverpool when he took over at Old Trafford in 1986), but if you think he is going out on a losing note you can think again. Glaswegian streetfighters don't quit.

FC

7 ROMAN ABRAMOVICH

PREMIER LEAGUE DEBUT (OWNER):
Chelsea v Liverpool, 17 August 2003

PREMIER LEAGUE CLUB (OWNER):
Chelsea

PREMIER LEAGUE MATCHES (OWNER):
Chelsea 342
Total 342

PREMIER LEAGUE HONOURS:
3 (2004-05, 2005-06, 2009-10)

COUNTRY:
Russia (born Saratov, 24 October 1966)

CHELSEA OWNER and Russian oligarch Roman Abramovich, one of the 100 richest men in the world with an estimated fortune of £8.4 billion, stands as concrete proof that, if you spend enough cash, any team in the world can be successful. Fans of Rochdale, Lincoln City, Crewe, and possibly many other clubs too, remain envious that the team he chose as the vehicle to prove this theory was Chelsea Football Club.

Why Chelsea? When Abramovich bought the club in 2003, he may have thought that no matter whatever happened on the road to achieving obscene amounts of moolah in Russia's post-communist fire sale of state assets, at least he could not possibly be less popular than the club's former chairman – the outspoken Ken Bates. In that respect alone, he's been a massive success, just by virtue of keeping his mouth shut.

The only slightly more difficult task was turning Chelsea into a global brand that could keep step with the likes of Manchester United, Barcelona and Real Madrid. His first move was to sack manager Claudio Ranieri, who failed to win Chelsea's first title for 49 years by finishing a meagre second in 2004. How expectations change. No longer was Chelsea to be seen as the dandy team of luxury performers who'd chosen the club only for its proximity to the clubs and boutiques of the West End. Chelsea, it seemed, was now a *bona fide* contender.

Jose Mourinho, who had just won the Champions League with FC Porto, was duly shipped in with a brief to win not just the Premier League, but the Champions League too. If he'd done it with a minnow like Porto, surely he could repeat it with a financially fuelled, emerging monster like Chelsea? Up to a point, yes. League titles came in 2005 and 2006, as well as an FA Cup and two League Cups. But Champions League success eluded Mourinho, who tended to work better with lower-profile players, and not necessarily the likes of Andriy Shevchenko (£31 million) and Michael Ballack (free transfer).

Stamford Bridge, despite Chelsea's newly elevated status as one of the elite, wasn't big enough for both egos and Mourinho left the club in late 2007. He was replaced by Avram Grant, the Russian's earlier appointment as director of football. Grant was promptly fired when Chelsea finished second to Manchester United in the league, and lost to them in the 2008 Champions League final.

Stamford Bridge then became as much a lure for big-name international managers as it had

> ## THE MOMENT HE BECAME A LEGEND
>
> When he fired Jose Mourinho and became one of the few figures in football with bigger gonads than the 'Special One'.

> ## WELL I NEVER ...
>
> Abramovich owns the largest yacht in the world, the 557ft aptly titled *Eclipse*. It has two swimming pools, a couple of helicopter pads, a mini-submarine and a missile-defence system, bullet-proof windows and armour-plating for the master suite. Well, you can't be too careful.

been for players – Luiz Felipe Scolari, interim manager Guus Hiddink, and Carlo Ancelotti (who won the Double but neglected to claim a European trophy) all came and went, despite Abramovich continuing to fund expensive signings, including Fernando Torres for a British record £50 million. It's doubtful Ancelotti's successor, André Villas-Boas, took out a long-term rental lease in London.

Just as well, as he didn't even complete his first season at the club. With Chelsea's campaign meandering along, and an ageing squad seeming to be past its best, Roberto Di Matteo was the eighth man put in charge of Abramovich's Chelsea, albeit on an interim basis. Somehow, the Italian inspired his team to a last hurrah, and in Munich fulfilled Abramovich's dream by bagging the Champions League trophy (as well as another FA Cup). Immediately, he was asking for a repeat, while the man who had led the side to European victory was left to wait to see if he would get the job on a permanent basis.

Such reckless hiring and firing has boosted Chelsea's image as the plaything of a billionaire who merely bought the team to add to his collection of yachts, private jets, luxury flats and limousines. Early TV shots of Abramovich failing to celebrate Chelsea goals like a Shed End loyalist added credence to the view that he didn't really care, though he later rectified this by learning to emote.

As a man, Abramovich remains reclusive, a shadowy and unshaven figure up in the stands who rarely talks in public. But he reputedly comes down to the changing room after every game he attends, and at least cannot be accused of being an absentee owner. Whether he intended to or not, Abramovich has become a fan.

IP

6 DAVID BECKHAM

PREMIER LEAGUE DEBUT:
Manchester United v Leeds United,
2 April 1995

PREMIER LEAGUE CLUB:
Manchester United

PREMIER LEAGUE APPEARANCES/GOALS:
Manchester U   265   62
Total   265   62

PREMIER LEAGUE HONOURS:
6 (1995-96, 1996-97, 1998-99, 1999-00,
2000-01, 2002-03)

COUNTRY:
England (born Leytonstone, 2 May 1975)

'BECKHAM CAN'T kick with his left foot,' George Best once remarked tartly. 'He can't head a ball, can't tackle, and doesn't score many goals. Apart from that, he's all right.' If he had lived a little longer, the terminally alcoholic Best might have been pushed to add that Beckham's ability to cope with fame, wealth and adulation meant that his career at the highest level lasted at least twice as long as his own.

While it's easy to see where Best was coming from, it's a selective assessment of a unique phenomenon. In highlighting Beckham's technical weaknesses, the former Manchester United maverick not only points up his own strengths, but Beckham's too. For what Best fails to point out is that Beckham's right foot is a tool of such artistry, agility and accuracy that it almost makes up for everything else that's missing.

A cockney Red thanks to his father's admiration of the very

Manchester United team to which Best belonged in late 1960s, Beckham signed with United at the age of 14 out of love. His joy at just being on the field in a red shirt was apparent throughout his Old Trafford career, where he won six league titles, two FA Cups and the Champions League. His craft centred around a right foot that could dip, swerve and weave a ball at corners and free-kicks, and deliver shots of devastating potency from 30 yards out.

Beckham's cross-field passing was immaculate, and he could instantly open up space and opportunities perfectly suited to United's deadly counter-attacking tactics, especially in away and European games. He was arguably the most consistent and precise crosser of a football since Stanley Matthews, and similarly was a creator of goals rather than a scorer, though his return of almost one every four games is actually slightly better than that of Paul Scholes. Knowing that he lacked the speed to beat opponents, and the defensive ability to tackle them, he compensated with a conscientious workrate that meant he could escape censure even when having a bad game.

His red card at the 1998 World Cup for a trifling flick at Argentina's Diego Simeone saw a downturn in the public perception of what was rapidly becoming the Beckham Brand. A pop-star girlfriend with a tabloid lifestyle, and a succession of variant hairstyles and fashion forays, ensured that the midfielder became famous as much for his posturing as he did for his play. A duly tasteless celebrity wedding to former Spice

THE MOMENT HE BECAME A LEGEND

On the opening day of the 1996-97 season at Selhurst Park, he took a short pass, briefly looked up from the halfway line, spotted Wimbledon goalkeeper Neil Sullivan off his line, and wafted in a perfectly flighted shot from 60 yards out. 'David Beckham, surely an England player of the future,' squealed an unusually prescient John Motson.

WELL I NEVER ...

Beckham suffers from ataxophobia (fear of disorder). 'I have to have everything in a straight line or everything has to be in pairs. I'll put my Pepsi cans in the fridge and if there's one too many then I'll put it in another cupboard somewhere.' He is also rumoured to have ornithophobia (fear of birds).

Girl Victoria Adams turned him into first a national, and then a global, institution. What he was missing in terms of intellect, David more than made up for in terms of a boyish smile and Grade A good looks.

Yet no matter how much money he made and how often the tabloid press aired his very public outings, deep down Beckham remained nothing but a football player. Despite the perpetual ads, the ticker-tape of ceaseless publicity, the reportedly massive earnings, and the glamorous moves to Madrid and LA, he always seemed most comfortable out on the field. Always keen to prove himself anew, Beckham wanted to keep playing for England (115 caps), and he wanted to keep on winning things for Real Madrid and the LA Galaxy. Despite setbacks and injuries at both clubs, he eventually did just that.

'This is what I do when I'm bored – new tattoos, new cars, new watches,' a younger Beckham admitted at the height of his Manchester United career. If money has no limits, what else are you going to do? Doubtless we could all think of a few good causes, and to be fair, Beckham has become a UNICEF ambassador and helped a number of charities, usually related to the help and/or protection of children, perhaps because, at heart, he's still a schoolkid who really just loves to chase and kick a football. Peel away the bullshit, and you're left with a charming if perhaps limited talent who just happened to help the Premier League sell itself to the whole world.

IP

> ## QUOTE
>
> 'The face of an angel and the bum of a Greek god. Rumour has it that his tackle is enough to not only take your breath away but possibly do you serious damage.'
>
> Gay magazine *Attitude* underselling its appreciation of Beckham as they name him as Top Fantasy Player in 1999.

5 | ALAN SHEARER

PREMIER LEAGUE DEBUT (PLAYER):
Blackburn Rovers v Crystal Palace,
15 August 1992

PREMIER LEAGUE DEBUT (MANAGER):
Newcastle United v Chelsea, 4 April 2009

PREMIER LEAGUE CLUBS (PLAYER):
Blackburn Rovers, Newcastle United

PREMIER LEAGUE CLUB (MANAGER):
Newcastle United

PREMIER LEAGUE APPEARANCES/GOALS:

Blackburn R	138	112
Newcastle U	303	148
Total	441	260

PREMIER LEAGUE APPEARANCES (MANAGER):

Newcastle U	8
Total	8

PREMIER LEAGUE HONOURS:
1 (1994-95); FWA Footballer of the Year
1994; PFA Player of the Year 1995, 1997

COUNTRY:
England (born Gosforth, 13 August 1970)

HIS GAME WAS all about muscle, commitment and an unerring eye for goal. Alan Shearer didn't just play a football match, he attacked it – looking daggers at the opposition, he scorned his slated victims, continually weighing the odds for a bout of man-to-man combat in the 18-yard box, an aerial tussle or a territorial feud to gain a precious square foot. Ultra-competitive, his concentration and opportunism were relentless.

Give him an inch and he'd barge you a yard; give him sight of the target and he'd strike directly with a minimum of fuss, his right boot and head, his barrel chest and elbows the weapons of choice. Alan Shearer didn't just score goals, he executed them without mercy – one of the greatest (and perhaps last) traditional, big, strong and unreservedly successful English centre-forwards.

Only once the net had bulged did his face crack, and then he'd wheel away to a devoted crowd. With his arm aloft – he was saying, 'Me. Again.' Occasionally he would do a funny little run. So, he was human after all, just scoring goals for his own amusement.

> ### THE MOMENT HE BECAME A LEGEND
>
> He scored a hat-trick on his Southampton debut against Arsenal, aged 17. He was the youngest player ever to do so in the Football League.

Not content with watching him go about his business so stubbornly, sports reporters became obsessed with 'The Real Alan Shearer', the mythological Geordie jester behind the jutting jaw and the 18-yard stare. 'At first I didn't even notice him as [former Newcastle United and England midfielder David] Batty chatted away in front of me,' reported Nick Varley from the frontline in *Parklife: A Search for the Heart of Football*.

'Then a disconcerting grin spread across Batty's face before he

> ### WELL I NEVER ...
>
> Despite playing for Newcastle United as a schoolboy, he failed his trial after volunteering to play in goal.

laughed out loud and shouted back over my shoulder. I turned around to see who it was aimed at and Shearer looked back, wearing an expression of utterly bemused innocence. Face as blank as a poker player's, he lowered his eyes to his paper and read as if that was exactly what he had been doing before ...'

What he was actually doing remains, necessarily, unreported.

Of course, no article has ever been written about Shearer without reference to his 'supposedly dour character'. Time and again, he has been asked about his Geordie roots, his sheet-metal worker father, and the strange circumstances surrounding the fact that he never actually seemed to be young at any point, or the grand double bluff of the 'Mary Poppins' image. Shearer has always politely declined or swerved the question with a delicacy for which he was not renowned on the pitch. He is a man who has claimed, variously, 'There is another side to me which people don't often see,' and also, 'My wife, Lainya, she could tell you a few stories.'

Today there are hundreds of thousands of youngsters who don't even know who he is – this bluff, bland non-pundit who inhabits the *Match of the Day* settee opposite the man off the crisp adverts.

For the record, it should be noted that Shearer's 260 Premier League goals remain the all-time record haul. The £3.3 million which carried him from Southampton to Blackburn in 1992 was a British transfer record that he repaid with golden goals and a Premier League title. After lifting the Golden Boot at Euro 96, Shearer's head told him Manchester United, but his big black-and-white heart, his boyhood hero Kevin Keegan and a world record £15 million fee said it just had to be the Toon. A third consecutive Premier League Golden Boot followed for 1996-97, but somehow it wasn't quite enough to carry Newcastle to the title.

Shearer is arguably Newcastle United's greatest-ever player; but more importantly than that, he's the Magpies' greatest-ever number nine. A professional role model, a giant. We'll draw a discreet veil over his brief and unsuccessful managerial career, but he remains an almost mythological creature on Tyneside.

'Then the water bomb sailed past and exploded with a plop at our feet ...' We're back with Nick Varley at the Newcastle training ground, this time interviewing Gary Speed on a bench below the balcony of the players' lounge. 'That'll be Shearer, won't it?' Speed laughed. It wasn't, it was Batty, but he thought it was Shearer. If it had been Shearer, he wouldn't have missed.

DH

4 STEVEN GERRARD

PREMIER LEAGUE DEBUT:
Liverpool v Blackburn Rovers,
29 November 1998

PREMIER LEAGUE CLUB:
Liverpool

PREMIER LEAGUE APPEARANCES/GOALS:
Liverpool   405 89
Total   405 89

PREMIER LEAGUE HONOURS:
None; FWA Footballer of the Year 2009; PFA
Player of the Year 2006

COUNTRY:
England (born Huyton, 30 May 1980)

AS CAREERS GO, Steven Gerrard can settle into his dotage comfortable in the knowledge that his befits the epithet 'illustrious'. Having made in excess of 400 Premier League appearances for his only club, Liverpool, gaining over 90 international caps and captaining his country, the only medal he is unable to produce is the one he desires the most – the one presented to the winners of the Premier League. And he hasn't given up on that one just yet.

This modest, quiet but surprisingly nervous player, known affectionately as 'Stevie G', has achieved renown for his surging midfield play, inspirational leadership, crucial goalscoring ability, incisive passing, robust tackling and box-to-box play. Zinedine Zidane described him as the 'engine room' of Liverpool and suggested that he 'just might be the best player in the world'. He was certainly the most complete midfield player of the so-called 'Golden Generation'.

His career, however, has not always been plain sailing. His list of injuries – back, ankle, groin, you name it – is so extensive he should leave his body to medical science. And when he has been fit, he has spent hours dealing with the controversy surrounding possible moves to rivals Chelsea, and an unsavoury but uncharacteristic off-field incident in December 2008 when he was embroiled in a bar brawl in Southport but acquitted of affray at Liverpool Crown Court.

His CV contains an impressive list of successes in the FA Cup (twice), League Cup (three times), the UEFA Cup and the Champions League in 2005, when his headed goal early in the second half instigated an amazing comeback from a three-goal half-time deficit against AC Milan.

It is sometimes forgotten that he also won the penalty, dispatched at the second attempt by Xabi Alonso, that resulted in the scores being levelled. The essence of the man, however, is best caught by his reaction to that first goal in Istanbul. Gripped by a belief that the impossible was suddenly within reach, he gestured to the thousands of travelling fans who had been wallowing in the trough of despond seconds before to get behind the team. That was leadership from the middle of the park and beyond the touchline. And it worked.

For his all-round contribution, he was made Man of the Match and later received the award of UEFA Club Footballer of the Year, which, when added to a lengthy list of other individual awards over the last 12 years, bears witness to his stellar contribution to football in general and Liverpool in particular.

Perhaps it is cruel rather than ironic that he cannot boast a Premier

League winner's medal, as he would certainly have made any of the great Liverpool teams of the 1970s and 1980s, but his rise has unfortunately coincided with Liverpool's decline in league competition, something which must have prompted him to flirt with the idea of a move elsewhere. But despite a very shaky start at Anfield, he stayed loyal.

Like Ian Wright and the late Gary Speed, he was overlooked at schoolboy level, despite joining the Anfield youth academy at the age of nine. His early time at Liverpool, he freely admits, was not very promising. On his first appearance from the bench in 1998, while warming up with the other subs, all of whom were roundly applauded by the Kop, he told the *Guardian* that he felt he could hear the fans asking: 'Who's this skinny little twat?' When he came on, shot through with nerves, he did little to incur anything other than instant scorn when slicing a cross into the higher reaches of the stands. Well, that was then. They know who the 'skinny little twat' is now.

GSt

> ## QUOTE
>
> 'It was difficult knowing one of your cousins had lost his life,' Gerrard has said about the death of his cousin, Jon-Paul Gilhooley, at the age of ten the youngest victim at Hillsborough. 'Seeing his family's reaction drove me on to become the player I am today.'
>
> **No better tribute perhaps.**

3 RYAN GIGGS

PREMIER LEAGUE DEBUT:
Manchester United v Sheffield United,
15 August 1992

PREMIER LEAGUE CLUB:
Manchester United

PREMIER LEAGUE APPEARANCES/GOALS:
Manchester U   598   107
Total   598   107

PREMIER LEAGUE HONOURS:
12 (1992-93, 1993-94, 1995-96, 1996-97,
1998-99, 1999-00, 2000-01, 2002-03,
2006-07, 2007-08, 2008-09, 2010-11); PFA
Player of the Year 2009

COUNTRY:
Wales (born Cardiff, 29 November 1973)

'LOOK AT RYAN Giggs, rolling back the years!' has been the standard exclamation of all television commentators whenever the Manchester United midfielder has beaten a player during the twilight years of his career. But Giggs doesn't need to roll back anything. The truth is, he's always been this good.

Manchester City may have won the Premier League title, but it will always rankle until long after his retirement that Giggs was 'lost' by the club as a teenager, following a spell at their school of excellence. But in truth, he has said he 'absolutely hated it' there, and turned up only because the coach of his boys' team, Deans FC, was a City scout. But then he would say that now, wouldn't he? Regardless, he certainly quickly made an impression upon Alex Ferguson, who said that when he saw the 13-year-old Giggs for the first time: 'He floated over the ground like a cocker spaniel chasing a piece of silver paper in the wind.'

Ferguson had been at the club for only a few weeks when Giggs came for a trial over the Christmas holidays in 1986, and one of his earliest aims was to ensure the club signed up the best local talent. Eleven months later, Ferguson showed up at his house with schoolboy forms on the boy's 14th birthday. Few doubted that Giggs *was* the best local talent.

Still, moving from City to United was typical of the player's changeling youth. He captained England schoolboys, even though he was eligible to play for only Wales at full international level. And at 16 he dropped his now absent father's surname of Wilson in favour of his mother's, so that 'the world would know I was my mother's son'. Later, he made the transformation from a daring, devilishly fast outside-left to central midfield elder statesman who was no less effective for an inevitable diminishment of his fledgling pace.

THE MOMENT HE BECAME A LEGEND

Giggs scored at Tottenham early on in the first Premier League season, a goal of staggering speed and skill that saw him latch on to the ball, beat one defender, nutmeg a second, then zip around the keeper to finish with a left-foot shot from a challenging angle. And there was so much more to come.

Had the player's career spanned only the 1990s, he would still own a top five place in the list of Premier League legends. He burst onto the first team scene with a series of performances that had the greyer generations marvelling at his old-time flair on the flanks, and youngsters agog at the kind of skills they'd seen only in archived footage of Stanley Matthews. Dark, dashing, handsome, and quick as a hare in a hurry, the newly spawned Premier League could not have wished for a more ideally moulded poster boy if they'd sent exact specifications to the footballer factory.

He scored against City on his starting debut (obviously), but an early goal against Spurs showcased the range of his nascent qualities and made the football world sit up and take notice. Flashing onto a loose pass, he bamboozled two defenders and swept past goalkeeper Ian Walker before scoring the kind of goal he'd repeat in various eye-catching ways against Queens Park Rangers the following season and many times beyond.

His winner against Arsenal in extra time of the FA Cup semi-final replay at Villa Park in April 1999 left Lee Dixon, Martin Keown and Tony Adams either lunging or prostrate on the turf after a 70-yard dribble and finish that was voted by Manchester United fans as the club's greatest goal of all time.

All this time, Giggs was busy providing goals for team-mates from the flanks, while not all his own strikes were the result of speed and deft foot movement. Chips, volleys, long-range strikes, textbook free-kicks, and even headers were part of his repertoire. And his skill as a clean, ball-winning midfielder who never shirked tracking-back duties has often been overshadowed by his inspirational creative gifts. His willingness to work for the team backs up claims that he is the most complete and consistent footballer in the history of the English game.

Of course, even a snake-hipped genius such as Giggs has not been immune to troubles and criticism. Although he racked up 64 caps for Wales, he was slated for his frequent international absences through apparent injury, with Welsh fans feeling that he always put club before country. He also suffered a short-term, mid-career loss of form at a time when he was dogged by hamstring injuries, but he changed his fitness regime (and his car to an automatic) to combat the problem and emerged better than ever. A fine goal against Juventus in the Champions League in a 3-0 away win in 2003 silenced any doubters who thought he was already past it.

When lurid revelations about Giggs' private life and extra-marital affairs came to light in 2011, including an alleged eight-year affair with his sister-in-law, it may have been a relief to some to discover that Giggs was human after all. He'd been touted as the model professional for so long, never having been red-carded in over 900 first-team appearances for his club (though he was once sent off for Wales), that some kind of downfall was perhaps inevitable. The player's attempt to use the legal system to gag media coverage of his affairs, however, badly tarnished his carefully nurtured image.

His form didn't suffer, however, and Giggs continues to break records while collecting honours, awards and accolades. To add to his 12 Premier League medals, he has two from winning the Champions League, four from the FA Cup, and three from the League Cup. He was twice PFA Young Footballer of the Year, the 2009 PFA Player of the Year, and winner of the BBC 2009 Sports Personality of the Year. The man who has scored in 22 consecutive top-flight seasons and 11 consecutive Champions League campaigns also boasts the most Manchester United appearances in the club's history, and was voted by fans as the team's greatest player of all time. And that's set against some pretty stiff competition.

IP

2 THIERRY HENRY

PREMIER LEAGUE DEBUT:
Arsenal v Leicester City, 7 August 1999

PREMIER LEAGUE CLUB:
Arsenal

PREMIER LEAGUE APPEARANCES/GOALS:

Arsenal	258	175
Total	258	175

PREMIER LEAGUE HONOURS:
2 (2001-02, 2003-04); FWA Footballer of the
Year 2003, 2004, 2006; PFA Player of the
Year 2003, 2004

COUNTRY:
France (born Paris, 17 August 1977)

THIERRY HENRY has twice been voted runner-up as World Footballer of the Year, but when he was creating and scoring goals for Arsenal at the peak of his career, he was arguably not just the best player in the world, but also the easiest on the eye, too. His consistently breath-thieving goals were of such effortless quality for so many seasons that many fans began to react with the same Gallic nonchalance as Henry himself when yet another 25-yard strike nestled into its immaculately conceived corner of the goal.

Henry was exceptional for a foreign player in England because his legendary status was fomented while he was actually in the Premier League, unlike many of the stars who swanned through Heathrow with their reputations, their egos, their hefty price tags and their dark-glassed agents as part of the luggage train. A promising young striker nurtured by Arsène Wenger at Monaco, he joined Arsenal from Juventus after an unsuccessful year in Serie A isolated on the left wing, a position that supposedly best served his speed and close control, but where he failed to find a comfort zone.

Many questioned the sanity of Wenger's reported outlay of £11 million on Henry in 1999, but the manager already knew the player well enough to recognise he would be cheap at twice the price, and that he was a natural-born striker rather than a flank player. Nonetheless, Henry struggled at first to fit in to the English game until, by his own admittance, he said he started to 'use my elbow' when going for the high ball, 'or I'm dead'.

THE MOMENT HE BECAME A LEGEND

In his second season for Arsenal, he scored the only goal in a 1-0 win over Manchester United at Highbury, taking the ball with his back to goal and, with one touch, teed it up for himself and then hit it with his second touch, on the swivel, from 25 yards out into the top corner in front of the North Bank. The kind of goal you can marvel at a million times.

Not that there was much point putting the ball on to Henry's head, given his grace and pace, and the skills he harboured within the sinews of his two fantastical feet. The ability to control a ball coming out of the air at any height or angle gave him a second's technical advantage over every other player in the country. On top of that was his ability to drift behind the back line and conjure up several steps-worth of spare space. Finally came the shots, as deceptive in style as the cool, quietly poised striker himself. Power was rarely the Frenchman's weapon of choice, because his science was an accuracy so finely honed that you almost suspected he had German-engineered crosshairs etched onto the front of his eyes.

The incredibly impressive stats of Henry's career must nonetheless take second place to the sheer artistry of his motion, the impossible magnetism of his close control, and the slow beauty of successive shots that were somehow squeezed just beyond the reach of groping goalkeepers repeatedly prone to shock by the audacity of his precision.

Tight angles were not 'impossible' to Henry, they were just another challenge, another chance to expand his repertoire of platinum-plated chips, clips and volleys.

Henry wasn't merely the opposite of everything represented by the lumbering oxen model of English forward play over the previous 100 years. He was the sophisticated ballet dancer on studs that once and for all consigned the old-fashioned virtues of slog, sweat and blunt force to the game's lower echelons of mud, blood and brutality where they belonged.

Still, let's reel off some statistics and be duly awed. In 1998, Henry had already become France's top scorer during its World Cup-winning campaign, and after picking up a Euro 2000 winner's medal he eventually went on to become his country's all-time top scorer with 51 goals. At Arsenal, he won two league titles, three FA Cups, and captained the side to the runners-up spot in the 2006 Champions League, as close as his club has ever come to being crowned champions of Europe.

He bypassed the goalscoring records of club legends Cliff Bastin and Ian Wright to become the highest scorer in the club's history, and became the first and only player to finish off 100 goals at Highbury. In all Premier League appearances, he netted 175 goals in just 258 games, the kind of hit-rate largely unseen since Gerd Müller and Pelé, and

QUOTE

'I remember after one game a fan asked me to sign my autograph on his arm. I said, "Give me a piece of paper or something, because it'll wash out on your arm," but he said, "No, I'm going to get it tattooed over your signature." I find that a bit hard to understand because after all I'm just a footballer, I don't save people's lives or anything ... I have to say when he came back and showed me, I was agreeably surprised. But I'm sometimes a bit ill-at-ease with that sort of thing.'

Henry confirms to *FourFourTwo* magazine that he definitely left his mark.

only rendered more normal in recent times by the proficiency of Lionel Messi and Cristiano Ronaldo as they bully inferior, poorly paid Spanish defenders.

Another aspect to Henry's game at Arsenal was his creation of chances for team-mates. His lifting of the FWA and the PFA Footballer of the Year awards after he had scored 32 times in all competitions in the 2002-03 season were not just down to his goals. He had also tallied 23 assists, because his passing skills were no less effective than his shots.

And the downside? Like Ryan Giggs with his alleged philandering, Henry left it until late in his career to make enemies, long after he'd left Arsenal for Barcelona. Most of those enemies are in Ireland, after his double handball put the Irish out of 2010 World Cup qualifying contention during extra time of a play-off game in Paris. It's a painful sight for admirers to digest, that slow motion tip-tap of the hand that set up William Gallas for the goal that took the French to South Africa instead of the more deserving Emerald Islanders.

Why would a player of such skill and calibre need to get away with such a trick? In short, why would a man who has achieved so much stoop to what looked like base, blatant cheating? The answer – that a professional does whatever it takes for the good of the team – seems far less than satisfactory, especially in the case of such an exceptionally gifted star.

Perhaps Henry's unsporting act can be explained, if not excused, as an instinctive reaction in the heat of a crucial game, which at least allows us to taint him with a smudge of imperfection. The act will ultimately be overshadowed, of course, by a history of highlights that beg us to forgive a lone and peculiarly out-of-place flash of skulduggery, and to place him on a pedestal marked 'Most Valuable Premier League Striker'. *Va-va-voom* indeed.

IP

1 ERIC CANTONA

PREMIER LEAGUE DEBUT:
Leeds United v Wimbledon, 15 August 1992

PREMIER LEAGUE CLUBS:
Leeds United, Manchester United

PREMIER LEAGUE APPEARANCES/GOALS:

Leeds U	28	9
Manchester U	143	64
Total	171	73

PREMIER LEAGUE HONOURS:
4 (1992-93, 1993-94, 1995-96, 1996-97);
FWA Footballer of the Year 1996; PFA Player
of the Year 1994

COUNTRY:
France (born Marseille, 24 May 1966)

'What a friend we have in Jesus
He's a saviour from afar
What a friend we have in Jesus
And his name is Cantona ...'

– Manchester United fans' anthem
to 'Eric The King', 1992–date

IMAGINE A TIME 2000 years distant, when every glinting village spread across the scorched English countryside will cluster around a tall stone shrine. There, under the sign of the wooden crossbar, devotees in white turned-up collars will meet at the weekend to reflect nostalgically on a greater power before a flickering silver screen.

To understand how a man can become a god, we must first appreciate how a disgraced outcast arriving on these shores in 1992 was able to achieve the status of latter-day saint before the turn of the millennium – and this mostly through playing football. Having chucked a ball at a Gallic referee, subsequently called each member of the disciplinary panel an 'idiot', received an extended two-month ban before promptly 'retiring', the 25-year-old French international martyr was personally persuaded by Michel Platini to go on trial – quite literally – with Sheffield Wednesday, in an attempt to salvage his football career. Not a promising start; but history shows us there have been worse in rival scriptures.

In an attempt to unravel the myths and catechisms of Cantonaism, let's consider King Eric's initial sphere of influence. What does it take to become recognised as the greatest-ever player in the world's greatest football league? The Right Stuff? Undoubtedly. The X Factor? Necessarily. Magic dust? Of course, and infinitely more besides. Cantona's differentiating factor was one of reach. In order to transcend football, you need the power not just to affect a plastic sphere pinging around an oblong of lime-green grass, but to stir a recognition of majesty in the soul of a man – the soul of everyman – made receptive to beauty by recently downing five pints of fizzy lager.

Yes, of course you've got to have the miraculous moves, together with the vision and the big-match nerve to perform when lesser mortals are pulling at the back of your shirt, funnelling back to kick your ankles. A supernatural touch and wondrous efforts of willpower can win football matches, but a higher, inspirational quality is required to personally deliver five league titles in six seasons, especially to two northern clubs previously labouring without success for decades – and then you'll need one hell of an excuse for the second-place failure, especially if your eight months on the sidelines were self-inflicted, triggered by one of the tabloids' favourite sins – otherness, or violence – worse still, a rebellious refusal to kowtow to the self-appointed powers that be.

Turning your ramrod back on the trappings of fame will help, moving in to working-class suburbs of first Leeds and then Manchester to rub shoulders with your people. But take heed: even in an age of burgeoning celebrity obsession, when an armful of Maori tattoo is taken as an indicator of personality and an ability to read an autocue is synonymous with charisma, best check your shining, honourable aura is in full working order before pulling on the shirt of the one club that inspires more love and 91 times more hate than any other – and then, instantly setting about making them all-powerful.

While clinching the last First Division title for Leeds and the first-ever Premier League title for Manchester United – their first championship win after 26 years in the relative wilderness – your sublime grace on the football field must somehow begin to win over the jeering fans predisposed to partisan hatred, and forge a direct spiritual link with tens of thousands in the stands. And also win over the TV multitudes of every footballing colour and creed, not just with football party tricks and exotic petulance, but by spouting an opaque personal philosophy, by kung-fu kicking onlookers in the throat, and by retiring in your prime.

So, a tall order ....

Yet when every commentator, social and sheepskin, routinely refers to your escapades using biblical language and imagery, you will have surely ascended to an exalted state. You do not make a comeback but instead undergo a 'redemption' (therepublikofmancunia.com); a European semi-final exit isn't a disappointment, but a 'cross to bear' (manutd.com); Manchester artist Michael Browne depicts you as Christ in neo-Renaissance oils, and a TV advert (for Nike) pits you not against an opponent, but against the Devil.

You are King Eric, 'the Messiah of Manchester United' (the *Guardian*).

> ## THE MOMENT HE BECAME A LEGEND
>
> Returning from his eight-month kung-fu ban to face Liverpool at Old Trafford, he set up a goal after two minutes and then converted a penalty – before eventually leading United to another Double.

> ## WELL I NEVER ...
>
> What Palace fan Matthew Simmons really said to Eric. Simmons reported telling him: 'Off you go for an early bath.' But witness accounts differed: in fact, he lurched down 11 rows to pitch-side to shout: 'You f*cking cheating French c*nt. F*ck off to France, you mother*cker.'

And make no mistake, that isn't the kind of 'king' that elevates a chinless blueblood to majority landowner in an ermine hat. It's 'King' as in 'The King', a title previously bestowed on untouchable icons such as Elvis Presley and George Best.

From the very beginning, when Cantona first arrived in England, he was recognised as extremely special. 'We've never seen so many people at a training session,' marvelled Wednesday boss Trevor Francis as the tabloids lurked, hoping for calamity. However, unconvinced of the Frenchman's ability and temperament, Francis asked to extend the trial by another week, while Howard Wilkinson, boss of table-topping Leeds, proved less picky. Wednesday's First Division push ended in a respectable third-place finish, while neighbours Leeds were boosted by Cantona's goals and assists to lift the championship trophy.

Then, almost incredibly, Leeds allowed themselves to be gazumped in identical fashion, their totemic outsider whisked away by the ultimate enemy after just 28 league matches. Cantona counts himself lucky to have arrived at Manchester United as their promising kids reached maturity; but everyone else knows it was Fergie's fortune to find the perfect tutor for his Class of '92, each responding in kind to the other's brilliance, Cantona thriving on his first tastes of responsibility, captaincy and togetherness.

He scored 18 goals to help secure their second consecutive Premier League title in a Double; but it was in United's doomed 1994-95 season that Cantona's standing as a martyr, a man of the people and a shining example took its strangest leap forward. Red carded at Palace, a moronic fan unwisely decided to launch a familiar volley of abuse at Eric, who responded as a vigilante freedom fighter akin to the native American chief tattooed over his heart.

Asked on the BBC's *Football Focus* in 2011 about the highlight of his glittering career, he responded, 'When I did the kung-fu kick on the hooligan, because these kind of people don't have to be at the game. It's like a dream for some, you know, sometimes to kick these kind of people.

> QUOTE
>
> 'Collar up, back straight, chest stuck out, he glided into the arena as if he owned the f*cking place. Any arena, but nowhere more effectively than Old Trafford. This was his stage. He loved it, the crowd loved him.'
>
> Roy Keane pays tribute to his predecessor as United captain.

So I did it for [the fans]. So they are happy. It's a kind of freedom for them.'

At the time, he was famously more circumspect. 'When the seagulls follow the trawler, it's because they think sardines will be thrown into the sea. Thank you very much.' You can get a T-shirt inscribed with this scripture credited to the 'Book of Eric, 7:95'.

'That's life,' he now recalls. 'That's me. Take it or not. I'm strong enough to come back.'

With order and 'godlike' (*Daily Telegraph*) genius duly restored, even concentrated by guilt, another Double and a final Premier League title followed in short order. Exit Cantona from United and, even more shockingly, from football.

In the intervening years, our charismatic guru has led the French beach football team, and has acted wonderfully on stage and the big screen, made headlines by speaking out against the corrupting influence of money in football, or by praising the virtues of the International Brigade. Back in Manchester to film Ken Loach's *Looking For Eric*, he wept openly at his ecstatic reception by 50 United fans wearing Cantona masks – 'Like a troop of Knights Templars who have just seen Jesus stroll by, swigging from the Holy Grail,' reported the *Independent*.

'I'm so proud that they still like me,' Cantona said. 'United fans are so loyal. We are bonded forever. I am still in love with United.'

In 2010, his revolutionary attempt to bring down western capitalism by encouraging mass withdrawals to 'kill the criminal banks' sadly failed. His running for French presidency in 2012 was taken seriously until he admitted a ruse to publicise the shocking state of public housing. Currently installed as director of soccer at the New York Cosmos, it's thrilling to realise Cantona has one eye on the United job, despite his declared distaste at the intervention of the Glazer family.

'If there was ever one player, anywhere in the world, that was made for Manchester United, it was Cantona,' says apostle Alex Ferguson. 'He'd travelled to so many different countries; there's a bit of the gypsy in some people. He'd been searching all his life for somewhere he could look at and feel: this is my home. And when he came here, he knew: this is my place.'

And what about the mysterious power that's felt, just looking into Eric's eyes or shaking him by the hand?

'I know,' says the gruff, grounded Glaswegian. 'It's daunting.'

DH

CLUB LEGENDS

ARSENAL

Paul Merson

Arsenal Premier League appearances/goals: 160 28
Premier League honours: None

NO MATTER how many of Paul Merson's 99 goals for Arsenal stick in the memory of the club's supporters, the defining image of Merson as an Arsenal player remains that of a man with his tongue hanging out, pulling a face like a clown, and pumping his arms up and down as he previewed another drinking spree.

You can buy signed, framed photographs online of 'The Merse' in this infamous pose. It reached a live national audience for the first time in 1993, when Arsenal beat Sheffield Wednesday 2-1 in the League Cup final at Wembley. Merson scored the equaliser with a shot from outside the penalty area, and then set up the winner with a dashing run down the left, his cross turned into the path of Steve Morrow, who couldn't miss.

This beer-soaked talent sums up why Merson was the kind of flawed hero that fans defiantly adore. He loved to go for goal whenever he got the chance, and he excelled in running at defenders, beating them thanks to his speed more than any fancy footwork. And yet he was an alcoholic who was also addicted to both gambling and cocaine.

Merson's latest autobiography is titled *How Not To Be A Professional Footballer*. It remains an anti-guide to an almost vanished era of maverick on-field flair and off-field naughtiness. He was the cheeky scamp who scurried down the wing, the loveable, local tearaway indulged by the faithful even when he left for Middlesbrough because they doubled his money.

IP

Mark Bosnich

Aston Villa Premier League appearances/goals: 178 0
Premier League honours: None

ASTON VILLA have won only two trophies since the dawn of the Premier League: the League Cup in 1994 against Manchester United, and then again in 1996 against Leeds. The goalkeeper on both occasions was fop-haired Australian Mark Bosnich, a classically crazy number one whose off-duty antics were rivalled only by his flamboyance on the field.

Villa's win in 1994 came thanks to a remarkable string of Bosnich penalty saves in the semi-final, second-leg thriller against Tranmere Rovers. The teams had ended all square at 4-4 on aggregate, but three diving saves at Villa Park put his team through to Wembley and were testimony to his agility and athleticism. At the crucial moment in sudden death, he first dived to his right to stop Tranmere winning, and then to his left to secure victory. No guesswork, just great goalkeeping.

Bosnich hit the headlines a few years later at Chelsea when he was banned from the game for nine months after testing positive for cocaine. In retirement, he sought treatment for addiction, while a series of glamorous girlfriends and unstable relationships helped to keep him in the public eye.

After leaving Villa, he may have won an Intercontinental Cup medal with Manchester United and had issues with the coaching staff, a recurrent problem that helped curtail his stay at Chelsea, but in Birmingham 6 postal district, a highly distasteful Nazi salute to Tottenham Hotspur fans notwithstanding, he remains the man who made over 200 appearances for the club and was among the last in a Villa shirt to pick up a major honour.

IP

www.avfcforums.com
www.avillafan.com
www.astonvilla-mad.co.uk

Gjorgji Hristov

Barnsley Premier League appearances/goals: 23 4
Premier League honours: None

A LEGENDARY moment in a club's or a town's history may not
necessarily reflect well on either. Barnsley enjoyed one season in the
Premier League, and nothing much they did on the field that year was
the stuff of legends. But there comes a time when a provincial English
town collides with the big, wide world beyond – and things turn ugly.

In fact 'ugly' was the word that the Yorkshire side's £1.5 million club
record signing Gjorgji Hristov supposedly used to describe the local girls,
when he told a Belgrade-based sports magazine that he didn't much
fancy the local ladyfolk. What's more, they all drank too much. Welcome
to Barnsley, Gjorgji.

The local girls were suitably outraged, and town barmaids offered to
stage a beauty contest for the Macedonian striker to judge. One
'appalled' local girl conceded, however, that Barnsley girls 'do drink a lot
of beer because you come out one pub and fall into another'. Hristov
sportingly judged the contest, even though it turned out that all he had
said to the magazine was, 'I miss Macedonian women. They are the most
beautiful in the world.'

That year Barnsley signed a lot of foreign players for its Premier
League adventure and, according to German goalkeeper Lars Leese's
biography, *The Keeper of Dreams*, little effort was made to integrate
them, although he did reveal how one local maiden made Hristov feel
part of the community. As he walked down the street one Saturday
night, she yelled at him, 'You Macedonian bastard, do you like these?'
She then lifted her T-shirt to show him what a Yorkshire lass is made of.

IP

www.bfcst.org.uk
www.barnsley-mad.co.uk

Robbie Savage

Birmingham City Premier League appearances/goals: 82 11
Premier League honours: None

MUCH-TRAVELLED Welsh midfielder and ballroom dancer Robert Savage enjoyed a reputation for late tackles and yellow cards, but when he was on the receiving end of a double dose of violence at the feet and head of Aston Villa striker Dion Dublin in 2002-03, he wrote himself a place in Birmingham City folklore.

It was a tense derby at Villa Park on a late winter's night, with Birmingham already in possession of the bragging rights thanks to a 3-0 win earlier in the season. In the second half, with the score at 0-0, Savage was taken out by a Dublin tackle so late that only those with widescreen TV actually witnessed the offender come to a halt, everybody else was watching the *News at Ten*.

It was a heedless challenge that deserved a straight red. An outraged Savage stood up and there was a full and frank exchange of views with the striker, who responded by delivering a full-on Glasgow kiss. Referee Mark Halsey showed Dublin the red card.

Fully recovered, Savage set up Geoff Horsfield's clincher by slamming his head into a hoofed Villa clearance that perhaps unintentionally put his team-mate in the clear and the away fans went loopy. He had set the stage for Birmingham's 2-0 win and the first double over the Villains since the year of the Silver Jubilee.

Savage was the kind of player you loved to have on your team, and hated when he played against you. He was no Eric Cantona, but his very presence could provoke the kind of extreme reaction that turned a game. At St Andrews, that made him a dirty angel.

IP

www.bcfcforum.co.uk

BLACKBURN ROVERS
Tugay Kerimoglu

Blackburn Rovers Premier League appearances/goals: 233 10
Premier League honours: None

A HARD TACKLER who can pass like a dream; a positional master upon whom team-mates can rely for cover in any quarter of the field; a selfless worker with a shot like a bazooka. Over the years, he may not have grabbed as many headlines as some of his showier short-term accomplices, but Blackburn fans have little doubt about the identity of their club's most valuable servant this century.

When Graeme Souness paid Rangers £1.3 million for the services of Tugay (as he is affectionately and simply known) in 2001, there was only a trademark headband to hint that this 31-year-old Galatasaray veteran would be anything other than a fill-gap.

But Tugay did more than snatch up the questionable headwear of Rovers legend Colin Hendry, he also played with a similar pride and determination. Gheorghe Hagi (the so-called 'Maradona of the Carpathians') had been right to label him one of the finest ball-playing midfielders in Europe – and not just among those nursing a 40-a-day fag habit.

For a player who scored so few goals in eight seasons, he has an astonishing CV of rocket strikes, every one seemingly from outside the area. But one beauty stands out in the memory: a sweetly timed, swerving volley direct from a corner that flew over the D, on to Tugay's boot and past Tony Warner in the Fulham net like an Exocet.

'I just wish he was twenty-five, not thirty-five,' said Tugay's boss Mark Hughes on that day in August 2005, 'because he is a fantastic guy, a great ambassador for himself and his country and the game of football.' And then he retracted his time-travel wish, having worked out that, '[Actually], if he was ten years younger, [he would not be at Blackburn] he'd be wearing a Barcelona shirt.'

DH

www.brfcs.co.uk
www.roverstalk.com

BLACKPOOL
Charlie Adam

Blackpool Premier League appearances/goals: 35 12
Premier League honours: None

A SQUAT, industrious midfielder with the silky touch of a high-class escort, the rocket shot of a backyard scientist and the eyebrow-raising passing skills of Ayrton Senna, Charlie Adam threw the entire football industry into disarray when he exploded into Premier League action in Ian Holloway's side of comedy northern seaside no-hopers back in 2010.

According to the expert pundits, the amusingly Tango-clad big-league debutants wouldn't get a single kick during the whole season against big-money, big-wallet, big-ground, big-rep opposition. However, the broadsheets' sports supplements' frustrated poets and novelists were quickly forced to revise their lengthy draft essays on the subject of class and the Golden Mile.

Just who was this large-bottomed apparent veteran who provided the 'Seasiders' with such a Titanic midfield motor, bursts of unexpected jet-ski speed and all-round crow's nest vision? 'He must be forty if he's a day! What's that? Used to play for Rangers in the Scottish park leagues? No wonder we've never heard of him! Is he by any chance related to Peter Reid, Everton's notoriously wide-beamed playmaker of old? Or possibly John Robertson, Cloughie's long-time flank weapon who allegedly trained on sixty Park Drive and chip butties well into his fifties?'

It's true, there was something magnificently old-fashioned about a Scottish player in English football – let alone one who could pull strings and run a top-tier football match like a starchy-aproned nanny in charge of a crèche of 21 sleepy toddlers. Shame he then went and signed for Liverpool, ruining everything for many nostalgic and romantic fans.

DH

BOLTON WANDERERS
Jussi Jaaskelainen

Bolton Wanderers Premier League appearances/goals: 379 0
Premier League honours: None

IN THE CASH-crazed, fast-churn whirl of the Premier League's booming business, there's little call to consider alternative methods of achieving results via stealth or shrewdness, via wise investment or good old-fashioned hard work. Money talks.

There's no official recognition of loyalty or consistency, so Jussi Jaaskelainen is unlikely to pick up a Lifetime Achievement Award from anyone outside of Bolton to go with his Barclaycard Goalie of the Year gong for 2002. But should football's virtual economics ever swing back towards reality, what price Colin Todd picking up a gold-plated Biro commemorating the best value-for-money signing ever made in Premier League history?

Back in 1997, Todd snared the Trotters' colossus from Finnish club Vaasan Palloseura for just £100,000. And Jaaskelainen stayed between the sticks for Bolton until the summer of 2012 – a massive presence, a hardy annual match-winner, a vain target for less imaginative investors. He eventually made 474 appearances in all competitions for the club, and during the 2011–12 season was the longest-serving foreign player in the top division, though relegation and post-season transfer to West Ham brought that run to an end. In 2009, he even quit international football on 56 caps for Finland to concentrate on prolonging his career at Bolton. He intends to settle in Bolton, the birthplace of his three sons, when he retires.

Jaaskelainen's greatest Premier League moment? That came away at local rivals Blackburn Rovers in October 2006, with Bolton 1-0 up and desperately running down the clock. Already known for saving Ruud van Nistelrooy's first Premier League penalty, he first stopped a Benni McCarthy spot-kick and then, after another two minutes' barrage, dived to his left to keep out another 12-yard effort by Jason Roberts. Forget the Lifetime Achievement Award, maybe they should just make him Mayor of Bolton.

DH

David Wetherall

Bradford City Premier League appearances/goals: **56 3**
Premier League honours: **None**

ALTHOUGH BRADFORD City fans won't thank us for pointing it out, over the years they have signed several big-name players from noisy neighbours Leeds United, who have proven to be some way past their best – the players and the club, as it happens: Paul Reaney, David Harvey, Trevor Cherry, Terry Yorath and, sadly, Lee Sharpe.

So it was with some trepidation that City fans looked forward to 1999-00, their debut season in the Premier League – especially when boss Paul Jewell topped off his *Dad's Army* acquisitions with the former Leeds centre-half David Wetherall (and full-back Gunnar Halle thrown in for good measure).

At 28, the one-time chemistry first-class honours graduate ('If you handed me one of my old textbooks, I probably wouldn't be able to understand a single word of it. I've forgotten absolutely everything I ever knew about chemistry and I've got no regrets; no way. No job is as enjoyable as being a footballer') had recently lost his place at Leeds but he still cost a club record £1.4 million.

It wasn't until the eighth game of the season that City picked up their second win, prompting former talkSPORT and Sky pundit Rodney Marsh to promise to shave off all his hair at Valley Parade if they managed to avoid the drop. However, when the going gets tough ... Wetherall's defensive partnership with Andy O'Brien began to shape up, and a nine-match unbeaten home run soon ensued.

With relegation still looming in their final game, at home to Liverpool, Wetherall headed home a perfect Halle free-kick early on, then retreated to help cling on – becoming the only man to play every minute of every game in that Premier League season. Bradford stayed up, and rent-a-mouth Rod's barnet was soon history.

DH

www.claretandbanter.co.uk

Dave Burnley

Burnley Premier League appearances (fan): 38
Premier League honours: None

'OH, I KNOW all about you,' said the prime minister. Dave Burnley (name changed by deed poll in 1976) had just been introduced to Tony Blair by, and was guest of, Number 10's director of communications and fellow Turf Moor devotee Alastair Campbell. There was a hint of tremulous disbelief in Blair's voice as he came face to face with a man Campbell had previously only spoken about in hushed tones – a man with a single-minded determination that even the famously obsessive spin doctor found remarkable.

Unable to drive and born 75 miles away in north Staffordshire, where he still lives, Mr Burnley has not missed a Burnley game home or away since 1974 and has had over 100 jobs and 75 different occupations from cleaning toilets to working in a bank in an attempt to provide the necessary flexibility to work around the fixtures and finance his *raison d'être*. He has travelled 180,000 miles to watch them at Turf Moor and a further 300,000 to watch them away. He estimates it has cost him over £90,000.

He has been beaten up over 20 times, usually in Wales, and in Burnley's Premier League season notched up his 15,050th pub ('Football and beer has kept me on the straight and narrow'). He has missed both his sisters' weddings (most recently to watch his team lose 5-0 at Spurs in September 2009), but, incredibly, in a succession of foredoomed relationships, found time to father a child, a daughter he named Clarette in honour of the team's colours. Almost inevitably, the self-styled 'extreme fan' lives with his elderly mother.

Doubtless Burnley 'til he dies, when he actually manages to shuffle off this mortal coil, he has asked to be placed in his seat on the Longside at Turf Moor for one last game although the club are believed to have health and safety reservations.

BB

CHARLTON ATHLETIC
Alan Curbishley

Charlton Athletic Premier League appearances (manager): 265
Premier League honours: None

JUST AS Curbishley's career as a once prodigious, latterly wily up-and-downer was winding down as player-coach during his second spell with Charlton Athletic, he was promoted and entrusted to continue his work as joint-manager with Steve Gritt – far exceeding his brief when he led the long-homeless Addicks back to The Valley.

This alone would have ensured a place on the club's eternal Roll of Honour, but when the managerial post was made his own in 1995, it transpired that the man known to the fans as 'Curbs' had hardly even started. Over a 16-year period since his return as a player, he guided Charlton into the Premier League not once but twice, and succeeded in establishing what had been a lowly Second Division club into one with Europe in their sights.

What's more, he did so on a shoestring budget, bringing through kids he'd coached himself – Scott Parker, Richard Rufus, Luke Young – often selling them on at a profit and investing the cash in talent he was able to inspire to new career highs – Chris Powell, Darren Bent, Clive Mendonca.

The dramatic high point of the Curbishley years was undoubtedly one of the greatest football games of the Premier League era, perfectly demonstrating how much it means to reach the greatest league of all. Having fallen in the play-off final the previous season, the Addicks faced Sunderland at Wembley at the end of 1997–98.

With five minutes to go in a mesmerising, ding-dong battle, they trailed 3-2 before Rufus took it to extra time with his first career goal. At full time the sides were locked together at 4-4, Charlton proceeding to their great Premier League adventure via a cathartic 7-6 penalty victory that 'Curbs' could hardly bear to watch.

DH

Roberto Di Matteo

Chelsea Premier League appearances/goals: 119 15
Chelsea Premier League appearances (manager): 11
Premier League honours: None

EVEN BEFORE the drama of Chelsea's 2012 Champions League title (not to mention the FA Cup a fortnight before), Di Matteo was always going to be the front-runner in this category – just ahead of Dennis Wise and Claude Makelele. He was a big-game player, a selfless midfield dynamo that could score when absolutely necessary – cometh the hour, cometh the man – and, in much the same way he stepped into the breach after the dismissal of André Villas-Boas.

Signed for £4.2 million by Ruud Gullit for Chelsea in 1996, he scored on his debut as Chelsea cranked up their bid for world domination. The next year he scored just 42 seconds after kick-off in the FA Cup final against Middlesbrough with a bespoke 30-yarder – it was the fastest-ever goal in an FA Cup final at the time and, according to Boro fan Bob Mortimer, 'the little f*cker killed the game'. In 1998, he scored again in the League Cup final before also playing in the successful European Cup-Winners' Cup final.

Injured for most of the following season, he returned to score the winner in the 2000 FA Cup final, the last one at the old Wembley. No wonder he said, 'It's a shame they're tearing the old place down – it has been a very lucky ground for me.' His career was curtailed by injury but his managerial career is in the ascendancy – he has already achieved in two months what Arsène Wenger has been chasing for 16 years at Arsenal.

A loner rather than a gregarious man, even Di Matteo was moved by the Champions League success. Asked straight after the match if he wanted the job full time, he dodged the question by answering, 'I'm going to have a big party tonight with the big trophy with the big ears.' That's no way to talk about the boss, but Abramovich will be familiar with Napoleon's dictum: 'I have plenty of clever generals but just give me a lucky one.' And, as if to prove the point, he awarded the little Italian a two-year contract in June 2012.

BB

www.cfcnet.co.uk
www.chelseafc.com

Steve Ogrizovic

Coventry City Premier League appearances/goals: 191 0
Premier League honours: None

STEADY, BIG-HANDED Steve 'Oggy' Ogrizovic had already won two European Cups by the time he signed with Coventry City, but as a reserve keeper on the Liverpool bench. His Liverpool appearances can be counted on one hand, but he made up for lost playing time by guarding Coventry's net just over 600 times in 16 years.

That alone is not the reason why Ogrizovic is a Coventry legend. Neither is it his winner's medal in City's only ever major triumph, the 1987 FA Cup final. It's not even his astonishing strike direct from a goal-kick in a mid-1980s league game against Sheffield Wednesday, or even his spectacularly malformed nose. Actually, it was a single save against his old club Liverpool, which effectively kept his side in the top flight.

Coventry's annual relegation struggle was a staple feature of the Premier League's early years. When Liverpool came to Highfield Road in April 1996, they still had a chance of winning the title. The Sky Blues, of course, were battling against the drop. Noel Whelan gave the home side an early lead, and they held on to it deep into injury time against an uncharacteristically toothless Liverpool attack.

But then ravenous young Scouse striker Robbie Fowler was clean through on goal, with only 'Oggy' standing between him and a precious point. The shot was hard, but the keeper was quickly off his line and equal to it. Coventry finished the season on 38 points, as did Southampton and, eventually relegated, Manchester City with an inferior goal difference to both teams.

As so often in the 1990s, Ogrizovic was the thin sky blue line between City and the second tier.

IP

www.skybluestalk.co.uk

CRYSTAL PALACE

Aki Riihilahti

Crystal Palace Premier League appearances/goals: 32 4
Premier League honours: None

ALL FANS LOVE a hard-working defensive midfielder who leaves it all out
on the pitch, maybe even more than the thrilling winger or the prolific
striker. Not because they enjoy watching him more, or think he's a better
player, but because they can relate to him. They admire the fact he
makes up for a lack of pure skill with a surplus of sweat, always slogging
for the badge.

That's the kind of player that Crystal Palace fans treasured in Finnish
journeyman Aki Riihilahti, but it's not the real reason that he's a legend.
Riihilahti gains that status by sheer force of personality. In an age when
footballers are pressurised to never say anything of interest to the press,
Riihilahti's website columns came to stand out as a lighthouse of free-
thinking philosophy.

The occasionally fractured nature of Riihilahti's English added to the
quirky charm of his world view. 'Do I exist if I don't always play fluent
football?' he would ask one week. 'Lot of entertainment values are
sacrificed in the altar of required points tally,' he mused as Palace
scrapped their way through a relegation battle. Riihilahti compared TV-
dictated morning kick-offs to 'celebrating Christmas in October'.
Offended by the attitude of England fans towards their own team, he
asked, 'Why are you pissing into your own tent? Many of you seem to
voluntarily want to put celery into your own food.'

A Finnish flag emblazoned with his name was posted behind one of
the goals at Selhurst Park for the whole of the 2004-05 Premier League
season. And one of the ten things that the Finnish sage learnt about
playing in the Premier League? 'You can sometimes get Molton Brown
body wash with your bath. In the Championship, you were lucky to get
warm water and a toilet that didn't smell like last month's Chinese
takeaway.' He remains a cult original.

IP

www.holmesdale.net

DERBY COUNTY
Stefano Eranio

Derby County Premier League appearances/goals: 95 7
Premier League honours: None

WITH 20 ITALIAN international appearances under his belt, three league titles with AC Milan and extensive previous in the rarefied atmosphere of Champions League finals, there was never any doubting Eranio's class. Here was a slick, turbo-charged Bugatti wheeled direct into the centre circle of Derby County's brand-new Pride Park. The question was why the 30-year-old had left it so late to make a name for himself in English football and whether he could hack it physically in the hurly-burly of the Premier League.

Over the course of four years and 95 Premier League games with the Rams, fans were sent into ecstasies by Eranio's vision and passing, coupled with a preternatural ability to materialise in the right place at the right time. Part of a great side that included other quality imports Igor Stimac, Francesco Baiano and Paulo Wanchope, Stefano delayed hanging up his boots at the end of the 2000-01 season, responding to Jim Smith's pleas to stay on, and only retired when Smith was sacked.

The first goal he scored for Derby, against Barnsley in August 1997, made instant history. After an abandoned game and two defeats, the nervy Rams were struggling to get off the mark at the new ground. When debut boy Francesco Baiano was brought down in the box, he grabbed the ball but his penalty was saved. Granted a reprieve due to the goalkeeper moving before the ball had been struck, Eranio took responsibility to become the first to hit the back of the net at Pride Park, securing their first home points – on the way to a respectable ninth spot.

Eranio is now back at AC Milan, sharing his magic with the Under-15s.

DH

Tim Cahill

Everton Premier League appearances/goals: 226 56
Premier League honours: None

HOW COULD someone so small, who has scored so many goals with his head, not become a club legend? That's the question. The simple answer is, stay calm. He is. It was between him and his manager, David Moyes, but as one Everton fan put it: 'Who would you rather sit next to on a Trans-Atlantic flight?

A gritty, archetypal pocket battleship used to playing as an attacking midfielder, the 5ft 10in tall Australian stepped up to play as an unlikely striker when all four of Everton's first-choice strikers were ruled out through injury at the end of 2008. Cahill duly scored winning goals to secure 1-0 victories away at both Middlesbrough and Manchester City. All very good, but better was to come the following month at Anfield.

Everton had already lost the first Merseyside derby that season, going down 2-0 at Goodison Park thanks to an on-fire Fernando Torres. And so when Steven Gerrard put Liverpool ahead midway through the second half with a low, long-range effort, it looked as though a taunt-provoking clean sweep would blot the blue side of Stanley Park's record books for that league campaign.

With four minutes left, however, Mikel Arteta delivered a flat, hard free-kick from the left side of the penalty area, and Cahill stooped to divert a cheeky, close-range header into the Liverpool net in front of his own fans. Cahill clenched his club badge between his teeth and ran to the corner flag to deliver his trademark 'boxing' celebration. The score remained 1-1 and, best of all, Liverpool were prevented from going top of the league.

IP

www.grandoldteam.com

Clint Dempsey

Fulham Premier League appearances/goals: 184 50
Premier League honours: None

JUST AS A woman often has to deliver a 150 per cent performance to prove herself in a man's world, so an American player earning his cash in England has to go a few extra yards to stand out in the old country, and show that the Yanks can play with their feet as well as their hands. Few US players, let alone Premier League stars, grew up in a Texas trailer park, but Fulham's Clint Dempsey has run those extra yards and more.

'The Deuce' is a versatile international who can play either as a wide or central attacking midfielder, or as an all-out striker, and has not only become the leading all-time US scorer in the Premier League, he was the first to score a hat-trick. In truth, he had already won over the Craven Cottage regulars long before his three-goal outing against Newcastle in late 2011, and even before his sweet chip that took Fulham past Juventus on their way to the 2010 Europa League final.

In fact, it was Dempsey's very first goal for Fulham that confirmed his special spot in West London football history. Having moved from Major League Soccer at the start of 2007 for £2.5 million, he found himself in a struggling side which, by the time it faced Liverpool at home in the penultimate game of the season, had not won for three months, and was staring relegation in the face.

Payback came when Dempsey created and scored the only goal of a 1-0 win, running at the Liverpool back line before playing a neat one-two with Liam Rosenior and dragging the ball into the corner of the net. The sun-soaked fans went, as his countrymen might put it, 'nuts' and, despite a loss the following week, Fulham stayed up by one point.

IP

Phil Brown

Hull City Premier League appearances (manager): 67
Premier League honours: None

FOR ALL HIS eccentric outbursts, the serial charges of misconduct, and his largely unsuccessful record as a football manager, fired by three clubs, Phil Brown will be idolised by Hull City fans for one thing above all – he's the only manager in the club's history to have taken them into the top flight, from a second-tier relegation place to charging shoulders with the elite. He even managed to keep them there for a second season.

In that respect, the game that made Brown a legend was the Championship promotion play-off win over Bristol City at Wembley in May 2008, but it may be the game a year later for which the perma-bronzed Brown will best be remembered.

Hull's first season in the Premier League was over, and even though they had just lost 1-0 at home to Manchester United, Brown was in a chirpy mood because Newcastle United, losers at Aston Villa, had gone down instead. How best to mark such a momentous day?

Naturally, Brown took to the field with a microphone and began to wail out a bastardised version of the Beach Boys' 'Sloop John B': 'I don't want to go home/ I don't want to go home/ This is the best trip I've ever been on ...' He sang, surrounded by photographers and sounding like Shane MacGowan on a particularly harrowing bender.

You could call it embarrassing, tuneless and inappropriate, but at the very least it shows Brown in all his glory – full of himself and craving attention, yes, but above all oozing passion for a club he'd taken to heights rarely enjoyed by provincial clubs in the big-time, big-city age of the Premier League.

IP

www.hullcityindependent.net
www.hullcity-mad.co.uk

Matt Holland

Ipswich Town Premier League appearances/goals: 76 6
Premier League honours: None

FELLOW IPSWICH legends Alan Brazil (Scotland) and modern-day 'Tractor Boy' Jason Scotland (Trinidad & Tobago). Both familiar names to any Suffolk-based pub quiz addict, along with the likes of Joe Jordan (Scotland), Mike England (Wales) and, of course, Matt Holland (Republic of Ireland). But in Ipswich the enthusiasm for the Irish up-and-down ball-player runs far deeper than an accident of either name or of birth. The long-time skipper is remembered as a model of loyalty, consistency and drive.

In these namby-pamby days of squad rotation, cheap red cards (cf. anybody tackling a United player at Old Trafford) and potential hospitalisation for minor abrasions, it isn't rare to find a player soldiering through six complete campaigns. It's impossible. Even the inspiration that is Matt Holland had to have one match-day off in the six years from 1997-2003 – although, to be fair, he was playing for his international team of choice. As for loyalty, Matt turned down a £4.5 million move to Aston Villa after Town were relegated in 2002, before moving on to Charlton and yet another ever-present season.

Signed from Bournemouth for £800,000 in 1995, Holland resumed his skipper's role at Portman Road and led Ipswich via the play-offs into the PL (Premier League or Promised Land, you decide) – and then straight into Europe with a fifth-place finish. While his glam career moment was a 25-yard screamer against Cameroon in the 2002 World Cup, Matt himself remembers that first top-flight season's 5-0 'Demolition Derby' against Norwich as the game that undoubtedly sold the most commemorative videos.

'We hit the ground running,' he told the local *Green 'Un.* 'And I don't think Norwich could believe what was happening. The fans at the time had some bad derby memories, so it was great to do something that made up for it. It was just a great all-round performance and a perfect day.'

DH

www.TWTD.co.uk

LEEDS UNITED

Lucas Radebe

Leeds United Premier League appearances/goals: 197 0
Premier League honours: None

THIRTY YEARS ago, it would have been unthinkable for the massed ranks of Leeds United fans to hold up a black South African player as representative of everything they loved about their club. Such was the depth of engrained racism on the Elland Road terraces back in the 1970s and 1980s – and, despite many fans' nostalgic quibbles about the influx of cash and 'family atmosphere' football, there's no denying the power of the Premier League's great clean-up act.

'People look at me in the street and say "footballer" not realising I am human as well,' Radebe comments on the modern game's obsession with celebrity. 'People think we are invincible. They say: "You live a great life. Can I touch you?" But things that happen to them happen to me.' It is the overbearing truth of the statement, together with the grounded humanity of Radebe's story, that helped make the player a Leeds idol, and a nonsense of blind bigotry. No less than Nelson Mandela called him 'my hero'.

Radebe arrived in Leeds in 1994, having previously been shot in the street when he had been considering leaving the Kaizer Chiefs. Throughout the years of Leeds' early Premier League success, 'The Chief' was a huge presence in the backline, turning down moves to Manchester United and AC Milan. Later, injury saw whole seasons pass Radebe by, while the tragic loss of his wife Feziwe, aged just 34, left him to bring up two kids alone.

Leeds band the Kaiser Chiefs, a local brewery's Radebeer and club mascot 'Lucas The Kop Cat' were all named in his considerable honour. Radebe's greatest match at Elland Road? His heartbreaking 2005 testimonial at the end of his 11 years' service, which was attended by 37,886 fans.

DH

motforum.com
www.leedsunited-mad.co.uk

Muzzy Izzet

Leicester City Premier League appearances/goals: 222 33
Premier League honours: None

PICKED UP FOR just £800,000 from Chelsea when Glenn Hoddle and Ruud Gullit were too busy signing megastars to notice the East End kid in the reserves, Muzzy Izzet's special trick was arriving in the box at just the right time to crack home a cross. He played for Leicester for eight years up until 2004, and even made a World Cup squad with Turkey, but it was his contribution on 19 October 1998 that made all that possible.

Leicester City might have beaten Leeds away in their previous game, but now the Yorkshire giants were threatening to steal away from the Foxes a commodity infinitely more precious than three points. It looked like Martin O'Neill, the club's wilful, eccentric inspiration, was on his way to replace George Graham. 'DON'T GO MARTIN' pleaded the *Leicester Mercury* placards for the night match against Spurs.

Having led the club to the Premier League in 1996, won the League Cup and anchored his boys in the top half of the table, it now looked to be slipping away. Meetings with chairman John Elsom were taking place before and after the match, which seemed almost incidental to City's plight – until O'Neill emerged from the tunnel to a tumultuous welcome.

Behind to a Les Ferdinand strike early on, O'Neill's canny, underrated side equalised through Emile Heskey to cue up a spectacular decider – in every sense – in the 85th minute. A free-kick was acrobatically hoofed out of danger by Sol Campbell but looped up only to fall on Izzet's deadly right boot 25 yards from goal.

Kaboom. Top left corner. He charges, arms pumping, towards the manager, who is already in mid-air ... By the time O'Neill lands, he has decided to stay.

DH

www.foxestalk.co.uk
www.talkingballs.co.uk

Jamie Carragher

Liverpool Premier League appearances/goals: **484 3**
Premier League honours: **None**

THAT RARE case of a local-born, one-club player, Liverpool's Jamie Carragher actually grew up as an Everton fan (like Fowler, Owen and McManaman), but has nonetheless racked up close to 700 appearances for the red side of the city. There's been barely a minute in all of those games where he's looked anything less than fully committed.

He may have scored more own goals than actual goals (including a brace into his own net against Manchester United at Anfield), but that reflects Carragher's purpose on the pitch, which is to be back in place defending his lines. His loyalty and love for the club alone would already render him a legend, but his most iconic performance came in one of Liverpool's most famous triumphs.

Late in the second half of the 2005 Champions League final against AC Milan, with a tiring Liverpool having come from 3-0 down to level at 3-3, it was Carragher who held things together at the back with two heroic tackles. The first came with 12 minutes left, when he prevented the Brazilian Kaka from converting a Hernan Crespo cross. The second came eight minutes later when he lunged in to stop well-placed Ukrainian striker Andriy Shevchenko from winning the game for the Italian side.

Liverpool hung on through extra time, when Carragher played through severe cramps, and won on penalties. It seems only fitting that the defender should have anchored their greatest result in the past two decades. Asked that same year if he wouldn't want to move to a bigger club, a bemused Carragher replied, 'Who's bigger than Liverpool?'

IP

www.thisisanfield.com

MANCHESTER CITY
Shaun Goater

Manchester City Premier League appearances/goals: 52 13
Premier League honours: None

BERMUDAN STRIKER Goater was already revered by Manchester City fans before their 2002-03 return to the Premier League, having proven his goalscoring chops across three divisions in City's up-and-down era around the turn of the millennium. But his final campaign for the club cemented his place in City folklore, thanks to his goals against the champions-in-waiting from across the city.

'The Goat' scored his 99th and 100th goals for the sky blue two-thirds of Manchester in the final ever derby at Maine Road. With the score at 1-1, he dispossessed Gary Neville close to the touchline in the United penalty area, and then slotted home a tidy finish past Fabien Barthez from a tight angle. The camera caught a shell-shocked Neville attempting to spit, but merely dribbling saliva all over his shirt.

Just to finish things off, Goater reached his century in the second half with a cute lob over the French keeper to make the final score 3-1, but he still wasn't finished with United.

In a rare example of an astute Kevin Keegan tactical move, Goater and Ali Benarbia came on as substitutes in the return match at Old Trafford with five minutes left and City 1-0 down. Benarbia's first touch was a free-kick to Shaun Wright-Phillips, while Goater's first touch – nine seconds after entering the field of play – was to head home Wright-Phillips's cross for the equaliser.

Best of all for City fans? It was Manchester United who'd brought Goater to England and signed him in the first place, but he never made the first team before moving on to more fruitful fields.

IP

www.mancityfans.net
www.bluemoon-mcfc.co.uk

MANCHESTER UNITED
Gary Neville

Manchester United Premier League appearances/goals: 400 5
Premier League honours: 8 (1995-96, 1996-97, 1998-99, 1999-00,
   2000-01, 2002-03, 2006-07, 2008-09)

IT IS IMPOSSIBLE to imagine Gary Neville in anything other than a
United shirt. A solid right-back with a wicked cross, a serially capped
international, as well as being club captain for five years, you might say
that Gary Neville's status as a club legend was steadily built over time.
But nothing he did with his feet in a 20-year career with United will
have endeared him as much to the Stretford End as the day he stuck one
to Liverpool fans.

It was in early 2006, and United were having a tough time of it at
home to one of their greatest rivals, creating little and defending
desperately, sensing that a point would be a lucky return. They were
extremely fortunate to steal the game at its death thanks to a Rio
Ferdinand header.

Lucky or not, there was no restraint to United's celebrations. Neville
in particular, who had been taunted throughout the game by chants from
the away support, was in no mood to be gracious, and let his joy be
known directly in front of the stunned Scousers. Although his roars and
gestures brought him a £5000 fine for misconduct, every true fan knew
that he was only showing what they all felt, and would have gladly done
in his position.

'The stick is part of the game,' reasoned Neville. 'One week you take it
on the chin, the next you give it out. I have to put up with Liverpool
fans singing plenty of songs about me, none of them tasteful, and I
struggle to believe that I have caused them any grave offence with an
exuberant celebration.'

You can bet most United fans hoped that he had.

IP

MIDDLESBROUGH
Steve Gibson

Middlesbrough Premier League appearances (owner): 456
Premier League honours: None

IT'S TEMPTING to wonder whether any of the Premier League's more celebrated/ infamous chairmen have ever spent time wondering about their image in the eyes of the fans. All that cash burned, and nary a word of thanks from the hoi-polloi ...

Well, maybe they should rethink, reform, and take a leaf from the book of Steve Gibson at Middlesbrough – the only Premier League chairman whose name is chanted around the smart new arena he effectively built with his bare hands, driven by the insane passion of a genuine fan that any one of us would recognise (and feats we would quite possibly repeat, if we earned more than, ooh, 10 or 20 million quid a year).

When he was a kid, Gibson used to go to Ayresome Park with mate Chris Kamara off the Park End Estate. For the uninitiated, that's gritty grassroots for you. By 1986, the Boro likely lad was prospering in chemical haulage, and single-handedly saved the club from bankruptcy. He's supported managers from Bryan Robson to Gareth Southgate with more than money – with his very soul.

His greatest moment in the spotlight came in 2004 when he was granted the Freedom of Middlesbrough after the club broke their century-long trophy duck (the League Cup against Bolton) – next stop the UEFA Cup final in 2006.

Boro may have been languishing in the second tier in 2012, but Gibson could still do no wrong, pleading with the fans to forgive his mistake in firing Gareth Southgate, and to back the club in hard economic times: 'We are here because of the fans, they are everything. There is no point having a club if we don't have the fans.' Nice soundbite, perhaps. The difference on this occasion is that not only is it true and he means it, but he actually gets it. Can you say that about the chairman of your club? Didn't think so.

DH

www.oneboro.co.uk

Nolberto Solano

Newcastle United Premier League appearances/goals: **230 37**
Premier League honours: **None**

IT WAS ALMOST Christmas Eve, babe, in the drunk tank some know as Elland Road. In 2001, Newcastle and Leeds United were the kind of teams that nurtured title pretensions. On a snowy, blowy evening, they produced a pre-Christmas cracker that warmed up even the bare-chested Geordies in the away end, and it was the gifted Nolberto Solano – the Premier League's first-ever trumpet-playing Peruvian – who placed the final fairy on the tree.

Newcastle had come back from 3-1 down in a pulsating game that had seen Leeds striker Mark Viduka break the nose, and then almost the leg, of Newcastle's Nikos Dabizas. Viduka inexplicably escaped with a yellow card, then put Leeds 2-1 in front, followed by an Ian Harte strike. But by the 90th minute Newcastle had levelled thanks to local lads Robbie Elliott and Alan Shearer.

Solano had been causing Leeds trouble all night with his cheeky back-heels and trademark dead-ball trickery, but it was a typical piece of industrious counter-attacking that saw him speed down the right wing with just seconds left on the clock. Kieron Dyer fed him a sinewy pass, Solano out-ran the fallible Harte, and then icily finished from a tough angle past Nigel Martyn to seal the 4-3 win.

This provoked his 69-year-old manager Bobby Robson into an impromptu jig on the touchline but, that moment aside, he was not a huge fan of luxury players and sold Solano to Aston Villa two years later. With Robson gone, the 'adopted Geordie' from the Pacific Coast returned for a second spell after just 18 months, to a Toon that truly appreciated his blend of modesty, diligence and pure South American skill.

IP

www.newcastleunited-mad.co.uk

NORWICH CITY

Paul Lambert

Norwich City Premier League appearances (manager): 38
Premier League honours: None

'**PAUL WAS** our number one choice,' said City's triumphant chief executive David McNally in 2009. 'It's all about ability, experience, track record, drive, hunger, commitment and [a] winning mentality.' The Norwich fans should have known all about his winning mentality, as his Colchester United team had routed them 7-1 in the game that prompted the dismissal of manager Bryan Gunn.

Lambert was in charge for the next City game, but most fans believed that to be a knee-jerk and unambitious appointment of a low-profile manager. That was, of course, to ignore 40 Scottish caps, sundry titles and cups with Celtic, and even a match-winning midfield role for Borussia Dortmund in the 1997 Champions League final. They were similarly dismissive of his lower-league coaching successes with Wycombe and Colchester. 'More bloody dross' was the reaction of one fan that lingers in cyberspace.

In retrospect, it was promising how Lambert had returned to Germany to take his coaching badges; how he'd fallen under the influence of Martin O'Neill at Celtic and followed in his footsteps at Wycombe. Promotion to the Championship for the Canaries was duly achieved, immediately followed by deliverance to the Premier League – albeit as apparent no-hopers ('MISSION IMPOSSIBLE TO KEEP NEW BOYS UP' – *Daily Star*).

And so to Lambert's greatest moment as Norwich boss: the entire 2011-12 season, during which his tactical thinking and man-motivation made up for absent billions. A team without stars ran for each other and passed in style. It was like watching Blackpool, without the final implosion. With Grant Holt's goals to the fore, they competed on every level for drive, commitment and positive thinking. And to think we ever doubted.

Can he now bring the same 'ability, experience, track record, drive, hunger, commitment and [a] winning mentality' to Aston Villa? Time will tell.

DH

Steve Stone

Nottingham Forest Premier League appearances/goals: 118 16
Premier League honours: None

'BULLDOG'S' TEN years in a Forest shirt witnessed a quantum leap in expectations and stature for the speedy, snappy Geordie winger. He made the transition from being an injury-prone teenager playing centre-midfield in Cloughie's youth team, via hundreds of games terrorising and tormenting various full-backs for the Forest first team, to England recognition and an eventual £5.5 million move to Aston Villa when relegation arrived at the City Ground in 1999.

Before he even made his first-team debut, Stone had broken a leg on three occasions, but fought back and blossomed into hyperactive prominence in Frank Clark's promotion-winning side of 1993-94, tearing down the wing to deliver ammunition and tackling back like a man possessed. In their first season back in the Premier League, Forest finished third and qualified for the UEFA Cup – Stone was the beating heart of the side.

As his hair quickly thinned, Steve laboured for Forest like a young Samson in reverse, deservedly winning a place in Terry Venables' England squad for Euro 96, after which the muscular, bustling flanker's coiffure seemed to give up the ghost completely. Another bad knee injury quickly put paid to his input for 1996-97, he missed the whole season, and Forest were relegated as a direct result.

The big-hearted Geordie won't mind us sharing the moment most Forest fans mention in relation to their hero – his hilarious all-time disastrous open-goal fluff against Reading in 1997 – as they instantly shot back to the big time. Set up by Kevin Campbell, eight yards out and with the keeper waiting for a bus on the other side of the box, he opted for a sand wedge rather than a putter and took out an innocent bystander.

In retrospect, Stone's best years were behind him when he made his exit from Forest, aged 28. Subsequently, his injuries finally caught up with him, and he retired in December 2006. He now works for Newcastle United as part of the backroom staff.

DH

Andy Ritchie

Oldham Athletic Premier League appearances/goals: 34 4
Premier League honours: None

> 'Wooooaaaahhhhh ... [wave hands in the air]
> Andy Ritchie's magic, he wears a magic hat
> And when he saw the Oldham, he said "I fancy that"
> He could've stayed at Man U, but they are full of shite
> And when he saw the Oldham, he said "f*cking dynamite".'

IT IS SOME measure of the affection felt for Andy Ritchie in the
Metropolitan Borough of Oldham that the above-sampled anthem is still
regularly voiced at Boundary Park, even though Ritchie once played for
the hated Manchester United, and then the even more hated Leeds
United. 'He's got no hair, but we don't care ... Andy, Andy Ritchie.' Once
a schoolboy prodigy (the most highly regarded in Europe at one point),
Ritchie matured late, joining Oldham at 27, but he was destined to set
the club alight in two spells totalling nine years service, then three as
boss.

With his sky-high work-rate, utter fearlessness and an eye for 100+
club goals, he ran through metaphorical walls to spawn a mythology of
heroic feats: like the time he was taken off for stitches in a head gash,
only to return and nod in the winner; like 28 goals in a season on
Oldham's way to the Premier League's curtain-raising season; and a
starring role in the 1994 FA Cup semi that saw them just a minute away
from beating Manchester United in extra time.

But Andy's ultimate fan recommendation came in 2002, courtesy of
Zinedine Zidane and Bobby Charlton's favourite player, Paul Scholes.
'Andy Ritchie was the best,' said Scholes. 'I used to watch Oldham and he
scored the goals and was head and shoulders the best player. Andy
Ritchie was my first hero, and then Frankie Bunn. They are still my
heroes. You don't change, do you?'

DH

www.oafc.co.uk

Pedro Mendes

Portsmouth Premier League appearances/goals: 58 5
Premier League honours: None

PEDRO MENDES was involved in English football for only four seasons, but he certainly made his mark – and on two occasions for the most unfortunate reasons. He first came onto the radar after a 50-yard speculative shot for Tottenham at Old Trafford was cleared from the back of the net by Roy Carroll while the referee, Mark Clattenburg, neglected to award a goal. The next time he attracted national press coverage was altogether more serious.

He was rendered unconscious by Manchester City defender Ben Thatcher in August 2006, after a challenge so grievous Greater Manchester Police became involved. Mendes required oxygen at the side of the pitch and had a seizure on the way to hospital. Incredibly, he was back in action two weeks later.

Having been signed for Portsmouth by Harry Redknapp in January 2006 with two other Spurs players (Sean Davis and Noe Pamarot) for a combined fee of £7.5 million, the manager noted, 'I always knew I had to put a team together that will get us out of trouble and back on track.'

In March, Portsmouth were drawing 1-1 with Manchester City at Fratton Park. The long-distance rocket was Mendes' weapon of choice, making goalkeepers look stupid just a sideline. He had scored the first on the hour from 25 yards, and then repeated the feat in injury time to end an eight-game streak without a win and kick-start a strong run of results (losing only two of the next nine games) to stave off relegation.

Before leaving for Rangers in a £3 million move, he starred in the 2008 FA Cup-winning team that beat Cardiff City at Wembley and, last year, four years after he left, he put his own money into the Portsmouth Supporters' Trust to help the fans effect change at the troubled cash-strapped club. He will never be forgotten at Fratton Park.

BB

www.pompey-fans.com
www.portsmouth-mad.co.uk

Trevor Sinclair

Queens Park Rangers Premier League appearances/goals: 102 10
Premier League honours: None

WHEN YOU THINK of Trevor Sinclair in a QPR shirt, there is only one image that comes to mind. It's the FA Cup fourth round at Loftus Road and QPR are winning 2-1 against Barnsley, but down to ten men. The ball comes to John Spencer wide on the right, he hits a speculative cross behind Sinclair who, already three or four feet in the air, executes a perfect overhead kick from just outside the box. In fact, he is so far from goal he is already on his feet before it hits the net.

Even the Barnsley fans applauded. In fact, the only person in the ground with reason not to enjoy the goal was Gavin Peacock, who had opened the scoring for QPR with a brilliant goal after taking the ball in his stride, drifting past a couple of players and belting one into the top corner. Nobody remembers that, though. Similarly, nobody remembers that when Sinclair joined QPR from Blackpool for £600,000, they had just finished fifth in the Premier League and were the top club in London.

With Les Ferdinand and Darren Peacock, and with Gerry Francis as manager, Rangers had the makings of a decent team – they had recently beaten Manchester United 4-1 at Old Trafford on New Year's Day 1992 – and the addition of Sinclair promised an exciting future, but the team struggled and was eventually relegated. The assets were sold off but, despite lucrative offers from bigger clubs, Sinclair stayed to help with the push for promotion.

It never materialised, and after 167 league appearances and 16 goals he left for West Ham in January 1998. He is, however, still revered in that part of West London, and in 2008 he was voted by the fans on to the all-time XI best QPR squad of players, alongside Rodney Marsh and Stan Bowles.

BB

READING

Graeme Murty

Reading Premier League appearances/goals: 51 0
Premier League honours: None

THE POSITION of Reading 'Club Legend' simply has to be reserved for the only player who served the club throughout the Coppell era and, as with so many in this section of the book, captained his club during a successful period in their history. Graeme Murty, a reliable and intelligent right-back, spent over a decade at the Madejski Stadium and was a key player in the side that won the Championship with a record 106 points in 2006 and achieved top-flight football for the first time in the club's history.

Less than prolific, it was perhaps nonetheless fitting that Murty should score on the final day of the season, against Queens Park Rangers, to secure the three points. It was only his second goal since he joined from York City for £700,000 in 1998 and was, of course, a penalty in the 84th minute.

The first season in the Premier League was an unqualified success and, although heavily tipped to go down, Reading finished eighth and one point away from UEFA Cup qualification. Far from being out of his depth, Murty added to his one Scottish cap (won in 2004) when he was called up for the Kirin Cup in Japan. He also signed a two-year extension to his contract and was named BBC South's Sports Personality of the Year.

Reading were relegated the following season, but Murty's best years were behind him ('I don't want to be the footballer who knows a great deal and who is good on the ball but can't run and lumbers around') and in 2009 he was released following the departure of boss Steve Coppell. Already voted into the club's all-time XI on the official website, as the club noted, 'Graeme was a fantastic captain and the memories of him lifting the Championship trophy will never be forgotten by any Reading fan.'

DH

SHEFFIELD UNITED

Brian Deane

Sheffield United Premier League appearances/goals: 41 15
Premier League honours: None

A TALL AND classically robust striker, Sheffield United's Brian Deane is a Premier League trivia question favourite for having scored the new league's first-ever goal, five minutes into the season's opening day at home to Manchester United. His close-range header from a flicked-on throw-in was the kind of poacher's tally that marked a style based on instinct and aggression.

Deane, however, was already a Bramall Lane legend thanks to a brilliant brace he'd scored just a few months earlier at home to Liverpool. The first involved him dispossessing eccentric custodian Bruce Grobbelaar 40 yards from goal before calmly lofting the ball in from distance. The second saw him fight off left-back David Burrows to track down a long through ball before exquisitely dummying Grobbelaar for the second. Final score against the then record English and four-time European champions: 2-0. He took that form with him into the bright new dawn of the Premier League.

Deane had been bought from Doncaster Rovers for £40,000, but was sold on to Leeds at the end of that first Premier League season for almost £3 million. When he returned to United four years later, the entire ground greeted his second debut against Sunderland with chants of 'Deano! Deano!' They were shocked when he moved to Benfica half way through the season, but he had added another 11 league goals to the 82 from his first spell at the club.

'I remember the day when this club sold Brian Deane and Jan Arge Fjortoft,' said fan and later manager of the club, Neil Warnock. 'It was like when President Kennedy was shot – that's how deeply I felt.' Over-dramatic, perhaps, but few United fans felt any different.

IP

www.unitedite.co.uk

Benito Carbone

Sheffield Wednesday Premier League appearances/goals: 96 25
Premier League honours: None

FEW PLAYERS have turned out for as many clubs as Carbone (18, in case you were wondering), a long-locked Italian midfielder who journeyed much, but was by no means a journeyman. The longest stop in his peripatetic career was at Sheffield Wednesday, a club more in need than most of some continental flair. They had, you will remember, missed out on Eric Cantona by demanding he extend his trial period.

For three seasons in the late 1990s, Carbone brought a touch of playmaker's magic to South Yorkshire, in a team that was steadily sinking towards the lower tiers. Although consistency wasn't his strong point, when he was good, he was spectacularly good, and memories of his improvisational flair survive at most clubs who fell victim to his talents.

Manchester United, for example, dropped two points at Hillsborough in 1996 in a 1-1 draw where Carbone was the central engineer of all Wednesday's creativity, scoring his side's only goal in a game that the Owls dominated, and should have won. But it was a far more audacious strike that won him a place in the annals of legend, on the opening day of the following season at St James' Park.

Standing just inside the Newcastle penalty area, Carbone controlled a long pass on his chest with his back to goal. When the ball dropped to his right foot, he chipped it back up to himself, before volleying it over his head into the corner of the Newcastle net with one of the all-time greatest bicycle kicks. Even the home fans applauded.

Wednesday lost 2-1, but who remembers the Newcastle goals (apart from perhaps Faustino Asprilla, who scored them both)?

IP

SOUTHAMPTON

Marian Pahars

Southampton Premier League appearances/goals: 129 42
Premier League honours: None

WHEN MARIAN PAHARS signed for Southampton in March 1999 for a fee of around £800,000, he was known as 'the Latvian Michael Owen', back when it wasn't a bad thing to be compared to the young England striker. They were similar in both style and stature, and it wasn't long before 'the little Latvian', as all television commentators were compelled to call him, had carved a name for himself on The Dell's wall of fame.

Pahars joined a team in trouble and, just a month after making his debut, he found himself in the starting line-up on the final day of the 1998-99 season, with the Saints needing to beat Everton to stay in the top flight. They went into the fixture on a run of four games unbeaten, all of which he had played in. In a team packed with attacking talent – Matt Le Tissier, James Beattie and Mark Hughes were also in the line-up that day – it was Pahars who stole the show.

The first goal was the kind of strike that became his calling card over the next few seasons. Receiving the ball in space at the top of the area, with only goalkeeper Thomas Myrhe to beat, Pahars lashed a left-foot shot into the net with such power that the keeper barely had time to mouth the words, 'What the f*ck'.

The second was better still. Beattie's run down the right produced a hard, low cross that Pahars met with a potent, bullet-hard near-post diving header. 'He's probably a bit better than we thought,' admitted his manager, Dave Jones. After that, nutmegging Jaap Stam and scoring at Old Trafford must have seemed a breeze.

IP

STOKE CITY

Rory Delap

Stoke City Premier League appearances/goals: 133 6
Premier League honours: None

IN AN ERA when only a handful of wealthy teams stand a chance of winning the title, the most satisfying role for the also-rans is that of spoiler. Football purists may turn their noses up at 'the likes of Stoke City', but the likes of Stoke City take great satisfaction in rubbing those turned-up noses in the thick mud of the six-yard box using whatever weapons come to hand.

One of Stoke's greatest weapons has been Rory Delap, and what pundits unfailingly call his 'trademark long throw-in'. If it pains you to watch the English-born Irishman propel yet another round leather missile into the mixer, just put yourself into the shoes of a Stoke fan. This is the highlight of their weekend.

And whose nose better to bloody than those highfalutin aristocrats of the passing game, Arsenal FC? In their first Premier League season in 2008, Stoke beat the Gunners with two goals of the lowest pedigree, both from throw-ins launched by Delap. The first required the merest of glances by Ricardo Fuller. The second was perhaps the most gloriously ugly goal in Premier League history.

Delap's delivery was headed on by Ryan 'Reckless' Shawcross into the path of Nigerian midfielder Seyi Olofinjana. The player seemed to stumble into the ball and hit it with his chest. As he continued to fall, he then stabbed it with the top of his left shoulder, and that was just enough to get the ball into the net.

An Arsenal player stuck his arm in the air, vainly appealing for something. Surely they can't allow goals like that? Oh yes they can, in Stoke-on-Trent.

IP

www.potters-online.co.uk

Kevin Ball

Sunderland Premier League appearances/goals: 43 3
Premier League honours: None

CLUB LEGENDS, players rather than managers that is, tend to fall into one of two categories: skilful mavericks or battle-hardened loyalists who would die for the cause. Kevin Ball very definitely falls into the latter category, and for that reason is adored by the Sunderland faithful. After a sustained period at Portsmouth, where he was also respected as a fully committed professional, he moved to the North East for £350,000 in 1990 and stayed there for the rest of the decade.

A typical Kevin Ball tackle would arrive from the blindside at speed, more often than not he would get the ball, sometimes he would get the ball and the player, and very occasionally just the player – one tackle in particular stays in the mind ...

After leaving the Stadium of Light and a brief period at Fulham (signed by former Sunderland team-mate Paul Bracewell), he washed up at Burnley. In a tempestuous local derby against Blackburn, he hit David Dunn with such force that he was shown a straight red. When he got home he shrugged, 'Another suspension' to which his wife replied, 'You could have been facing a prison sentence for that.' But that was Kevin Ball.

He was one of the few players who moved up the pitch as he got older, having started as a centre-half and then becoming a bulldozing midfield general. Although he still tackled like a centre-half, it would be unfair to characterise him as just a hardman. At Sunderland he had leadership qualities enough to captain them to the 1992 FA Cup final against Liverpool and two successful promotions to the Premier League in 1996 and 1999. He made 339 league appearances for the club and was rewarded with a testimonial against Sampdoria before the start of the 1999-00 season. Never a prolific scorer, 27,506 fans saw him miss the sudden-death penalty that handed the game to the Italians. But not one of them cared.

BB

SWANSEA CITY

Brendan Rodgers

Swansea City Premier League appearances (manager): 38
Premier League honours: None

MANY A NEUTRAL Premier League fan prone to old-school nostalgic tastes will have felt a bittersweet pang of regret to see the outstanding underdog bosses from the 2011-12 season immediately sever links with their self-made sides to join bigger clubs.

At least the initially unfancied Alan Pardew's victory in the LMA Manager of the Season stakes saw him cling on to his Newcastle post; but the unexpected success of Roy Hodgson's WBA saw him exit for international duty before the season was even over, closely followed on the path to the big time by Norwich mastermind Paul Lambert and Swansea's high-impact pass-and-mover Brendan Rodgers.

What joy to hear the tone of the commentators and expert summarisers hiccup and then flip from casual patronage to startled respect throughout the course of Swansea's first season in the Premier League. What a pleasure it was to watch Swansea's odds-on shots for an instant return to Championship obscurity grow in tandem with their reputation as a mini-Barcelona – with Rodgers' adherence to such an elegant *modus operandi* paying highest dividends with a glorious 3-2 win over mighty Arsenal, then their famous upset to beat eventual champions Manchester City.

The chief Swan having deserted the nest, fans will take solace from his outstanding legacy of sweetly passing, furiously supportive team players, and the chance to pick another gem, just as the one-time obscure Irish stopper was plucked expertly from the job scrapheap after an indifferent showing at Reading.

'There's been lots of emotion, lots of tears, lots of thinking,' said Rodgers. 'But the professional challenge of managing Liverpool was too great to turn down and, hopefully, in time that will be recognised.'

DH

Luc Nijholt

Swindon Town Premier League appearances/goals: 32 1
Premier League honours: None

UNHERALDED Dutch holding midfielder Luc Nijholt was signed by Swindon Town before their defensively generous 1993-94 Premier League season, when they shipped exactly 100 goals. In a year that saw them finish bottom and win only five games, one of the high points was a 2-2 draw at home to Manchester United.

Swindon twice came from behind to claim an improbable point, and the first of their two goals was a wanton strike from Nijholt from 25 yards. True, it took a big deflection off Roy Keane that foxed Peter Schmeichel, and it was the only goal that Nijholt scored in two years at the club. But ...

But if you could translate into words the almost audibly astonished burst of celebration that followed, it was not far removed from: 'We are Swindon Town, and f*ck me but we've just scored against Manchester United!'

It was a bad-tempered game and, to most, best remembered for Eric Cantona's red card after he stamped on John Moncur – the small town underdogs really got under the skin of the defending champions on that sunny afternoon in the West Country. To Swindon fans, however, it's not just Nijholt's goal which made him a legend that day. It was his attitude.

Swindon's approach showed United utter disrespect. Twice in quick succession, Nijholt came in late on the combustible Keane. Self-styled 'Guv'nor' Paul Ince came over to have a word. Not once, but twice, Nijholt faced off with Ince, pointing to himself and no doubt challenging the England midfielder to come and have a go if he thought he was hard enough. Turns out that he wasn't and he backed down. United went home a man down and with two points less than they'd bargained for.

IP

www.thetownend.com

Ledley King

Tottenham Hotspur Premier League appearances/goals: 268 10
Premier League honours: None

IT WASN'T just the topicality of Ledley King's name appearing in the news in the summer of 2012 that tipped the scale sentimentally in his favour as Tottenham's representative 'Club Legend'. After 16 years with the club, having joined as a trainee in 1996, he was finally out of contract. The 31-year-old was facing up to retirement, while his rightful place was at Euro 2012, alongside his former Senrab junior team partner John Terry.

Tottenham through and through, the large kid from Stepney proved himself to be an honourable, selfless anomaly. King was one of his generation's greatest stoppers, with outstanding natural gifts of speed, timing and unshakeable power, reading the game like a seasoned pro from an early age and going on to win international honours as well as the respect of fans and opponents alike.

And he had the verifiable courage of a lion, putting his own health and future on the line week after week as he fought back against recurrent metatarsal breaks and horrific knee injuries. King's doctor described him as 'superhuman' and as a player who has 'defied science' – he ordered him to quit four years ago. Fortunately for Tottenham, he chose to ignore the diktat.

Ledley soldiered on, his proudest moment coming in 2008 with a stirring testament to his greatness from boss 'Arry: 'There's no cure. There's no cartilage, nothing to operate on. It's just bone on bone, so it's just a question of managing it. It swells up after games and it normally takes seven days to recover. He rarely trains, he mostly just goes to the gym to keep himself ticking over. But even if he only plays twenty games a season, he's worth having because he's so good we have a much better chance of winning [if he plays].'

DH

www.thefightingcock.co.uk
www.tottenhamhotspur-mad.co.uk

Graham Taylor and Elton John

Watford Premier League appearances (manager and owner): 38
Premier League honours: None

'"CANDLE IN THE WIND" remains one of my favourite songs,' Watford manager Graham Taylor once said. 'But Elton [John] and I had an agreement that I would tell him nothing about music if he told me nothing about football, and it worked well.' In fact, it worked very well. In fact, it worked very well twice.

In 1977, some time between 'Crocodile Rock' and 'Song For Guy', the youthful Taylor was lured by the Watford-owning pop star from a successful management stint at Lincoln City to take the reins at the Fourth Division Hertfordshire club. He took them up to the top flight in three seasons, and an FA Cup final in 1984.

Twelve years later, having done well at Aston Villa and slightly less well as England manager and at Wolves, Taylor returned to the club, recently rebought by Elton John but languishing in the third tier of English football, and once more led them upwards, this time to the Premier League in successive seasons. 'I told him he was coming home,' said the bespectacled ivory-botherer. 'Everybody loves him here.'

But Taylor felt out of place in the modern game, and the 1999-00 season saw Watford win just six games before going straight back down. 'These days you spend two million pounds before you realise the player can't even trap a ball,' he lamented. '[The only good thing about being a manager] is, when you're out on the training pitch with your players. No phones, agents, media or directors, just you and a group of players committed to improving themselves.' Few more unlikely partnerships in football have worked as well, and Elton John underlined his respect for a man he considers to be a 'dear, dear friend' by naming Taylor as one of his six Gay Icons for a photography exhibition at the National Portrait Gallery in 2009. Did he not like that? Why should he not like that?

IP

www.gloryhorns.co.uk

WEST BROMWICH ALBION
Youssouf Mulumbu

West Bromwich Albion Premier League appearances/goals: 115 11
Premier League honours: None

HE MAY HAVE more than his fair share of vowels in his name, but that
has not stopped Baggies fans comparing him to a man with an even
more impressive 50 per cent vowel-to-consonant ration: 'Mulumbu
woah, Mulumbu woah, he comes from Africa, he's better than Kaka.'
Articulatory phonetics to one side, however, this shows the degree of
respect with which Mulumbu is held at The Hawthorns and how rapid his
acceptance since he first arrived at the club from Paris St Germain in
2009.

He made his debut in April, but was signed on a one-year permanent
contract for £175,000 just three months later, and then for another year
a month after that. You might call Youssouf Mulumbu an impact player.
There would be several Premier League opponents who would not
disagree with you. A tenacious tackler and goalscoring holding
midfielder (if that is not an oxymoron) from a council estate just outside
Paris, Mulumbu is in the mould of his former PSG team-mate Claude
Makelele.

An international for the Democratic Republic of Congo (despite
representing France at Under-20 and Under-21 levels), he is a superstar
who is mobbed in the street and requires a bodyguard whenever he
returns to his homeland. He has, however, recently retired from
international football 'to extend his professional career' and has
benefited from the decision – while also alerting a host of top European
clubs, rumoured to include Atlético Madrid and Bayern Munich, that he
won't be caught up in the African Cup of Nations.

He remains loyal to Albion, however, for the time being. 'Albion have
given me a big opportunity and I don't want to disrespect the club,' he said
after winning both the fans' and players' Player of the Year last season,
and signing yet another new and improved contract. But whether he
leaves or stays, he will always be remembered for his last-gasp winner
against Villa in April 2011 – their first victory over their rivals in 26 years.

BB

Julian Dicks

West Ham United Premier League appearances/goals: 110 21
Premier League honours: None

OVER TWO lengthy spells with West Ham United, captain and left-back Julian Dicks earned himself the love of Upton Park through hard graft and a refusal to give up on any ball, no matter how many weeks late he might turn up for the tackle. He was possibly the last top-flight professional to regularly play with his socks down by his ankles.

Despite appearances to the contrary, there was a more skilful side to the defender's gritty repertoire, reflected in his healthy tally of 50 league goals for the club. He had a knack with penalties and free-kicks, and his left peg packed an almighty force into his strikes on goal. If Hammers fans could pinpoint one particularly juicy Dicks performance, they'd opt for the gusty winter's night in February 1997 when a relegation-threatened West Ham entertained their hated London neighbours, Tottenham Hotspur.

After Teddy Sheringham had given Spurs the lead, Dicks levelled with a well-placed header from a corner-kick. Later, with the score at 2-2, he delivered a free-kick on to the head of new signing John Hartson to put the Hammers ahead. And once David Howells had cancelled out that goal, it was up to Dicks to win the game when the home side were awarded a penalty with less than 20 minutes left.

Dicks stepped up and hit the ball into the top corner with such power that, had it not been for the net, the shot would probably have decapitated the first spectator in its path. West Ham hung on to win 4-3 and jump out of the relegation zone, setting themselves up to eventually avoid the drop by two points, led to safety by their Harley-riding, slap-headed hero.

IP

Roberto Martinez

Wigan Athletic Premier League appearances (manager): 114
Premier League honours: None

FOR EVERY PEP Guardiola there is a Jose Mourinho. For every Brendan Rodgers there is a Roy Keane. That is to say that great players do not necessarily make great managers, and sometimes a journeyman player can have the necessary skill-set to make it as a top-drawer manager – think Arsène Wenger, Alex Ferguson and, now, Roberto Martinez. The only difference is that the journeyman player has to work that much harder.

The Spaniard turned up at Third Division Wigan Athletic in summer 1995 to join compatriots Jesus Seba and Isidro Diaz – inevitably dubbed 'The Three Amigos' – as chairman Dave Whelan, a former professional footballer and self-made millionaire, embarked upon a reckless mission to make his club a top-flight team within ten years. Martinez ended up spending six seasons in the North West before moving on to play for Motherwell, Walsall, Swansea City and Chester City.

Latterly, he became captain of the clubs he represented, before an offer of a managerial job at Swansea presented itself in 2007. He took it. A year later they went up into the second tier as League One champions. Whelan came calling. He needed a manager for a Premier League team and presented him with a cast-iron three-year contract. Martinez remembered the promises that Whelan had made and kept when he joined as a player, thanked Celtic for their interest and decided to take the job at Wigan. He has since turned down Aston Villa to stay there.

His short-term task has been to keep the club in the top flight by adapting his tactics to his players, rather than the other way round. A self-confessed workaholic ('The moment you feel you need a day off, you are in the wrong business') he masterminded victories over both Liverpool and Manchester United last season to provide a comfortable seven-point cushion above the relegation zone. Sometimes loyalty is its own reward.

BB

www.wiganer.net

Robbie Earle

Wimbledon Premier League appearances/goals: 244 45
Premier League honours: None

WHEN YOUNG Robbie Earle was toiling in Port Vale's midfield for nine years back in the 1980s, his industry and class caught the eye of practically every fan and reporter who deigned to dip a toe into the quagmire of Third Division football; but big-league bosses were clearly looking for more upscale prospects in environs more glamorous than Burslem. Except for Joe Kinnear, that is.

Switching to the top tier's ultimate outsiders in 1991, Earle's fortunes would perfectly mirror those of Wimbledon for a further nine years, providing a thorn in the side for big spenders and inflated egos, while winning the midfield livewire admirers on an international basis – he won 33 caps for Jamaica and appeared in the 1998 World Cup finals in France.

Unafraid of hard work, yet possessed of a criminally underrated cultured side, Earle became the very embodiment of the Crazy Gang spirit, burning new members' flash suits almost as often as he confounded opponents unwise enough to expect nothing more precise or beautifully timed than a toe-to-toe battle. Earle was a great team player with outstanding individual attributes and an eye for goal – and he wasn't alone. As Robbie himself has pointed out, 'If we were in the Premier League now doing what we did twenty years ago, Joe Kinnear would be Manager of the Year every year.'

Propelling the Dons to a record sixth place in 1994, scoring 11 goals in 1995-96 and earning the club captaincy in 1996, Robbie's own favourite moment came in 1999, finishing a move he'd started himself with a spectacular overhead kick, out-showboating even George Graham's Spurs side of millionaire strollers. He retired in 2000 and the Dons were relegated at the same time.

DH

WOLVERHAMPTON WANDERERS
Alex Rae

Wolverhampton Wanderers Premier League appearances/goals: 33 5
Premier League honours: None

AS A NEUTRAL onlooker, you might think the inspirational Paul Ince or long-serving Jody Craddock would tip the scales as the Wolves fans' Premier League era favourite – and they're certainly on the right track with their qualities of dogged digging deep for the cause; likewise the proud, dignified hardman Mick McCarthy. Wolves have spent only four seasons in the big league, and they've all been rough rides, with no room for luxury passengers.

Maybe that's why no player sticks in fans' minds quite like Alex Rae – born on the wrong side of the tracks in Glasgow, introduced to English football at Millwall, he fell victim to alcoholism during his days at Sunderland – and bounced straight back to star with real passion, tigerish tough tackling and even moments of elusive culture in 2003-04's single season in the sun. Fans of a certain vintage called Rae a throwback to the fearless Scottish foot-in midfielder that inhabited every decent side in the 1970s – the ultimate accolade.

Rae scored a belting 25-yard volley away at Bolton that lit up *Match of the Day*'s Goal of the Month and, momentarily, the Wolves faithful's hope of survival. And then there was the legendary match against Leicester at Molineux in October 2003, when Wolves found themselves 3-0 down at half time and won 4-3, Rae heading the equaliser with something approaching orgiastic ecstasy.

Too good to go down on goal difference with 33 points? No, not really. After one season back at the top, they went whence they came, with Leeds United and Leicester City. Rae, however, was nominated the fans' Player of the Year for his work-rate and immense presence, and even ended up top scorer in all competitions, with eight goals to the good. As they used to sing, 'He's got no hair but we don't care, Alex, Alex Rae.'

DH

www.wolveswebfansclub.co.uk

THE WRITERS (and their favourite Premier League moment)

Richard Arrowsmith (RA) • Cantona's deadpan celebration after his sublime chipped goal against Sunderland during the 1995–96 season.

Bill Borrows (BB) • Manchester City's winner against QPR in 2012 and, simultaneously, the look on the faces of the United fans at the Stadium of Light.

Frank Carney (FC) • Any tackle by Villa's Martin Laursen, the greatest centre-half the Premier League has ever seen.

Derek Hammond (DH) • Stan Collymore's debut hat-trick for Leicester City, March 2000. Broke his leg four days later, what might have been …

Damian Mannion (DM) • The opening day of the 1994–95 season when Jürgen Klinsmann announced himself with a goal and a celebratory dive.

Chris Mendes (CM) • Jamie Mackie's 2012 winner at the death to beat Liverpool. QPR subsequently avoided relegation by one point.

Ian Plenderleith (IP) • Still waiting. Chelsea and Liverpool relegated on the same day with own goals from Cole and Suarez respectively.

Gary Silke (GS) • January 1998. Tony Cottee scores only goal to earn O'Neill's Leicester City victory over Manchester United at Old Trafford.

Graham Stephenson (GSt) • Gary Neville feeding Shaun 'The Goat' Goater in 2002, the last Maine Road derby. Of course, he scores.

Richard Winton (RW) • Dabizas still doesn't know what happened. All he remembers is Bergkamp going one way in 2002 and the ball another.

ACKNOWLEDGEMENTS

Johnny Aldred, Gavin Crossley, Dave Cottrell, Dan Davies, Hazel and Clive Davenport, Jaison Davies, Grant Fleming, Steven Gill, Dave Hall, Michael Harris, Andrea Johnson, John McDonagh, James Mannion, Tim Southwell, Elizabeth Stephenson and Andy McConachie at footballcardsuk.com – the UK's number one memorabilia shop, with over 30,000 football cards on offer online.

Nick Noble and Phil Dorward at the Premier League. All the presenters at talkSPORT, Scott Taunton, Moz Dee, Lord Peter Gee (and 'Creative') and Alice Furse.

Joanne Edgecombe, Rhea Halford, Ian Marshall and Rory Scarfe at Simon & Schuster, and to John Skermer for checking the proofs.

And, of course, Jonathan Conway at MCA Associates.